South to the Caribbean

HOW TO CARRY OUT
THE DREAM OF SAILING
YOUR OWN BOAT
TO THE CARIBBEAN

The Author

Brunelle *in the British Virgins*

BILL ROBINSON

~~~~~~~~~~~~~~~~~~~~~~~~~~~~~~~~~~

South to the Caribbean

HOW TO CARRY OUT
THE DREAM OF SAILING
YOUR OWN BOAT
TO THE CARIBBEAN

W · W · NORTON & COMPANY
NEW YORK LONDON

Published simultaneously in Canada by George J. McLeod Limited, Toronto.
Printed in the United States of America
First Edition
Library of Congress Cataloging in Publication Data
Robinson, Bill, 1918–
    South to the Caribbean.
    1. Yachts and yachting—Caribbean area.
2. Sailing—Caribbean area. 3. Caribbean area
—Description and travel—1951– I. Title.
GV817. C37R6 1982   917.29   81–3990
ISBN 0–393–03265–5   AACR2

W. W. Norton & Company, Inc. 500 Fifth Avenue, New York, N.Y. 10110
W. W. Norton & Company Ltd. 25 New Street Square, London EC4A 3NT
1 2 3 4 5 6 7 8 9 0

Contents

~~~

CONTENTS

Preface

~~~~~~

There is that dream.

It is a dream of an island looming purple on the horizon as the boat slips across the cobalt of tropic seas with trade-wind clouds overhead and flying fish skimming away from the bow. It is a dream that can be partially fulfilled, on occasion, in cruise ships or a week or two of chartering, but a basic element of it, really, is to be at the wheel of your own boat—time schedules irrelevant and all else in the world forgotten. How often, for so many of us, on a commuting train, in a traffic jam, in the slush of a miserable winter day, have the eyes glazed over while the dream took hold? Escape; adventure; humdrum cares forgotten.

And how often, when the glaze cleared and humdrum cares resumed, have a host of practical considerations laid the dream to rest? Rockwell Kent, the sailor-artist who took the cutter *Direction* to Greenland in the 1920s, where she was wrecked and salvaged, wrote a fascinating book that told of these adventures. He called it $N \times E$ and prefaced it with a little fable. In it a commuter suburban husband, to whom the "little round of his activities became unendurable," schemed and dreamed for years of an escape to Paradise in the South Seas. In secret he built a boat, and the time finally came when his wife had to be confronted.

"What——" arms akimbo, "do you think you're going to do in that boat?" Kent had her ask.

"I was going," the husband answered, "to sail to Par—— to the South Seas."

"You are not."

"And there," Kent finished the fable, "ends one of the saddest stories in the world."

Fortunately, I have a different kind of wife, so this book is dedicated to Jane and to our working out of that dream.

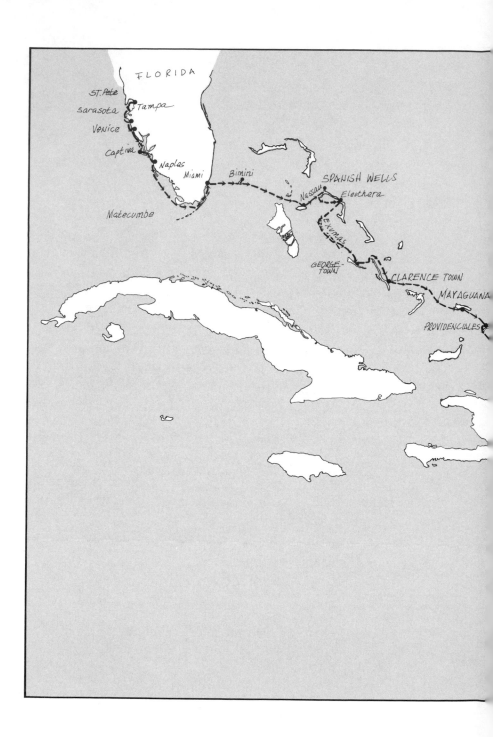

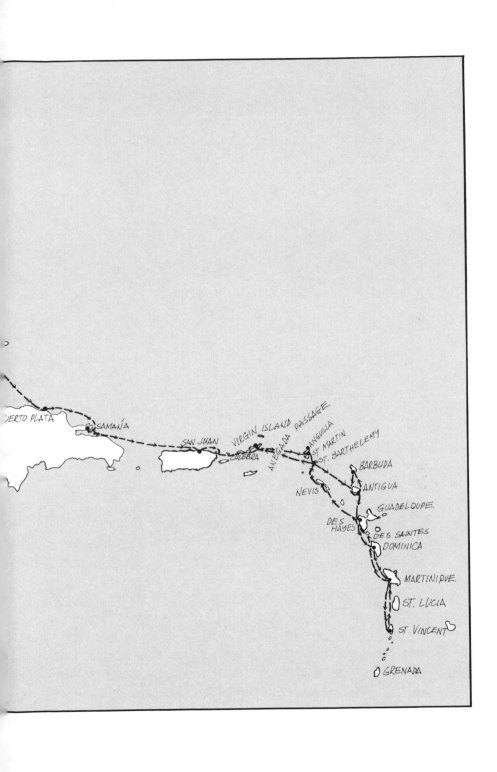

South to the Caribbean

HOW TO CARRY OUT
THE DREAM OF SAILING
YOUR OWN BOAT
TO THE CARIBBEAN

1. A Thrilling Start

~~~~~~

"I christen thee *Brunelle!*"

Jane's words were whipped off into the darkness by the wind amid the cheers of guests at the christening party as they huddled in parkas and foul-weather gear around the bow in a slip at St. Petersburg Yacht Club. The froth of exploding champagne and slivers of broken glass had hardly disappeared to leeward in the rain before everyone made a dash aboard and below to escape the thirty-five-degree temperature made even more brutal by a forty-knot northwester. Everyone but Jane and me, that is. I hadn't had the camera ready at the moment of impact, and she had to fake it a couple of times more for posterity, teeth chattering, as she cried, "Get it over with!" (and the picture didn't turn out).

Thus began our adventure of tropical escape.

There was a good side to the situation, though. It would be hard for the weather to get any colder. This was January 2, 1979, and a stinging cold front slicing across the Gulf of Mexico from somewhere in the colder reaches of the Rocky Mountains had blown away the balmy calm of New Year's Day. We had asked about twenty people to *Brunelle's* christening, which didn't seem like such a large party when we figured it would spread around the cockpit and on deck, but twenty people below in a thirty-seven-foot cutter with a tri-cabin layout made for an atmosphere reminiscent of a Haitian refugee sloop. Somehow, feeling like the Marx Brothers in their famous stateroom scene in *A Night at the Opera,* we managed to pass the champagne and other assorted liquids over and under and around without too much spillage, and the cheese and crackers and other goodies disappeared on schedule.

The guests cozied up on the settees like New York subway riders and tucked themselves away in odd corners of the bunks, and our most elegantly attired guest, complete in yachting blazer, white pants, and club tie, found the after head to be the most convenient place to hold court. This was Pokey Wheeler, a veteran Great Lakes sailor who now winters in St. Pete. I first met him after the 1958 Chicago-Mackinac Race when he brought his guitar aboard *Hilaria* (I was a crew member) for a songfest. He had one memorable song about a timid, browbeaten mouse who got drunk, and it ended with the punch line "Bring on the goddamned cat!" Every time I rendezvous with Pokey I make him sing it, as per this occasion, though the after head was not the best stage for bringing his performance to the whole crowd.

Our shipmates for this maiden cruise were Hugh and Winkie Livengood and Ted and Helen Tracy. Winkie, Helen, and Jane have been the closest of friends from early childhood, and the six of us have cruised together often. It takes friends as old as this for six to cruise in a boat under forty feet, and they are the only people, besides family, we would consider doing this with. They didn't know anyone we had asked to the party, but they said after it was over that they felt they knew all of them quite intimately. Passing champagne in something like a rush-hour tangle breaks barriers easily.

A center of attention in all this crush was a small framed picture of a square-rigged ship under full sail which I had mounted on the bulkhead in the main cabin. This was the original *Brunelle,* a ship owned in my grandmother's family out of Hull, England. My grandfather had been captain of her more than one hundred years previous to her namesake's commissioning. She was an unusual vessel in several ways, some of which might have seemed poor reasons for naming a boat after her. She was very fast, and grandfather often delighted in roaring past steamships when he had a good reaching breeze and *Brunelle* had a bone in her teeth and was hitting as high as sixteen knots. However, she was loosely built, and her planking would work. When she was charging along like this you could look over the side and watch the planking ripple; the carpenter had to go the rounds each day and knock in the bolts of the chainplates, which were constantly working loose. Other captains would be hired and would get about as far as the Orkneys only to take her to port and refuse to go farther; then grandfather would be summoned once more by his in-laws to resume command.

Despite this problem, he had a great affection for her and sailed her all over the world; he made a model of her and had an artist paint her under full sail when he retired. I have inherited the model and the painting—it is a photo of the painting that hangs in *Brunelle*'s saloon today. I also have grandfather's parallel rules that he used aboard her.

Eventually, her construction problems led to her demise. In a January voyage in the North Atlantic, she worked badly in a series of gales, and the leaks caused her cargo of grain to swell so much that she developed a list and became uncontrollable, losing her rig. All hands were rescued, and the hull never sank, finally drifting ashore on the coast of Brittany. While this may not seem like a happy omen for a namesake, she never did sink, and she was the pride of the family fleet and a lovely vessel. With the sturdy CSY construction of the new *Brunelle*, I didn't worry about the hull working or rippling, and since it is a distinctive name, we decided to use it.

I wish I knew the original derivation of the name. I have a nice theory that I could pass off as true, since there is certainly no one around today to refute it, but I have to admit that it is completely unsubstantiated. My theory is that it is a feminization of the name of Isambard Kingdom Brunel, the great inventor and engineer who was responsible for a host of firsts in many engineering fields in England during the nineteenth century—such as building bridges, tunnels, and aqueducts—and who is best known as the designer and builder of the ship the *Great Eastern*, one of the astounding engineering feats of all time. The story of Brunel and his ship was told a few years ago in a fascinating best seller called *The Great Iron Ship*.

In my fantasizing, I have it that grandfather's pride and joy was designed by Brunel and named after him through the feminization of his name. It makes a good story, but, considering the weakness in her construction, Brunel might not be too proud of the connection. In any event, *Brunelle* is the name Jane shouted into the icy wind, and I liked to think that it was distinctive and unduplicated in the yachting world.

The champagne that fizzed off into the darkness after Jane's healthy whack on the bowpiece was not the same brand as the stuff that we were serving at the party. In an excess of frugality, I had shopped around for a christening bottle and found one at $3.98. I couldn't imagine there being anything cheaper and was well satisfied with this find until I happened to see the same brand marked down to $2.98 (post New Year's special) at another store. I bought it, and the $3.98-bottle went into the bottom of the refrigerator—forgotten for many months. I then bought some slightly higher priced stuff to serve at the party.

Despite the conditions, the party seemed to be a success, and there were no bodies found in odd corners the next morning when we settled into the business of putting *Brunelle* in full commission and, it was devoutly to be hoped, taking off on the first leg of the cruise. Despite additional errands and chores still to be done, we wanted to give the Livengoods and Tracys some sailing on Tampa Bay and get them at least as far as Sarasota.

One look across the yacht club sea wall at the bay beyond took care of that idea for the next day. The cold front had blown the rain of the night before away, and we now had a bright, clear day that might have been delightful for skiing, but not sailing. The wind was still close to forty and so was the temperature. We had an alchohol heater for the cabin and had scrounged up some flower pots to put over the burners on our propane stove. The combination acted in an amazingly efficient way to disperse the heat around the cabin.

Even with all this, the ladies decided the boat was not for them and repaired with their knitting and needlepoint to the potted-palm ambience of a nearby hotel lobby—not exactly the most dashing surroundings in the world and cool enough even there for them to keep their coats on while they knitted and needled, and the white-haired denizens of the hotel, bundled like Eskimos, tottered by on their canes or were wheeled past in chairs. What a thrilling start to a cruise.

2. Questions

With a start like this, it might seem proper to raise the question, What were they in for? In fact it had been raised by Jane and me, and our family and friends, many times while the "dream" was being turned into reality—starting with placing the order for *Brunelle* in March 1978 after having seen the prototype of the model, a CSY 37, at the Miami Boat Show.

It was not exactly a new dream. Back when I was a newspaper sportswriter in my thirties and our children were in their early teens, I had planned to quit my job, sell the house, buy a boat, and take off for a year when I hit forty. Sportswriting was a very pleasant life with no pressures except the financial ones of living on a shoestring, and I had a great deal of time to spend with the children during the daytime. Soon, however, they would want my money, not my time, and sportswriting ultimately lacked both financial advance and personal gratification. Covering sailing (and taking part in it) was fun and allowed me to set my own schedule for the entire summer, and football was exciting, but a lifetime of Saturday nights at Seton Hall basketball games, with Roller Derby, Golden Gloves, and a few other charmers thrown in, did not appeal. The dream of "escape" was a virulent one.

This dream was temporarily erased when I landed a job as associate editor of *Yachting* at age thirty-nine. Instead of dropping out to go sailing, I could do a great amount of it in the name of business, albeit in short takes of a week or two at a time. I had always wanted to work on a magazine in preference to a newspaper, and I had saved every copy of *Yachting* since I had started getting it—practically as soon as I learned to read. The dream did not die; in fact, the job might be called a dream one in itself, and it was, for twenty-one very rewarding years.

The prototype CSY 37 off the CSY plant

However, my full-time involvement as editor ended on January 1, 1979, and I became semi-retired, with the title of editor-at-large. Jane said this referred to my waistline, while I preferred to think it opened up the world, and the deferred dream, to me. My time would be my own, even though I would continue to contribute columns and articles to the magazine.

We were in a good position at least to break loose, if not exactly to drop out. It was one of those rare stages in life when we had very few strings or entanglements. It is amazing, as the years pass, how each era, as you move into it, seems to promise freedom from some previous involvement in the diapers-to-nursing home cycle, but the freedom never comes. Between job, children, and the ebb and flow of generational responsibilities, entanglements never cease. No sooner are your children out of the nest, with tuition bills finally off the budget, than the older generation's geriatric concerns become a problem. You wonder whether this will be solved before your own geriatric problems begin, and then the grandchildren come along as a fascinating new interest. How is it ever possible to break away from these Chinese puzzle boxes of continuing demands and do something as self-centered and impractical as taking off on a cruise to the "Paradise" that Rockwell Kent's timid commuter so ardently desired (and that I had always kept in the back of my mind, ever since that earlier plan)?

So often, it never is possible, but for us, twenty years later, it finally seemed that there was an interval when none of the responsibilities we did have were demanding enough to stop us from going. And, after all, we were not planning to disappear over the rim of the sea for ever and aye. We would go for a few months at a time, leaving the boat where she could be looked after while we came home to tend to the practicalities of life and catch up with family and the growing grandchildren.

I am probably not very unusual in that most of my serious planning (and daydreaming) is done in those hours between 0400 and the time when proper sleepers are supposed to wake up. Comparing notes with contemporaries, I have found that most men in the later stages of the male menopause experience this same phenomenon once their prostate, or whatever, prods them awake for that 0400 visit to the head.

From then on, sleep is elusive and the small, dark hours are given over to tossing and turning, physically and mentally.

My tossing and turning produced the idea of circumnavigating the Caribbean in the new boat, not exactly as challenging as circling the whole world, Cape Horn and all, but a suitably adventurous and ambitious project for semi-retireds in their sixties. Then, of course, the next few sessions in those same hours brought the problems and questions crowding in. Even though we were beyond long transoceanic passages, a project like this was quite a challenge; while one half of me planned and dreamed in a ferment of excitement, the other half began to fret over all the obstacles, and the things that could go wrong.

To start with, for those in our age bracket, the general question of physical capability had to come first. No matter how healthy you feel at the moment, this is something to think about for anyone over sixty. As of the conception of the project, we were both in excellent health for our age, but not without a cloud or two on the horizon. Jane had had a heart attack and double-bypass heart surgery four years previously. She has been absolutely fine and free from complications ever since, a modern miracle of medicine we can only be tremendously grateful for, and there is no reason for her to hold back from doing anything she wants (except smoking), but it did happen.

I have had nothing like that in my own medical history. A mysterious attack of vertigo while cruising a couple of years ago has not recurred; other than that I simply have a few creaky joints: one bad knee from being bow-legged and playing squash racquets for forty-five years, and two stiff shoulders. One is from a squash injury which healed itself, and the other came when I was knocked over and landed on it hard. This happened during the rescue by the boat I was on, *J & B*, of the crew of the sinking SORC entry *Mary E* in the 1976 Miami-Nassau Race. One of the *Mary E*'s crew lost his balance just after being pulled aboard and hurtled across the cockpit to lay a perfect body block on me, knocking me on my shoulder on the leeward deck. The deep bruise that resulted has left that shoulder permanently stiff.

I never was very agile moving around on deck and I really have to move with care now as the result of the way these creaks slow me down—and as the general result of advancing age. Just something to think about.

Then there are teeth. For some reason, my teeth always seem to act up when I travel. I broke one on the Hawkesbury River in Australia, had an abcess during Antigua Race Week, and broke another one eating an apple from the "Welcome" fruit basket on a Saturday afternoon at the Hotel Grand Bretagne in Athens. I once got through a week's cruise in Maine on a continuous overdose of aspirin for an aching molar. Sometimes Jane has these problems too.

All this reminded me, as I considered our dream cruise, of a yachtsman who retired to St. Lucia with his wife back in the 1950s, when it was still a rather unusual thing to do. "It's great here, and we love it," he said when we once dropped in on them during a charter cruise, "but there's just one problem. My wife has a lot of dental troubles, and every time she gets a toothache, it costs me about four hundred dollars. We have to fly to Barbados, which she won't do alone, spend a couple of nights in hotels because of the plane connections, and usually end up doing a lot of shopping, just to have a tooth looked at."

I also remembered what I had gone through to solve some of my own dental problems. The hotel personnel in Athens found a nearby dentist, even though it was Saturday afternoon, who built a new tooth for me in about two hours, explaining in his best Greek-accented English that he had studied at "Ooneeversaty SickahGO" (a city in Illinois if you didn't quite get it). In Antigua, aspirin wasn't enough to kill the pain, and neither was Cavalier Rum, so I inquired in desperation about a local dentist.

"Yes; we have one," I was told. "He's Chinese and his name is Dr. Fong."

"Can he take care of it?" I asked.

"Oh, he'll pull it out," was the breezy answer. "His motto is 'Dr. Fong pull your fang!' "

This word sent me back to the ineffectual aspirin, but help was at hand. I was crewing in a boat owned by a Puerto Rican gynecologist, and he finally solved my problem by giving me some pills that I understood him to say were to help women through labor pains.

Fortunately, they didn't make me pregnant, and by inference, this leads to another consideration—the question of the conjugal couch. One might be in the "September Song" years in this regard but far from ready to call it quits. What of the natural impediments inherent in shipboard life: lack of privacy, and so forth? Would not such draw-backs create problems in this department?

And then there were the supposedly well-meaning people who had read *The Bermuda Triangle* and believed its preposterous nonsense.

"How do you dare go into the Bermuda Triangle?" they would ask in all seriousness. "And how about all those hijackings, and revolutions, and piracy, and drug smuggling? You'll have to take guns with you, but they probably won't do you any good." (I have never had a gun in my house or on a boat and do not believe in them as a solution to anything. I can't imagine my ever using one effectively in the remote circum-stance where one might possibly help.) The only valid worry of this sort would be the political instability of the Caribbean Islands and coun-tries.

On a more practical plane, I was well aware of the problems of maintenance and repair. I have written before of "Robinson's Law," which is that there is never a time on a fully equipped boat when everything will be simultaneously in working order. On *Brunelle* this went into effect the first day, when the fuel gauge went out (I have never been shipmates with one that worked)—and to this day has remained that way, a continual proof of the law.

Mechanical skills have never been my forte, to put it politely. When left completely to my own devices, and at my own speed, I can solve simple problems sometimes, and I am great at poking a screw-driver at an engine and staring at it very hard, willing it to behave while muttering incantations. I have, however, basic lack of confidence and a proven knowledge that it is much easier to take things apart than it is to put them back together again, which leads to problems. Would I be putting us into uncalled-for difficulties by heading out into the blue under this handicap? I had very little hope that outside help would be readily available in some of the places we were heading for, and, especially in those 0400 toss-and-turn sessions, I have a very vivid imagination for all the things that can go wrong. Perhaps over the years as an editor I had read too many articles about the terrible things that have happened to people—along with learned articles of advice on what to do in everything from a dismasting to Tampax jammed in the head. I have lived through enough crises of varying proportions in fifty-plus years of cruising without having to be told about all the problems that can arise. So many articles of advice in boating magazines and how-to books seem calculated to scare any sensible soul as far away as possible from the boating scene instead of even hinting vaguely that it can be fun. At 0400, I sometimes tend to agree with them, but I always feel better when the sun comes up.

Studying the manufacturers' manuals and instructions that come with the various pieces of equipment is no help at all. Collected in an impressive volume about the size of the Manhattan phone book, *Brunelle*'s are full of vital information—like who handles their spare parts in Madagascar, along with diagrams and schematics that tend to blur out in the key parts and look like a textbook explanation for nuclear chain reaction, but are of very little help to the layman. I don't know why boat builders don't put together a simple manual, written in direct, layman's terms, that tells the average owner about the things he might be capable of doing and should know about.

My best recourse when mechanical problems arise is the friendly fellow yachtsman. I seldom go up and make a direct request, like, "Will you fix my bilge pump?" My approach is more subtle. I usually start with something like, "Have you ever had trouble with your bilge pump?" Or perhaps, "Do you know anyone around here who repairs bilge pumps?" If the guy takes another sip of his beer and looks glassy-eyed, I move on to another boat, but very often the response is a satisfyingly macho, "Oh, having trouble, Bill? Could I have a look at it? We had that trouble once in Hatchet Bay, and I think I know what it might be."

Hard as it is on my ego, I humbly accept the offer; it is surprising how many owners do know how to bleed injectors, change the diaphragm in a pump, or fix any of those other things I can take apart but not put back together. This system is better than my trying to digest manufacturers' instructions. We call it the Friendly Yacht Service Co.

There were other things to think about even later in the day than 0400, such as speaking Spanish with port officials, mail and other forms of communication, diverse currencies, and the practicalties of life back home—like paying bills and leaving our house empty. Since we would not be in the boat all the time, we were not pulling up stakes and selling out. We would also have to find places to leave *Brunelle* every few months while we came north. Daughter Martha and my office assistant, Rosie Curley, would combine to work on my finances, and we arranged a house sitter—a man on temporary assignment at a Bell Lab near us—thus taking care of at least two of the worries. And perhaps, after all this, we would run into disillusionment over what tourism has done to the Caribbean since our first visits in 1958.

Some of the time we would need crew for longer passages, and we planned to have guests for a week or so at a time. Would making connections be a problem? Schedule keeping in a cruising sailboat is an iffy business, especially since we would be going to windward for one thousand miles from Florida to the Virgins—the first place where you can relax and say that you are really in cruising country after leaving the Bahamas. This would be our first main objective, and a "break point" where we could leave the boat for the hurricane season.

All this led to a whole new set of considerations. What route should we take to get to the waters where 'islands loom purple on the horizon'? Since we would be starting from Tampa, where *Brunelle* was a-building, we had two basic choices. One was to assemble a deep-water crew and take off from Miami, passing through the Bahamas as quickly as possible and heading eastward into the open Atlantic from the north end of Eleuthera. We could hope to pick up a norther at the start, arrive at the trade-wind area in the general longitude of the Virgins, then turn right and reach down to a landfall there. This would mean more than a week of watch standing in open-sea passaging, and I vetoed it for three reasons. First, although we could probably find a crew to do it, this would take a great deal of organizing. Second, neither Jane nor I really wanted to stand watches for that long a time. And third, we wanted to make our way in leisurely fashion down through the Bahamas and Turks and Caicos, as we had never been beyond the Exumas and really wanted to see the far Out Islands, as well as Hispaniola.

Most of this could be done in single-day passages for the most part, though not entirely, but it would be almost 100 percent on the wind in an area where the trades have some real heft. I compartmented the trip in my mind into separate sections—each one with a worrisome area to be negotiated looming like an obstacle in a hurdle race.

I thought of each one as a "worry box" in my mid-night musings, and they started rather close to the beginning of the voyage. The west coast of Florida from Tampa to Naples was simple, but from there to the Keys, around the southern tip of Florida's mainland and across Florida Bay, would be more than a one-day passage. The choice of overnight stops was fairly daunting, in fact almost nonexistent. Then there would be the Gulf Stream from Miami to Cat Cay or Bimini. I had crossed it sixteen times by sailboat and countless times in Navy subchasers, and the percentage of easy passages had been very low. To any boat owner with a sense of responsibility and an imagination, this fifty-mile leg is always to be taken seriously; the Great Bahama Bank's sixty-mile expanse beyond Bimini is another item to think about carefully.

Island-hopping on through the Bahamas has no challenges to match these—the longest stretch is never more than 45 miles all the way to the Caicos—but from there it is 90 to 150 miles to Hispaniola, depending on your departure point. This is usually directly into the trades where they are noted for their boisterous authority, and then it is another 100 miles along the forbidding north coast of Hispaniola to its eastern end, again directly into the trades. The next leg is the Mona Passage; it is 180 miles from Samana, the last port in eastern Hispaniola, to San Juan across this notorious stretch of turbulence. Tales have been written of marriages ending on a Mona Island passage, and the charts contain cheery warnings like "confused seas and unpredictable currents here," and "this area is to be avoided when possible."

This route has been dubbed the "Thorny Path" in the guide

books—I think Carleton Mitchell first coined the phrase—and it was our choice for our voyage of romantic escape. As described above, one could certainly have doubts about it, but it seemed the better of the two choices open to us and certainly more interesting.

All those worry boxes did lurk in my mind, although I tried to isolate them and only think about the next one ahead. Then, of course, there was Anegada Passage, the eighty-mile open-water stretch from the Virgin Islands to the Leewards that had to be negotiated—to windward of course—if you wanted to go on down the arc of islands toward South America. After that it was downwind into political uncertainty.

So here were all these questions and 0400-worries. Was it silly to take them on? Should we just poke around the west coast of Florida and the Keys and forget about that dream of the islands? Obviously we did not, or this book would not exist, but they were with us, inevitably, as we went on our way. I can't imagine an owner who does not sail with doubts and uncertainties in his mind, aware when he embarks on such a project of the problems and possible pitfalls. I was no exception. At the beginning, far from backing off, we were really excited about meeting the challenge and finding solutions to the problems. Otherwise, it would all have remained just a dream.

3. MSDs, Tables, and Other Items

Although I really wanted to be sailing, there was plenty for me to do in our weather-enforced stay in St. Pete. While the ladies knitted and purled amid the potted palms, many items of commissioning were still to be attended to. For one, I had to go to Tampa and get a radio operator's license. Tracking down the office through a change of address and driving over the causeway across Tampa Bay, I was doubly glad *Brunelle* was still in port. The bay was a froth of whitecaps so close to each other that they almost blended as one sheet of foam, shot through with wind streaks. The northwest gusts rocked the rental car, and the palm trees and casuarinas on the little islands bent to the whipping wind.

Brunelle (37'3" × 29' × 12' × 4'9") had been built at the CSY plant in Tampa, where most of the commissioning process was done. In the few days before the New Year, Jane and I had checked over the 1001 items that go into a newly commissioned auxiliary—a process as complicated as setting up a new household, with the addition of some nautical items. We had brought a full auto load of gear from our old boat down from her resting place in North Carolina, where she was awaiting a buyer, but we still had to comb the chandleries, supermarkets, and department stores of Tampa for things like a swimming ladder, pots and pans, dish towels, galley utensils, toilet articles, condiments, charcoal, courtesy flags for all the countries we planned to visit, flashlights and batteries, and a virtually endless list of miscellany. We also brought our old Avon inflatable dinghy, which we carry lashed on deck. Oars only; no outboard.

CSY boats are sold directly from the plant, so we were dealing with the plant commissioning crew, not a local dealer. One salesman, who happened to be an old friend named Ford King, was our shepherd

We carried an Avon inflatable dinghy on deck

in putting all this together and in getting all sorts of little finishing touches done by the plant workmen. While we would be loading some of our purchases aboard, a man would be installing shock cord along the bulkhead above the refrigerator—to hold up the top-opening lids to the three compartments when you were using them. Another mechanic would be fiddling with something on the engine, with the hatch to that compartment wide open in the cockpit, and a man with a varnish brush would be touching up something in the forward cabin. Over all this, the bimini top, an absolute essential for where we were going was being fitted.

Everyone would be terribly polite as we squeezed by each other amid mounds of equipment, and the general impression had to have been that it would never be finished and that all the stuff we were bringing aboard would never fit. With the holiday weekend approaching, it became a question of getting everything done before the plant

A Bimini top would be essential where we were going

crew disappeared for their three-day break and the Tracys and Livengoods arrived. Also, I had to be given a check out on all the equipment and special features. This was supposed to take at least one whole day, or maybe two, but we finally found time for it late one afternoon, when the workmen had disappeared at last.

We didn't want to spend the weekend at the empty plant in an industrial area, so the "shakedown officer" came with us as we moved the boat the five miles or so across the bay to the more congenial surroundings of St. Petersburg Y.C. While Jane steered, he went over the boat from bow to stern with me tagging along, notebook in hand. He was a young, enthusiastic sailor who really knew his stuff, and I'm afraid he assumed a lot more mechanical knowledge in me than I had. One of the hazards of being editor of *Yachting* has been that everyone imagines I know everything about everything to do with boats (and there is always great glee whenever I am caught in one of my not-infrequent louse ups); this young man went ahead at a lightning clip in his explanation of all the gear.

I scribbled frantically in my notebook as I followed him around, and I am still trying to decipher what I wrote. Fortunately, the deck gear, rig, and sails were all pretty familiar to me and presented no problems, but, again, it was all those mechanical things that gave me pause. At least I could tell the refrigerator compressor from the engine (it is green and the engine is red), and we got the inspection done and had her safely snugged in at the yacht club in time for the officer to get home for supper, leaving us with our gear piled around us and my illegible notes in hand. We then had one day to ourselves before the guests arrived to stow all our gear and achieve a semblance of organization.

The layout of the CSY 37, known as Plan A (as opposed to a Plan B which I shall describe later) is a tri-cabin layout, with a stateroom forward, a main saloon, with a nonconvertible dinette to port and a settee to starboard that forms upper and lower bunks, and an after stateroom to port. The galley, with its propane stove, is to starboard of the companionway to the cockpit, which is all the way aft; the refrigerator, the tops of whose three compartments make a long work counter, is forward of the galley, between it and the settee. Each stateroom has its own head and shower. The forward stateroom has two bunks that can be made into a double with a filler piece, and the settee in the after cabin converts to a double through a series of contortions that have to be seen to be believed. This is a minor drawback, though I can now convert and un-convert the bunk with no sweat in a matter of seconds; the only other criticism I have of the layout is that both heads are to port. This presents a problem when the boat is well heeled over on the port tack. It would be nice to have a leeward perch on either tack.

This is better than Plan B, though, in which the lone head is in the place that gave it its name on old sailing ships, right up in the forepeak. Aft of this is an enclosed stateroom with double bunk and a hanging locker opposite; the rest of the cabin is one big saloon, with a settee that goes upper-and-lower like ours, a big dining area, and the galley and a nav station across the after end of the cabin. With the raised-deck construction of a CSY 37, this makes for an impressively

We pulled away from the CSY plant at Tampa

spacious saloon. She would be fine for marina living and in-port entertaining, but I shudder to think of using that head while thrashing to
windward offshore. Knowing that we would have guests aboard frequently, we much preferred the Plan A layout, and we chose light-
colored woodwork and upholstery and off-white bulkheads to give a
sense of light and space.

In it, we found a surprising number of places to stow things as we
gradually disposed of the mounds of stuff all around us, and I kept a
stowage list as we went. The only mistake we made was to be too
optimistic about stowing cans in the bilge. It was, of course, beautifully
clean and dry the first day aboard but became a bit damper after a few
passages offshore, and the cans suffered. Modern aluminum cans are
very light and flimsy and do not wear well in a damp atmosphere. After
several months, many of the cans of beer and soft drinks had developed
pinhole leaks, and all carbonation evaporated.

We also found that the refrigerator compartments were so capaciously deep that Jane could not reach anywhere near the bottom of them to retrieve stuff. There were no shelves in them, so one of our forays into the markets was to buy some of those wire baskets used for drying dishes. Two of them were jammed into each compartment for orderly stowage of food, and Jane did not have to stand on her head and hang by her heels to get what she wanted. We couldn't find a proper-looking swimming ladder in Tampa or St. Pete and settled reluctantly for a plastic folding job.

And so we were in pretty good shape for our guests and for the christening party. We had the shock cord to hold up the refrigerator lids, we had added clothes hooks and a retaining section of shock cord on the bulkhead just inside the companionway for foul-weather gear, and we had installed extra shelves and racks in the appropriate places for books, magazines, charts, and binoculars. There were a few things we didn't know how to dispose of, including the tool kit, which has remained forever on the sole in the after cabin, but almost everything had its home—*Brunelle* was beginning to look a bit more like home to us.

There were two major problems, though. The first concerned the heads, and the second had to do with the dinette table. In accordance with the ridiculous requirements forced on the boating public by the EPA in the matter of the euphemistically labelled MSDs (Marine Sanitation Devices), a boat could not be released from a builder's yard unless she was equipped with approved devices. I won't go into a lengthy discussion of the tiresome subject here. I have written editorials and nauseam on the subject, pointing out both the infinitessimal effect boats have on water pollution compared to municipal and industrial contributions and the completely impractical solutions in the matter of devices.

We had to have a type of electric macerator-chlorinator (at a goodly sum to buy and install) that I guess is a perfectly effective piece of equipment, but in a moderate-sized auxiliary with no generator the electrical drain on the batteries while operating the devices is staggering, and they also make a noise like a subway train roaring through a tunnel. I figured we would have to run the engine to keep the batteries up whenever a head was being flushed, not exactly an adjunct to gracious living—especially for those ladies who like to pretend that they never, no never, go to the head at all and ardently desire complete secrecy and anonymity when they do. This may sound silly, but we have had plenty of them as guests over the years. As soon as possible after the infernal machines were installed, we found a mechanic who could disconnect and bypass them, since we would be heading into offshore waters, where they were not required. It will be a simple matter to reconnect them if and when we return to "civilization." In the two days we lived with them, Jane developed such a phobia about the fuss and noise that she would walk half a mile to find a head on shore rather than use the one on the boat, and a bucket was substituted for nightime emergencies. This sort of thing also developed a form of feminist resentment over my ability to go topsides and use what we sometimes refer to as "God's Great Mens Room"—the rail—for nocturnal calls.

When I got back to the boat from Tampa, the ladies were getting a bit tired of the potted palms and wheel chairs, and we all repaired to the boat to work on the still unsolved problem of the dinette table. When I first saw the boat at the Miami Boat Show, I commented that the dinette table was ridiculously inadequate for four people, much less six, which would sometimes be the guest complement in CSY's charter fleets; there had been some talk of doing something about it. When we first saw *Brunelle,* however, she still had the same little table, which had about a two-and-a-half person capacity. There was a sheepish admission from CSY personnel that this had been overlooked in the press of meeting production deadlines.

Without coming right out and saying it, they were able to remind me with polite subtlety that I had already caused them considerable extra difficulty in production because of *Brunelle*'s color scheme. All CSY boats have beige topsides and a maroon sheer stripe, but I was able to persuade Jack Van Ost, head of CSY and an old friend, that I could have something different. My two previous boats had had light blue topsides, and I really wanted the same color again. First of all, it is very practical in not showing dirt, and it is a very pretty nautical color.

Also, I really did not want to look just like all those charter boats in the Caribbean. There was wailing and gnashing of teeth in the production department at the plant, but Jack had given his word, and blue she was to be. We finally settled on the exact colors via telephone—with Ford King in Tampa and me in New York—using a copy of *Yachting* as a color chart. We picked the blues on certain pages for the topsides and sheer stripe, and that was the way the gelcoat people arrived at the colors. (Actually, the royal blue sheer stripe had to be done with Imron paint.)

On top of the production people's wails, the sales department then found that many of the prospective customers they were taking through on plant tours said that they wanted a blue boat too and were quite put out that it would not be possible. They were told that this was a one-off experimental job, but that did not mollify them, so *Brunelle* finished her trip down the production line wrapped in butcher paper to hide her individuality.

This was not used as a direct excuse for CSY not having re-designed the table, but I was given to understand, in the nicest way, of course, that I had already been something of a pain in the neck. But, they would do something about the table now. With the six of us in attendance, we had a meeting with 90 percent of the production brain power at CSY to see what to do about the pesky thing, a slight strain in the cabin capacity again. As we went over possible solutions, I tried to get across that this was really needed for their charter boats, not just for me—to make up for the blue topsides business.

The dinette has a curving, L-shaped settee that starts at the mast and wraps aft around the table. It does not convert to a bunk, which is a real blessing. Convertible dinettes are as cantankerous and unmanageable as any item I can think of in the nautical world, usually leading to loud curses and smashed toes as someone tries to wrestle one into position at a late hour of an evening that has been based on alchoholic consumption.

All very well, but how to expand it? Not a furniture designer by trade or inclination, I had merely suggested that they devise some sort of folding leaf or slide-out panel; in theory, it seemed like a simple problem. When we got down to taking a close, hard look at it, we saw that a sliding panel would need some sort of leg support, which would be impossible to fold up against the bulkhead, and would also be in the way of people sliding along the settee to go to or from the galley. A folding leaf seemed like a better idea, but it would have to be supported by a removable bar between it and the overhead. No problem!

Everyone retired with wide smiles and in no time, a folding leaf that fit snugly on top of the existing table appeared; it was a heavy panel of Formica-covered plywood, the same thickness and weight as the table itself. The fiddle on the inboard edge of the table was removed, and the leaf was attached with a piano hinge. In the middle of it was a fitting to take a butterfly nut; a similar fitting was installed on the overhead. A metal bar, with flanges at each end to go over the fittings and be held by the butterfly nuts, was also provided. Presto: we had a table for six.

At least until breakfast the next morning we did. We ate ashore that night, and the next morning I started setting up the table for the six of us to eat. I attached the metal bar to the fitting on the table first and then reached up to affix it to the fitting on the overhead. In this balancing act, I let go of the bar by mistake; and as it slipped out of my hand and fell, it neatly levered the bottom fitting off the table.

Try again. Ford King had been attending to this and all our other little problems, and his face fell a mile when he saw what had happened. This time, he had the fitting through-bolted on the table, and it definitely would be impossible to pry it out. All very well, until we tried to fold the double table up against the bulkhead, its normal out-of-use position. The through bolts now made the whole package so thick that the hook to hold it in place at the top was no longer long enough. This brought a lengthy discussion on shimming the plate for the hook and other makeshifts, until I timidly came up with the suggestion to try a longer hook. Eureka!

A longer hook was found, and at the time the whole problem seemed solved, but you will find the saga of the table a continuing one as our voyage progresses. You would be surprised at what can happen to one simple table when it has been designed by a committee.

4. On Our Way

It was time to leave.

The wind had eased off, and the sun was beginning to win out over the chill in the air. The table was fixed (so we thought); the heads had been quieted down; we had said good-bye to our St. Pete friends and all the CSY people who had been so helpful (I think if we had stayed one day more, Ford King, good friend as he was and as thoughtful and helpful as he was, would have gone over the hill until we did leave); and we were ready. We had had a short shakedown sail in very light air on New Year's Day before the front came blasting through, but we really wanted to get sailing and to get on our way. The Livengoods and Tracys had been with us several days with a minimum of sailing and a maximum of errands and lobby sitting, and we hoped to get them at least as far as Sarasota, or they wouldn't have been able to say they had been cruising at all.

Tampa Bay was calm and shining as we headed out on it at noon the next day, and we soon had the sails up and were easing along toward the Sunshine Skyway in a mild southerly that had replaced the blustery northwester. Our target was the Buccaneer, a marina on Longboat Key just south of Tampa Bay. We had been in there on previous cruises and found it a very pleasant stop, with a good restaurant. The Intracoastal Waterway leads from Tampa Bay, through a drawbridge in the long causeway out to Anna Maria Key, to Longboat and Sarasota Bay. I had heard a rumor about some bridge in this area being closed to boats, and I asked the dockmaster at the yacht club, who said he had not heard anything about it. He called the Coast Guard for me and got the same story, and we therefore headed for the bridge in full confidence after a pleasant sail down the bay. We gave three blasts on the horn.

Somehow there are few sillier feelings in the world than to sit in front of a drawbridge blowing away on your horn and not have it open. We huffed and puffed and waited and waited in front of the Anna Maria Bridge but nothing happened, so I finally eased up as close as possible for a better look and found that there was no one in the bridge tender's hut, and scaffolding was all over one leaf of the bridge. A tiny sign said it was closed to boat traffic during repairs. I was reminded of a tale I had heard a few years ago of a lady single-hander who started out on what she hoped was a world cruise from Manhasset Bay, Long Island—a complete novice but all steamed up, and headed down the East River toward New York in her twenty-four-foot sloop. As she neared the Throgs Neck Bridge, which is a big, high-level fixed bridge with clearance for ocean-going vessels, she got out her horn, blew three times, and began to circle, waiting for it to open. She was still blowing and circling when a large tug boat that towered over her came under the bridge and charged by her; she suddenly got a better perspective and sheepishly continued on her way.

We felt about as silly as that single-hander must have, but there was no way to get through this bridge, the afternoon was drawing on, and the only thing to do was backtrack into Tampa Bay and head for the nearest anchorage inside DeSoto Point at the entrance to the Manatee River. This happens to be one of our favorite anchorages in the Tampa Bay area, so it was no great hardship to spend the night there, except for the silly feeling of having blown for a non-opening bridge and the disruption in an already well-disrupted schedule. DeSoto Point is supposedly where the explorer of the same name made the first landing on Florida's west coast and then ranged well inland, but it is hard to imagine how anyone with the gumption to get that far as an explorer would pick this isolated and inaccessible spot to come ashore. At any event, the point is named for Ferdinand, and there is a nice park there that keeps the surroundings in a natural state. On the other side of the cove, pleasant suburban houses line the shore, but there is a good away-from-it-all feeling in keeping one's focus on the point.

The river was alive with small fish worrying the surface, and thousands of birds wheeled over them in shrill confusion. Brown Pelicans, so ungainly when waddling on land or paddling around on the water and so beautifully controlled and graceful in flight, flew in single file low over the water, their long beaks dowsing toward the surface. They were alternately beating their wings and gliding in unison. It was just outside the Manatee that we had seen flocks of rare white pelicans wheeling high overhead in the sun. Our approach had also been through the usual convoy of porpoises, which are constantly around you in Tampa Bay, rolling under the bow and leaping alongside as though asking for applause.

A small auxiliary sloop came in soon after we did and anchored nearby. She was from Michigan, and the couple aboard—in comparing notes by calling across the water—said they had trailed her down and were just starting out on a cruise.

"Wow! Did you see all the sharks coming in here?" the husband asked. "There were big ones jumping all around the boat."

I said that no, we hadn't seen them, and didn't have the heart to ruin the excitement of their first day of cruising. The Great Lakes were never like this.

The Great Lakes also seldom have sunsets like the typical Gulf one that flared beyond DeSoto Point soon after we settled down to happy hour, anchor cup, or whatever name you care to give evening cocktails. There is something about the Gulf of Mexico that breeds special sunsets that have added panache since they are over water—in contrast to most East Coast spots. The mix of primary reds and yellows—with pastels in mauve, pink, light blue and a distinctive, clear, apple green constantly shifting and blending through the cloud patterns—makes an unusually riveting sunset, and we had a good show across the calm sheen of the cove.

The next morning was clear and warm, with a gentle northeaster, and we had our first chance to try out a new sail, one I had never been shipmates with before. This is a poleless spinnaker, especially designed for cruising boats. Ours was made by Charles Ulmer, who did all *Brunelle*'s sails, and he calls it a Flasher. Other sailmakers have their own names for their version of it. It is cut like a rather flat spinnaker and it tacks to the bowplate instead of being rigged on a pole. It is effective in winds from a quartering run to just forward of the beam

Breaking out the Flasher for the first time

at strengths up to about fourteen to sixteen knots, and it really makes a boat come alive. An owner is allowed a choice of colors on the multiple panels of the sail, and I chose just about every one available, creating a rainbow effect that is fairly startling.

The Flasher is not difficult to rig or control, though this was the first time that I had ever followed a set of printed instructions (in the brochure that came with it) in setting a sail. We got it up with a minimum of fuss, and we all broke into spontaneous cheers as the colors flashed (could be how it got its name) in the slant of morning sunlight. *Brunelle* surged ahead with a satisfying gurgle and whoosh under the bow, and we had a fine sail out of the bay through Passage Key Inlet.

Anna Maria's white beaches were close aboard to port, with a pleasingly tropical look to them; to starboard, tankers and freighters using the main ship channel past Egmont Key formed a hazy parade. The Gulf, a peculiar flat, pale green in its inshore waters, stretched wide and clear to the horizon.

In *Brunelle* the cockpit is aft, at the lowest freeboard on the hull, and it stretches from gunwale to gunwale with no side decks. In contrast to the high center cockpit of our previous boat, *Tanagra,* an Out Island 36, intimacy with the water had been restored; there was a wonderful sense of it sliding by with whispering ease, especially so as we were farther removed from the noise of the bow wave. There was also an impression of much more boat under you in steering from all the way aft. *Tanagra* gave us five years of great cruising, and we will always regard her with strong affection. We hated to give up the roomy privacy of her after cabin, but I had to admit to myself that there was a better feel to sailing this way.

The Gulf is a special body of water. It is big and wide and could be the ocean, but that underlying restlessness of a ground swell is missing. In calm weather, it is mirror flat; when it kicks up, the waves are shorter and steeper than deep-sea ones, and they can be especially vicious. On this day it was in the most benign of moods; the breeze was just right; the sun warmed our shoulders; and *Brunelle* swept along in free and easy freedom. This, finally, was it. We were on our way, and the bow slicing through the green of the Gulf was pointing south. No purple islands loomed on the horizon as yet, but we were aimed in their direction.

5. *Klunk*

As so often can happen with a morning shore breeze, our northeaster pooped out in early afternoon. We lolled through lunch hour off the white beaches and high rises of Longboat Key, with water-ski boats buzzing and circling inshore of us, and then turned on our power to head through New Pass into Sarasota and the civilized amenities of Marina Jack in the heart of town. The center of the high-pressure area that had followed the cold front was upon us, and no breeze came in the rest of the day to replace the morning northeaster.

That was it for the Livengoods and Tracys, who had to return north, and Jane and I continued by ourselves toward Naples and the next crew rendezvous. The calm of the center of the high was wiped out the next day by a strong southerly, as the high moved on and another one approached in the rather swift pattern of the movement of winter weather across the continent. No sense bashing our way in the open Gulf, so we powered lazily down the Intracoastal Waterway to Venice, recalling the pleasures of ICW trips in *Tanagra* between New Jersey and Florida. We were glad we had come this way when we saw the white horses charging by outside the pass (Florida–West Coast for inlet) at Venice and the metronome motion of the masts of boats negotiating the pass.

Venice Yacht Club was a snug and hospitable haven. Moored to the bulkhead, we were just astern of a Gulfstar 41 with the legend *Euphoria,* Buffalo, New York, on her transom. Jane studied it for a while.

"Do you remember a note I had on the telephone table at home?" she asked. I said that I had seen it but didn't know what it meant and had forgotten to ask.

"When I was telling Peggy Dyer about our plans, she said to keep an eye out for a boat, and I think that was the name—*Euphoria,* from Buffalo."

The Dyers are old friends who divide their time between Marion, Massachusetts, and Sarasota. Peggy had told Jane that a couple named Rabow in the next apartment in Sarasota was taking off on a cruise like ours, but, with the thousands of boats there are in Florida waters, we thought little about the possibility of running across any given one. In one of those coincidences, here they were, and I went over and introduced myself. They, too, had had the word to look out for us, but, since our bow was toward them, they hadn't seen *Brunelle*'s name yet.

This was the first of many encounters of this kind that are so much a part of the fun of cruising. In a day or two, strangers become "old friends," and then paths diverge. Sometimes they are never seen again, but occasionally there will be a surprise reunion after a year or more in some far-off port, and the friendship resumes as though there had been no interruption.

The Rabows are typical of many of the cruising people we met. They are considerably younger than we are but they, too, were striking out on an adventure "before it's too late," able to do so through Jerry Rabow having sold a company he owned in Buffalo and cutting ties with a way of life held for many years. Most of the cruising people we met were younger than us, and we envied them the chance to do it sooner in life than we had been able to—though I can't really complain about the number of cruising opportunities we have had in short doses through the years, thanks to my job.

Since we were both heading for the east coast of Florida and then the Bahamas, we agreed that it would be fun to cruise in company for a while and decided that the next stop would be Captiva, one of the barrier beach islands enclosing Charlotte Harbor and Pine Island Sound. During the night, the next front—foretold by the strong southerly sucking into it—came through with a heavy dose of rain as we rode snugly to the Venice Y.C. bulkhead. It was a milder front than the previous one, with a pleasant, cool-but-sunny morning-after and a fresh westerly that allowed us to do some sailing as we wended southward through the protected waters of Charlotte Sound. The basin of a resort called South Seas Plantation at Captiva was approached via a long avenue of stakes marking a channel across the flats, and then a right-angle turn to port toward the almost hidden entrance. Once inside, we found the piers very close together and hard to negotiate. We were after hours, with no dockmaster to direct us, but we finally found a slip near *Euphoria* and settled down for a quiet evening of comparing notes. In making the landing, I discovered that *Brunelle* had a habit of stalling when throttled down to idle, and that her twenty thousand pounds had a lot of carry to them when trying to fend off a dock. Embarrassment, but no damage.

This was a beautifully organized and maintained marina, with everything in perfect order; it also happened to be the most expensive one we hit on our entire cruise. I had checked in late in the afternoon with a night watchman and had not been given any information about the operation of the marina. After breakfast, I felt it was the proper thing in such a confined basin to go ashore to use the head, especially with our disconnected MSDs, but I found that the door marked Men was locked with some form of combination.

I was futilely punching at the door when a dock attendant came by, and I said, "How do you get into this place?"

He stopped, regarding me a bit suspiciously, and asked, "Are you a boater?"

This created a real dilemma. For years, I had carried on a campaign in the editorial pages of *Yachting* against the use of this term. Continuing tongue-in-cheek in a tradition started by *Yachting* old-timer Bill Taylor, I had pointed out that a "boater" was a form of straw hat and vowed time and again that the word would not appear in authorized use in *Yachting*'s pages. It was a losing battle—eventually even the Coast Guard started using the horrible term—but I had remained adamant. The word really grated on me, and here was this terrible dilemma. Should I stand on my integrity and years of editorial righteousness and give the fellow a lecture on nautical terminology, or should the other concerns of the moment be allowed to prevail?

They did, and I merely answered with a meek "Yes."

Nodding his head, he worked the combination, which I would

have been given if I had checked in before 1700 the day before, and let me into the premises. I must say they were dazzlingly clean, which cannot always be said about shore facilities at even some of the fanciest marinas.

South Seas Plantation lived up to its name in atmosphere. Well-tended lawns and palm trees, with low buildings spread over the whole parklike area from Gulf front to the bay, made for very pleasant surroundings, even if you did have to be a boater to get into their facilities. There was a problem, though. As I said, the marina slips were very close together, and the maneuvering space between the end of the slips and a sea wall opposite was also very tight. In fact, a powerboat across the end of our finger pier blocked the only way I could back out; we ended up trying to turn around in the slip, between our pier and the next, in an area that was perhaps a bit over forty feet wide—not much room for turning a single-screw thirty-seven-foot auxiliary in a fresh cross breeze. By repeated backing and filling I was making about a foot of progress each time, but it looked as though we were going to be there all day until a crewman on a large power yacht on the other side of the slip saw my efforts. As *Brunelle*'s bow came up close to his deck, he reached out and grabbed our pulpit; with another crewmate to help, he pulled the bow around until we could head out the slip. Freed at last, we headed out the dogleg entrance to the basin to the staked channel, and in my eagerness to be off, I forgot about the unmarked right-angle turn into the channel, cut the corner, and felt that sickening lurch that means you are aground.

Before we had a chance to do much about it, *Euphoria* came out of the basin, and, seeing us stuck, headed over to help. She had more draft than we did, and she, too, lurched to a stop a few feet from us, as Jerry Rabow and I looked at each other and exchanged shrugs and forehead slaps. The westerly of the day before had come around into the northeast and was cool and fresh in a sparkling sky; before two abashed and embarrassed skippers became extra mortified, we were both able to slue off into deep water with the help of the breeze swinging our bows.

And so we bid farewell to beautiful South Seas Plantation, and the rest of the day was a gem. The breeze held strong and clear in the northeast, and we could thread the intricate channels of Pine Island Sound and San Carlos Bay back of Captiva and Sanibel Islands under sail for all but one switchback. The two boats made the drawbridge between Fort Myers Beach and Sanibel in company, and we then headed down the open Gulf to Naples on a broad reach. There is no Intracoastal Waterway for this stretch, but there was certainly no need for it on this glorious day—our first really good sail in open water.

Brunelle and *Euphoria,* the latter named well for a day like this, surged along bow-to-bow over a sparkling sea, with the low winter sun slanting across the southwest sky and sending a path of glitter that engulfed us and artistically backlighted *Euphoria* to leeward. The miles reeled off, landmarks on the low coastline slipped astern, and there was a special excitement to being out there and becoming more and more at one with *Brunelle* as she tracked along in the small quartering seas.

If we hadn't had a crew pickup to make at Naples, as well as a fifty-hour check on the engine and a few more supplies to find, it would have been tempting to sail on into the twilight to Florida Bay under what would be a near-full moon, continuing right on to the Keys. Instead we powered into Gordon Pass at Naples, a narrow inlet that looked as though it could be trouble in an onshore breeze, and threaded our way north up the Waterway the few miles to Naples Y.C. Some of the fanciest and most impeccably kept waterfront estates I have ever seen lined the channel and lagoons shooting off from it on the port hand, while the mangroves and scrub of undeveloped land were to starboard.

Naples Y.C. is a moderately sized club with very few local yachts but a large restaurant business in its elegant dining room; the cooperation and hospitality were excellent as we waited for the Haights to join us and had a local mechanic check out the engine (and its nonfunctioning instruments) after fifty hours. They had ceased to operate on the way in from the Gulf, and for some reason known only to Westerbeke, whose 4-108 diesel was our power, the needles of the oil and water gauges remain in the middle of the dial (instead of dropping to zero) if they stop working or when the engine is turned off. If the tachometer

Euphoria *was artistically backlighted to leeward*

hadn't quit too, it would have been hard to tell that they were kaput and this seems a poor arrangement to my layman's mind.

The Westerbeke man adjusted the idle speed so that the engine wouldn't stall at embarrassing moments and supposedly fixed the instruments. He checked over the engine and made the fifty-hour lube oil change, and we would be ready to go as soon as the Haights arrived. *Euphoria* had left, amid hopes for a future rendezvous. By one more day, however, another front was building and there was no point in bashing into a strong southerly all the way to Florida Bay. It had rain squalls in it too, so we spent a couple of days enjoying the delights of Naples' geriatric Gold Coast. The beautiful elderly abound in this pleasant haven, so the restaurants are good and the shops and boutiques artfully enticing. It was a real tug of war to get our wives out of Lily Pultizer's, and they were quite disappointed that neither Jack Haight or I would buy a sport jacket whose decoration was a life-sized Tiger head, since we had been roommates at Princeton once upon a time.

In those days, his nickname was Doc, presumably because his father was a Reverend Doctor; eventually he earned the name for himself by becoming a Ph.D. Now everyone calls him Jack, but I still revert to Doc without thinking. He has been a history professor at Lehigh for over thirty years. His special field is United States–French relations in World War II, which has given him a wonderful excuse to take sabbaticals in Paris over the years. His wife, Debby, has spent every summer of her life at a small, private summer resort called Desbarats on the North Channel of Lake Huron, near the Soo, and they have had their own place there for many years. She, in fact, was named Deborah in honor of the place her family loves so much ("Desbarats" is pronounced Deborah).

The academic life has given them many opportunities to travel as well as to spend long, pleasant summers at Desbarats. They have a great many interests and enthusiasms, and it has always been stimulating to have them as cruising companions. Debby is the more experienced sailor, from her many summers of sailing at Desbarats, and she has a wonderful way of ordering Doc around a boat, prefaced by "Sweetie," which keeps him happily hopping to her bidding. Jane, who was brought up on horses and had never been on a boat until we got married, was quite jealous of this ability of Debby's, but she once did have a small revenge on me the one time since we have been married that anyone could get me on a horse. That was in visiting Petra, in Jordan, where the only access to that fascinating "lost" city is to ride a horse through a six-foot-wide gully, called a *siq,* for about half an hour. While I clutched the pommel of my beast's saddle and tottered in terror for the whole ride, Jane gave me a condescending laugh and trotted far ahead, her straight, confident back and "good seat" showing her disdain for my awkward lurching.

I had hoped to make a stop at Marco Island, a few miles south of Naples, to shorten as much as possible the Florida Bay run, but friends living there told me the channel was too shallow for an auxiliary and that a ketch drawing about five feet had hung up hard right in the middle of it a few days previously; we decided to take off directly from

Naples. By now, the latest front had whooshed by with its accompaniment of squalls and high winds and quickly left a flat calm behind it in the center of the next high-pressure area.

We powered south over a mirror-flat Gulf into a hazy, ill-defined horizon, chugging along all day in a void. Our cruising speed of 6.7 knots is 2250 RPM's, but 2000 has a more comfortable feel and gives us 6.3 knots. The choice of stops was either a creek called Little Shark River, which, according to the *Waterway Guide,* was one of the most popular havens for mosquitos in all the Everglades area, or, by pressing on after dark, the lee of one of the little islands in Florida Bay. One called Sandy Island would be the first we would come to, and the *Guide* gave it fair marks as an overnight anchorage. No one seemed to want to brave the mosquitos, so we kept going past the entrance to that creek late in the afternoon, hoping to make Sandy Island by about 2000, an hour and a half after dark.

Debby, who has a lively imagination, had recently read a newspaper account—one of those lurid exposé things—about the piracy and hijackings surrounding the drug smuggling trade in the Gulf of Mexico. It gave special emphasis to the swamps and creeks of the Cape Florida area as being particularly favored by the operators, and she had worked up a good case of the jitters. She eyed the low pencil of coastline to port with some suspicion and put me through a grilling about the possibilities of our running afoul of these people. I did my best to convince her that they would not be likely to have an interest in a slow, medium-sized auxiliary. They would want big, fast boats for long hauls, I said, and small, fast ones for pickups and drops along the coast. I did have to admit that the coast was an ideal one for making undetected drops.

She didn't act too convinced by my reasoning, but then another worry came along that was much more imminent. The shallow waters of the edge of the Gulf are infested with floating buoys marking pots for fish, lobsters, or crab—I'm not sure which. No matter what they mark, they presented a real hazard as the light began to fail, and they were growing more numerous as we closed with the entrance to the channel across Florida Bay known as the Yacht Channel. They were mostly Clorox bottles or plastic floats, low in the water and very hard to see in the best of light.

By now, we were committed to going on, so I trusted to luck as we forged across the glassy surface into the gathering darkness, wondering at the same time how drug smugglers managed to negotiate these waters in the dark without fouling their props.

Debby asked, "Shouldn't I keep a lookout on the bow?"

I had just said, "I don't think it would do much good; by the time you could see one it would be too late to warn the helmsman," when there was a heavy "Klunk," and the engine made a grinding noise. Doc was at the wheel, but I was next to the single-lever engine control and quickly slapped it into neutral.

Too late, though. *Brunelle* wallowed to a halt, and, looking over the transom, I could see a scruffy, slime-covered plastic buoy bobbing in our wake in the glow of the stern light. We had really caught one.

6. A Pot of Trouble

There we were, immobilized by a pot and completely becalmed. I could see Debby looking over at the thin line under the rising moon that was the coast she had such imaginings about, and a form of despair and indecision was my first reaction.

But not Doc. "Have you got a good knife?" he asked. "I'll go down and see if I can cut it loose."

"Do you really want to?" I said.

"Well, now that you ask, no," he answered, with an ironic laugh, "but I will."

"Jack, you shouldn't," Debby said. "Maybe there are sharks."

"Nonsense," he said. "I'll take a look, anyway."

This was the christening of the plastic folding ladder we had acquired, so we broke it out of the cockpit locker, tied a safety line on the brave swimmer, and on the knife, and he went over the side and under the stern while we hovered over him anxiously.

He broke the surface with a snort. "Wow!" he cried. "It's cold."

Back under he went, and in a minute, the float could be seen drifting away, trailing a short length of line. Jack came back out for air, puffing and blowing.

"It's really wrapped," was his hard-breathing report. "It's really tight, and snarled around the shaft. I know I can't do anything with it, but I did cut the line to the pot, so we're not hung up."

"Well come on out," Debby cried immediately. "You'll get too cold."

Easier said than done.

He swam to the ladder, which was attached to a hand rail amidships (the slight rake-in of the transom prevented use of it over the stern), grabbed the slippery plastic ropes that the steps were strung on, and tried to heave himself up. The ladder curved in under the hull, giving him an impossible angle for pulling himself up, his hands slid down the ropes, and he fell back into the water. Once more he tried and got one rung up, but he couldn't let go a hand to move it higher because of his slanted angle under the hull, and he hung there, muscles quivering as he shivered with cold. Eventually, with a supreme effort, he got one rung higher, where we could reach down and give him some support while he worked up to the next step. Shaking from effort and cold and shedding water like an angry dog, he made the cockpit, where Debby wrapped him in towels. Despite the lack of results on the propellor shaft, it was a noble effort and we were free to sail. Not a strong underwater swimmer, I had no desire to try it myself.

Cursing the ladder, and myself for stupidity in buying it, we pulled it aboard and sat there contemplating what to do next. The only thing possible was to try sailing, and then the question was whether to head back to Naples or to go on to the Keys. I looked up Flamingo, the only harbor of any description with some civilization in all the vast area at Florida's tip, and saw that its entrance was too shallow for us. Onward seemed best, so we chose the Keys.

We made sail while the girls made supper, and *Brunelle* sat on the glassy surface, over which hardly a ripple could be seen in the moon path. Her sails flopped idly, and we made no visible progress whatsoever. We ate glumly, with nobody saying much, alone in a calm void. One navigational aid winked at us far ahead, and the coastline was just visible. Once in a while we could hear the distant hum of a boat's motor but could see nothing.

Debby would say, "What's that?" and I knew what she was thinking.

In mid-evening, a few zephyrs stirred, also stirring our hopes, and we moved a little bit in the right direction. Since these stopped before midnight, I decided that the best thing to do was to anchor until either daylight or a breeze, whichever came first. We were in shallow water of less than fifteen feet, despite the distance from shore, and there was only the slightest surge on the billiard-table smoothness of the Gulf. In deference to my crew's nervousness about the area, and in hopes of reacting to a breeze if one did spring up, I decided to sleep in the cockpit; it was a long night of watching the moon sail by overhead and listening to the small gurgles the hull made with its slight, occasional movements. Now and then a motor hummed in the distance, but no one came close enough to be seen. Debby claimed that she hardly slept at all, listening for the clump of feet landing on deck and imagining all sorts of things while half-awake, and I was sure I hadn't had any sleep, though I must have dozed off now and then.

Dawn beat the wind. In fact there wasn't any until mid-morning, when a mild southerly filled in, and we weighed anchor and headed for the Yacht Channel. The radio had been talking about another front on its way across the Panhandle of Florida far to the north, and I hoped that the southerly would act like the ones that had preceded the other fronts that had come through—building up during the day and giving us a fast reach across Florida Bay to the Keys. I didn't want to arrive in the Keys, with their intricate channels and small harbors, after dark and under sail. I had studied the *Guide* and figured that Lower Matecumbe, where there was a marina close to the end of the Yacht Channel, was the best place to aim for.

It would have been a very pleasant day to be sailing if we hadn't had a few others things on our mind. We slipped through the greenish water nicely, ticking off the buoys as they slid by, the sun was warm, and the breeze was pleasant. It was just that there wasn't enough of it. Even though the NOA VHF weather radio kept telling us that the front was moving down across central Florida and had arrived at the Tampa Bay area, the breeze remained mild-mannered and gentle, perhaps eight to ten knots.

Somehow, we managed to pick up another pot. They still dotted the water like measles, and we kept a very careful watch, but this one was so crudded with grass that it was submerged; we didn't see it until I felt us slow down and saw to my horror that it was hooked on the rudder. Fortunately, it must have been an old, rotten rig, because it broke off before we had a chance to agitate, and we were sailing again.

While we reached placidly along in the sunlight, purple clouds began to build in the northwest, gradually raising big anvils of cumulus toward the sun. As the afternoon wore on and I kept track of our progress, I realized it was going to be a very close finish at Lower Matecumbe between our arrival, darkness, and, probably, the front. When we came out of the Yacht Channel, our course was a bit more to port in open water, and the wind had gone into the southwest, so we set the Flasher to get every last ounce of effort out of *Brunelle.* For a while sunlight slanted against the multicolors of the sail, but then the clouds moved higher and began to build as we slid along at what seemed an agonizingly slow pace. The weather station was still playing the same tape about the front being in Tampa Bay, but we had a pretty good idea that it was closer than that.

Scanning ahead, I eventually picked up the stakes for the entrance to Lower Matecumbe and began to breathe easier. It looked as though we had it made, though the light was fast fading. The breeze had dropped off even further, but, finally, we arrived at the channel entrance in the last half-twilight and doused the Flasher.

The narrow, staked channel ran in to the south toward the harbor for a few hundred yards and then made a ninety-degree turn to port toward the single pier of the marina. There was a small open area east of the pier that looked as though it had just enough room for *Brunelle* to turn in, and I planned to reach in under main, run in toward the pier from the turn, jibe in the open area, and settle in starboard side-to at the end of the pier. In the last light it had looked as though there was an empty space there.

"We've made it," I said to myself. "We've won the race."

With the darkness almost complete, but enough lights on the stakes and pier for us to keep our bearings, I made the turn in toward the pier—all set to slide up to it in decorous dignity.

In sports, it is a cliché that games like football and baseball are a matter of inches. In sailing, there is a matter of minutes, or even seconds, in which a boat can save her time on another in a handicap race, gain an overlap at a mark, or, even in cruising, hit a change in tidal current or a wind shift.

With us at Lower Matecumbe, it was a matter of a couple of minutes. Right after we had made the turn toward the marina, completely committed to our approach and with no room in the channel to change course until we got to the little basin next to the pier, the front caught us. With literally no warning, the breeze jumped from five to thirty knots, dead on our stern, in one blasting gust, and we had nowhere to go but straight ahead. If it had been a minute or two sooner, we could have turned and gone back out the main channel. If it had waited a couple of more minutes, we would have been safely at the pier.

But here we were, roaring ahead on the starboard jibe into a space that was much too small for us to maneuver at this speed. And, as we burst out of the channel into the turning basin, I saw that there were three concrete posts that were not on the chart; they were showing up white in the glow from the shore lights right in the middle of the basin, further reducing the maneuvering area.

"What are we going to do?" Jane asked. She is one of the calmest of females and almost never raises her voice, but this was more than a polite inquiry.

"Take the mainsheet. We're going to have to jibe," I yelled, "and we're going too fast to make a landing, but there's nothing I can do."

The Haights had gone forward to get the bow lines ready, and in the roar of wind and forward rush of the boat, there wasn't much I could communicate to them in time to be helpful.

As soon as we entered the basin, I veered to starboard to give us more room to turn in, but there was very little space on that side. If I went any deeper into the basin we'd be crashing among the concrete posts. In all my years of sailing I had never before been in such a complete box. There was no good way out of it. If I had had time to think, I would have been cursing the whole chain of circumstances, but all I could do was concentrate on the maneuver, judging the last second before I had to jibe to avoid running aground or hitting the posts. Also, at this stage of ownership, I was not thoroughly familiar with *Brunelle*'s turning circle at full speed, but I already knew from a couple of landings when the engine had stalled that she had plenty of carrying power.

I turned the wheel to port as quickly and sharply as I could, yelling "Jibe," and Jane trimmed the main as fast as she could. The sail slammed over with a crash, and *Brunelle* was headed for the pier like a runaway bull. There was a good-sized auxiliary with two small boats rafted next to it directly in our path, and forward of her, at the end of the pier, there just happened to be that one empty space. For a moment I thought that *Brunelle* would not round up enough and that we would smash into the nest of boats with results too horrible to contemplate, but she answered the helm enough, and Jane had let the main slack off enough, so that her bow started turning to windward enough to miss the boats. Now we were headed for the pier itself, still going about six knots—not exactly the recommended speed for an eggshell landing—and my part in the act as helmsman was finished. I yelled a warning as loud as I could to Debby and Jack, though I couldn't see exactly what they were doing, and there was a thundering crash as our starboard bow connected with a piling at the end of the pier. Although I couldn't believe what I saw, the piling completely disintegrated as though a bomb had exploded inside it, and, as I ran forward to do what I could about getting a line ashore, the force of *Brunelle's* charge took her around the end of the pier, with her bow headed downwind on the opposite side of it and the sail filling again. There was a sloop berthed just ahead of us, but somehow we shuddered to a halt a few inches from her.

Then I saw that Debby was at a piling on the other side of the pier end. She had taken turns around it with one of our lines, and was straining at it mightily, holding the boat fast at last. Doc had been rigging a line when we hit and hadn't seen what was coming, but she had managed to jump ashore at the moment of impact and had been able to get the line around the piling, which was fortunately a solid one (it turned out that the one we demolished had been a rotten one), and this quick action had saved further carnage and embarrassment. Doc was soon there to help her.

We were still in what might be called an awkward spot. The howling frontal squall was filling the main, and we only had that one line ashore. People were now on the pier, although we hadn't seen anyone while we made our headlong approach. Attracted by the crash, they had come running, and extra lines were soon rigged. To bring the main down, I had to sweat the boom in as far as I could to get the sail off the shrouds, and then it had to be wrestled down inch by inch while full of wind. A husky man from one of the boats at the pier had come to lend a hand, and we finally managed to get it down on the boom. By that time there was ample manpower to walk *Brunelle* back around the end of the pier and make her snug at the empty slip, although there was no longer a piling to make fast to.

I wasn't sure I wanted to examine our bow, but I knew I had to face up to it sometime; it was a wonderful relief to find that there was no hull damage whatsoever. The only casualty was the decorative fiber-glass trailboard at the bow. It had been torn loose, and some of the teak covering board above it was split, but, considering the circumstances, I breathed a great sigh of relief. Every time I looked at the nest of boats astern of us, I shuddered at the thought of what would have happened if our ten tons had plowed into them at six knots. And I thanked God for the rotten piling.

The first squall of the front had blown by, and the wind had gone northwest, while ragged clouds were breaking up as they raced across the moon. We still had a line to get off our propeller shaft and a trailboard to be repaired, but we were snug in port, and we could finally turn thoughts to a drink and dinner.

I don't remember a double martini ever tasting better.

7. *Across the Stream*

We were lucky. A young man who ran a water-skiing service at the marina said that he was a strong, experienced snorkeler and would be happy to take a look at our propeller shaft. With a great display of muscles and manly chest, he jumped in and went under the stern after promising to have it clear in a few minutes. Some thirty dives later, he was a blue, quivering mass of goose pimples, but he wouldn't quit, and eventually he came up with the last crushed and stretched piece of line. It had been a real snarl, wound tight on itself, and had to be cut out a few inches at a time. We wrapped him in blankets, fed him hot coffee, and finally persuaded him to take some money for his efforts; it was a great feeling to be back in business. One of the questions that had not popped up in my advance musings was my lack of ability underwater, but my theory about friendly neighbors wanting to show their superiority had been proven again.

In two days of alternately sailing and powering up the Waterway and Biscayne Bay, in the cool aftermath of the front we were in Miami in a guest berth at Biscayne Bay Y.C., gathering forces for our crossing to the Bahamas. The Haights had gone back to classes at Lehigh, and we were once again awaiting a crew change while having repairs done. The engine instruments had quit once more, and we had another session getting them working. For repairs of the bow that had won the battle of the rotten piling, I was recommended to a man who was working on another boat at the marina. He was an ex-airline pilot who had been laid off in a cutback by the company and had gone into the boat repair business for himself as Turnbow Marine. He looked much more like a young business executive than the conventional picture of a boat-yard worker, and he went about his work with neatness and dispatch, turning out a fine job at what seemed a reasonable price.

Jane dressed for cold-front weather on the Waterway in the Keys

The trailboards were not one of my favorite features on the boat, as I didn't think they quite came off in their imitation of the old carved boards of wooden vessels, but this one was back in place, and we looked decent again. I had also decided that the twenty-five-pound plow anchor provided was not big enough, and we replaced it with a thirty-five pounder.

On our way up Biscayne Bay, we had our first real beat to windward in a good breeze, and I had not been happy with the set of the roller furler jib, a high-cut one some people refer to as a Yankee. No matter how I twitched and pulled at it, adjusting the position of the

60

sheet block on the rail track, the upper part of the luff fell off rather badly and was constantly fluttering, and the boat would not point as high as I thought she should. We tried it by itself and in combination with the staysail, but it didn't work well either way. Since the sails had been made by Ulmer and since he had a representative in Miami, I asked him to come have a look; the solution was simple. We didn't have enough tension on the halyard, even though it seemed extremely taut. When it was taken up more, the sail set well, and we have been pleased with it ever since. The main and the staysail both seemed fine, and I felt much better about the whole rig now. I really like the roller-furling feature on a cruising boat. It is the lazy man's delight and a great safety factor—and the double headrig allows for a good choice of sail combinations according to wind strength and direction.

During the wait for our next crew to gather, there was another one of those frontal cycles that come through every few days in January and February. Our daughter Alice and her friend Weezie Potter took a week off from their jobs in New England to come with us, and, while we were waiting for the last member, John Yeoman, a young squash-playing friend from New York, to finish off a business trip to Atlanta by taking a long weekend with us, we could have powered across the Gulf Stream in that one day of calm that so often prevails when the center of a high is in the area. Instead, we basked in the sun at the yacht club marina and watched the rare sight of manatees (or sea cows or dugongs) wallowing around alongside us. I have heard the theory that these strange creatures were responsible for the mermaid legend, but it seems to me that someone would have to have been at sea for an awful long time to find anything alluring about a sea cow.

The trip around from Tampa had been the first of my worry boxes about the cruise (it would have been more of a worry if I had known how many pots there were in the Gulf of Mexico and Florida Bay), but now we faced the first major one—the Gulf Stream crossing, plus the continued passage to Nassau. Thousands of boats do it all the time, and I had done it many times myself, but it is one of those bodies of water that a prudent sailor always treats with respect. I had seen it absolutely placid in my first crossing by yacht in 1957, when the water was so

61

smooth that you could look far into the depths and see small fingerlings and jellyfish swirling about, but I had been battered by it in the subchaser Navy with the worst conditions I had seen in two years of sea duty. I had had its stinging salt in my eyes while standing on the flying bridge of an SC, and I had felt it down my neck many a time in the Miami-Nassau Race.

It was on my last previous crossing that *Mary E* had sunk in heavy seas while we stood by her all night in *J & B* after the rescue of her crew—the most uncomfortable twenty-four hours I have ever spent at sea—and I have never been able to take this fifty-mile stretch of "ocean river," hurtling its billions of gallons northward at two and a half knots or more, as anything but a real challenge.

In a way, the Gulf Stream symbolizes the ambivalence with which I, and I'm sure a great many more owners, approach an open-water passage. You love sailing, you love the challenge and the satisfaction of making a passage to a distant port: the freedom of it, the absorption in it to the exclusion of everything else in the world, and the sense of accomplishment that it brings. And yet, there are always those nagging reminders of things that can happen, of things that have happened in the past, lurking in your consciousness, and you can be pretty sure that at some time in the passage, if it is rough at all, you will say to yourself, "What in hell am I doing here?" Nobody but yourself makes you go to sea when you are in command of your own boat, and once out there your emotions are a strange mixture of the pleasure of being at sea and the desire to get where you are going safely and without mishap.

And to me, the maxim of "getting there" applies no more strongly anywhere than in the Gulf Stream crossing. It is one stretch of water I am always happy to have behind me, and all these thoughts churned through my mind when, with full crew aboard, we slipped out of the club marina at dawn on Saturday and headed across Biscayne Bay to Biscayne Channel and a departure from Fowey Rocks Light. The breeze was fresh from the southeast, with a forecast for it to hold all day, preceding another front that was due that night. The next day was Super Bowl Sunday, and the forecasts were mainly concerned with how it would affect the game. We just wanted the front to stay away until we got to the other side.

As we threaded the narrow channels from Biscayne Bay out to open water past the spindly fishing camps on stilts that dot the reefs, Saturday fishermen swarmed around us in their little outboards, along with some deep-sea sportfishermen, but we were soon by ourselves when we cleared the last buoys and pushed out onto the inky blue of the Stream, which was sharply defined at its edge under a hazy sky. The breeze was about seventeen knots and kicking up the usual steep chop but not as bad as if it were blowing against the Stream, when the chop can get really nasty. To allow for the Stream on a direct course of 085 °M we needed to steer at least fifteen degrees to the south; I allowed even more than this and decided to stay as close to the wind as we could, motorsailing at 1800 RPMs under staysail and main. Motorsailing is not the pleasantest way to go, but I figured that we wouldn't make enough speed under sail alone in this sea condition to lay Bimini, much less Cat Cay, where we were hoping to end up, before the Stream swept us well north.

It was a rough, bouncy passage, and the dodger front that snaps onto the Bimini top was an effective help in keeping us dry. *Brunelle* proved herself generally a dry boat in this first brush with a sloppy sea and proved it time and again thereafter, but some spray is bound to come aboard with this much wind and sea. The only person to get wet was Jane, who was sitting on the windward side of the cockpit just below the little well deck where you step down from the raised deck of the cabin top. This little "bathtub" has a scupper drain in it, but the hole is outboard. With the boat heeled over, water that comes in gradually collects on the leeward side of the well, and eventually there was enough for it to slop over on an extra lurch to leeward, giving Jane a good sitzbath as she screamed in surprise. Since then we have learned to watch for this little booby trap.

The breeze increased as the day warmed, and the sun played hide-and-seek through scudding clouds. The seas grew higher, and we plunged into them with considerable force. She wasn't pounding and never has, but the bow was smashing through hard, with a lot of water forced by it; after a while there was a strange thumping noise from up forward. We slowed down and headed off for a minute, and John went up and discovered that the port trailboard, not the one that had been damaged at Lower Matecumbe, had partially broken loose. The main bolt holding the forward end of it was still attached, but the after end had gone adrift. There was space between the bottom of the board and the hull for water to be forced up, but no opening at the top for it to be released. The pressure of being to leeward in a head sea had torn the after end of it free. John got a line on it so it wouldn't swing around, and we went back to our plunging progress.

As it continued to get rougher, I thought Weezie might be *Brunelle*'s first seasick case. She paled and drooped and had that resigned look on her face, but hung on bravely without mishap, though she didn't take any of the hard boiled eggs, celery, or fruit that Jane handed out at midday.

We have a tradition while cruising of a beer at 1100 and cocktails at noon. I was the only one who wanted a beer, but I could see Jane measuring me as the sun approached the yardarm, wondering whether I would stick with tradition under these conditions. On starboard tack, the galley is to windward, making it difficult to handle ice, glasses, and bottles, but I felt that I should meet the challenge without any special show of difficulties and somehow managed martinis, laboriously but successfully. Gauging the amount of vermouth is a trickily challenging business when the boat is lurching and leaping; it helps to have the gimballed stove as a working area.

About 1400, a thin little lump of greenish brown appeared on the horizon, and it looked suspiciously like Bimini, not Cat Cay, as we brought it up a bit more. The RDF confirmed the suspicion, picking up Bimini's strong signal from right where the land was, and it was obvious that the fresh southerly had increased the speed of the Stream and combined with our own leeway to set us well north of Cat Cay, not an unusual happening. From this sighting it took us till 1700 to get into the harbor, as we were even north of Bimini and eventually had to douse sail and power south outside Bimini's raging bar. By now the wind was almost south and over twenty knots, obviously clocking around in its prefrontal swing, and the seas were steep and sloppy as they peaked on the sudden shallows of the bar. The passage into Bimini is all the way at the south end of the bar now, although it had been across the middle the last time I had been there. Now the whole bar was a tumbled boil of white, and there was obviously no way to get inside it except to round that southern end. A passing sportfisherman pointed the route to us, and we finally swung to port and rolled our way along the beach in the bright blue water inside the bar, with surf crashing on both sides of us.

That wonderful feeling of easing at last into calm water after a rough passage had an extra kick to it here as we slid into the harbor and looked back at the spume and spray flying across the point, and I could be especially thankful that the front, which was obviously on its way, had not caught us outside on a lee shore. There are times when the bar would be impossible to negotiate, as we saw the next day.

We found a slip at Blue Water Marina, one of the many busy ones in this crowded sportfishing center. It was a fine, secure feeling to be at a concrete pier, with all services, while the wind hummed louder and louder in the rigging and moaned in that strange, ghostly fashion that is only produced by casuarinas. A big stand of these tall Australian pines lined the shore and broke some of the force of the wind as it increased steadily through the night.

Next to us was a little twenty-three-foot sloop with sitting head-room, and the young married couple aboard had a restless, uneasy manner as they did boat chores. They were obviously upset at the weather, and, when we got talking to them, admitted that they had been there for ten days and were a bit tired of Bimini. They were weekend sailors from a small lake in Oklahoma, where their boat was usually moored. It was their first boat, and they had learned about sailing as they puttered around the lake.

Adventure called, however. Husky and solidly built, the husband is a construction worker. They had decided to use the free time from a seasonal gap in employment during the winter by trailing the boat to Florida and heading for the Bahamas. In crossing the Gulf Stream, they were both seasick, and they had lost their bearings by the time they made a night landfall at Bimini. Unable to find the entrance, they

Surf from a Gulf Stream front on Bimini's beach

anchored off the bar and began calling on CB radio, the only kind they had aboard. Eventually, they managed to raise a woman ashore on Bimini and, after much back-and-forth, established their position. The woman said she would find someone to lead them into the harbor the next morning, and they spent a wild night tossing at anchor before their rescuer appeared.

Since then, they had not been able to work up any enthusiasm for going anywhere else, as the succession of fronts we had been having kept them locked in port. Soon they would have to do something, as their time was running out, but this was certainly no day for it. Even in the protection of the slip, the little boat heaved and rolled restlessly, and life aboard must have been a bit confining.

This was Super Bowl Sunday, which dawned bleak and rainy, with low clouds flying against a high overcast of gray, and the shallow waters of the bank off to leeward were a streaked pattern of white. It was also

Seagulls huddled on the pier when the front hit

Weezie's birthday, and the best present we could give her was to stay
snugly tied up and let it blow. I made the half-mile walk to the custom's
office at the seaplane ramp and had to pay eighteen dollars to enter the
Bahamas because it was a Sunday. (It is free on weekdays.) For all the
custom's man could have known, I could have stayed there a month
without checking in, but I had done the proper legal thing.

On the way back, I crossed over the island, which is about one
hundred yards wide and runs in a north-south direction, to look at the
sea on the Gulf Stream side, where nature was putting on an awesome
show. Out at sea, the dark line of the Stream was almost black under
the lowering sky, and a wall of bruised-looking clouds, shot through
with shreds of gray, towered over the horizon. Closer inshore, the water
became a vivid contrast in pale, luminous green, where the waves reared
high and then curled and crashed in a smother of foam that swirled
over the beach all the way up to the bank I stood on. To the south,
the bar was a solid line of white as far as the eye could see, and no boat

could have come in from offshore on this day. The wind, in the thirties and with stronger gusts, lashed the palm trees behind me into a clashing clatter, and the air was filled with fine spray from the surf.

Out in the Stream, separate rain squalls were breaking out of the purple clouds, and I could see that the front was just about here. There have been few times when I have seen one approach so graphically, and I had just made my way back to *Brunelle* when the wind whined up another fifteen knots or so and great sheets of rain flew horizontally across the marina. Seagulls gathered on the finger piers, huddled with backs to the wind, and even in the marina stray gusts set up little swirls of whitecaps. It was a great day to be in port.

8. Where's the Light?

If Super Bowl Sunday had been a great day to be in port, the next was an even greater one to be sailing. The squally front had been followed by a gradually clearing northwester, cool but not biting, that restored the sun to the pale waters of the Great Bahama Bank.

While the front raged, we had spent a lazy day at the Blue Water Marina. Jane and I read and listened to the football game, and the younger generation found that the Compleat Angler, one of Bimini's many convivial bars, had the game on TV, with a good portion of the island's population, both transient and resident, crowded in to watch it. They reported that the Bahamians in the throng were much more interested in the cheerleaders, bands, and halftime show than they were in the exploits of Terry Bradshaw and company. By the time the game was over, the party had progressed to the point where it could have been the Little League Championships from Williamsport, Pennsylvania, for all anyone in the Compleat Angler cared.

Jane and Alice had combined on a birthday feast for Weezie, which was ready when they came back from the bar—a lavish roast beef dinner starting with caviar hors d'oeuvres (complete with sour cream, chopped egg, and onion) and ending with a cake Alice had smuggled aboard. The evening tapered off in a pleasantly boozy sort of songfest, and there were a few cobwebs to sweep away in the fresh breeze of the morning.

The day started under high, gray clouds, but the forecast was good, so we powered out of the harbor and made our way onto the bank below South Bimini in the vicinity of the wreck of a concrete ship that makes a conspicuous landmark. Off Gun Cay we altered course to the eastward at 098°M and started the run of forty-six miles across the unmarked waters of the bank to Russell Beacon, the next navigational aid.

The Great Bahama Bank is a vast marine plateau that is largely underwater, in depths varying from a few inches to two fathoms or more. Here and there, it rises above the water, forming the low islands of the Bahamas, and stretches for over three hundred miles from Bimini in the north almost to the coast of Cuba in the south and beyond Ragged Island in the southeast. Cut through by the deep blue of the Tongue of the Ocean between Andros and Nassau, it extends eastward, at a greatest width of two hundred miles, to Long Island, the Exumas, and Eleuthera. North of the Northwest and Northeast Providence Channels that are its northern border is the companion Little Bahama Bank, upon which Grand Bahama and the Abacos sit. These two banks play a vital role in all the civilizations surrounding the North Atlantic basin. If they were not where they are, the return circulation of the waters pushed into the big bowl of the Gulf of Mexico by the trade winds would not be forced into the narrow strait between the banks and Florida, creating the "jet" effect of the Gulf Stream that sends its warmth all the way to the British Isles and Scandinavia. Without this influence, the northeast United States and all of Northern Europe would be no more habitable than Labrador and Greenland.

Aside from this geographical importance, both the Great and Little Bahama Banks provide some of the most fascinating sailing anywhere. The waters over the white sands of the bottom have a clarity, sparkle, and luminous translucence virtually unmatched in the world (certainly in the most frequented cruising areas), and it is a very special sensation to sail through them. The boat seems almost to be suspended in air rather than water because of the unusual clarity, and the pastels of the varying depths, in pale greens, blues, and creams, are a continuous delight to the eye. The bottom is always in plain sight as you skim along, with an occasional starfish, clump of grass, or rock as a punctuation mark on the expanse of white. In some areas coral heads and reefs show their colors, and there are grassy patches here and there. Sometimes the bottom is flat and featureless and at other times there are series of ridges, or whorls and corrugations, forming patterns. When the water is calm, there is an optical illusion that the bottom is going uphill, and you are sure that you will run aground in the next few yards. In fact, the continuous sight of the bottom takes some getting used to before a nervous skipper can settle down and accept it, and eyeball navigation is an essential part of bank operations. Only experience can teach the subtle shadings of color that come with varying depths and types of bottom or coral head. Tidal currents sweep the bank in unpredictable directions, depending on the wind, which makes a guessing game out of some of the longer legs without check points.

Crossing the Great and Little Bahama Banks in favorable weather can be one of the true delights of cruising, but conditions are not always benign. A strong breeze kicks up a short, steep, nasty chop over the banks because of the shallow water, and over the years I have heard many a horror tale of boats unable to make headway against the chop of a strong easterly, taking twenty-four hours or more to make thirty or forty miles. Anchoring on the bank to break up an overnight passage is fine if the weather behaves, but it is a rugged experience when a sea is running. On my first crossing of it in a motorsailer drawing six feet, we anchored in the center of the bank on a night of complete calm— so still that it was the only time in my life when I was conscious, as I sat on the flying bridge after everyone else had gone below, of absolute silence. Until you experience this, you don't realize that you are able to hear sound of some description, perhaps just the ticking of a watch or the far distant hum of passing cars, at almost every conscious moment. A boat is seldom without noise of some sort, but there was no sound whatever in the great empty, star-filled stillness of the bank that night, and I have never forgotten it.

I have also not forgotten that we were set off course by one of those unpredictable currents and spent the next morning bouncing over a succession of sand ridges before we finally got our bearings and found our way out onto the Tongue of the Ocean. Another problem at night is the presence of native fishing and freight boats operating without lights, and the *Yachtsman's Guide to the Bahamas,* that absolutely indispensable book for cruising in the area, warned that there are a great many pots on the bank, a hazard to night navigation. After our

The Flasher was the perfect sail for reaching

experience in the Gulf of Mexico, I had no desire to tangle with any more pots, but the *Guide* went on to say that they were there mainly in summer and fall, so I breathed a bit easier.

In a slow auxiliary, the distances on the bank are just enough so that you are on your own and away from any refuge for longer than on the usual port-to-port passage; you must either anchor on the bank or keep going through the night. I planned to do the latter if no problems arose.

As we put Gun Cay light over our stern and headed out across the great open expanse of pale green, the clouds began to break up, and the breeze settled in nicely on our port quarter at about sixteen knots. Soon the sun was warming our backs and chasing the chill of the frontal passage from the air, and we broke out the Flasher on an ideal point of sailing for it and romped toward the empty horizon. It was perfect sailing, with an almost flat sea and the bottom sliding swiftly beneath us. This route was claimed safe for five feet of draft, which did not give our four-foot-nine all that much clearance. We refused to worry about three inches, and *Brunelle* reeled off the miles in very satisfying fashion.

Because of the many possible variables in a bank crossing, I can't say that I was completely relaxed as we surged along. It was, without doubt, a glorious sail, but behind the enjoyment there was always that same old nagging anxiety about the unfortunate things that could happen, and I wanted to get the passage over with, even though I delighted in the conditions. At the rate we were going, which I figured at a bit over six knots, I expected to pick up Russell Beacon just after dark (about 1815 at that time of year); as the sun sank redly into an empty horizon astern, I began to search the darkening wall of night over the bow for the first pinprick of light from Russell.

Nothing showed, and by the time full darkness descended on us, there was still no sign of anything man-made in any direction. The stars filled the sky to the very horizon in the clear Bahamian air, but no flash of white popped out of the east to reassure us, and there went the end of a perfect day. I couldn't imagine that we had been set so far off course that the light couldn't be seen at all, if not on the nose then at least somewhere. If we had been, there was no way to figure a course correction. In daylight, the nature of the bottom, with grass to the north and brown sand to the south, can be of some help, but night blots it all out; my only choice was to stand on as before, trusting that my course had been correct and that the light was not working—a not unusual situation in the Bahamas and all through the southern islands.

There was some reassurance when small freight boats appeared from ahead and passed us on a reciprocal course. It can be folly to assume anything about the course or actions of another vessel, but they did seem to be on a direct course across the bank. The next marker would be Northwest Channel Light, fifteen miles beyond Russell, and it was an anxious few hours as we swept on into the empty darkness. To complicate matters, the breeze began to fade as the center of the high moved toward us, slowing our rate of advance and delaying the expected time of picking up NW Light. As we wallowed down to four and then three knots, I debated turning on the engine, but if we were off course, I did not want to charge ahead into possible shoals and reefs at the Joulter Cays north of Andros, so we drifted along, peering forward and trying to will the light to show. Finally, with the breeze all but gone, it popped into view at 2230 right where it should be. So Russell had to have been inoperative.

I breathed a sigh of relief and turned on the engine, and the rest of the night was a power run in a total calm across the Tongue of the Ocean and Northwest Providence Channel, forty-nine miles from NW Light to Nassau. Remembering some turbulent passages over this route, I was not too unhappy about the calm. There was a little extra fillip to the night in that Alice and Weezie had never before done watch standing through a whole night, and they found the experience exciting. It was a dark one, but clear, and the stars were brilliant all the way down to the rim of the sea.

With the dawn, New Providence's low silhouette, topped by the ball of Lyford Cay's water tower, was there on the horizon, and we chugged toward it over a slaty sea of molten lead. Not a ripple broke the surface until we were almost to the entrance, when vagrant puffs began to fill in from the south, signalling that the center of the high

Nassau Harbor is always filled with a mix of vessels

had gone by and that another frontal cycle was about to complete itself.

There is always a sense of excitement in entering Nassau Harbor, with great white cruise ships towering over it at the Prince George Docks, the incredible dilapidation and clutter of the Haitian sloops anchored beyond the docks, and the glossy collection of yachts at anchor and in the marinas at the eastern end of the harbor's long, narrow open-ended cut between Paradise (ex-Hog) Island and New Providence. While the Bahamas were not our ultimate goal—we still had many horizons to cross—they are the final target for many cruising boats and a great place to cruise. We had a good feeling of accomplishment in being there and planned to hang around for a while and enjoy the cruising. The next worry boxes were pleasantly off in the future.

9. *Bahamian Interlude*

Nassau was a time for settling in. Up until now it had all been a rush and an agitation to get the boat together and make schedule around Florida and into the Bahamas. Now we had time to sit back and relax for a while. Specifically, we had to settle the sale of *Tanagra,* our Out Island 36, since the bank would own a good percentage of *Brunelle* until *Tanagra* was sold. She was being bought by Yacht Charters of Nassau, run by Captain Bud Geiselman and his wife, Rickie, who also operate East Bay Marina, hard by the Paradise Island Bridge in Nassau, where we were basing.

Not the most elaborate of Nassau's marinas by a long shot, East Bay is small and somewhat ramshackle, with a mix of locally owned boats, charter yachts from the YCN fleet, and transients, who are shoe-horned, rafted, and stacked in a manner most sardines would not tolerate. The Geiselmans and their two children live on a houseboat at the marina, so there is close supervision, and it is the most conveniently located of all the marinas—right across the street from East Bay Shopping Center, which even has a supermarket. The Bridge Restaurant is also across the street, and it is a walk of only a mile or so to downtown Bay Street if you do have business there.

Bud had brought *Tanagra* down from her berth at Oriental, North Carolina, a cold January trip down the Intracoastal Waterway. Most of the fronts that had pursued us around the tip of Florida had hit him with considerably greater authority and lower temperatures on his way down through the Carolinas, Georgia, and northern Florida. Now our two boats were a couple of slips apart at the marina, and we were awaiting receipt of insurance funds Bud was using to buy *Tanagra.* One of his charter boats had been lost over New Year's while crossing the bank from the Exumas back to Nassau. She had been dismasted, and

Brunelle *at East Bay*

the broken section of mast had punched a hole in the hull, sinking the boat. Fortunately, she was cruising in company, so no one was lost, but the wreck could not be located by air search, and the insurance on her was being used to replace her with *Tanagra.* The transaction involved receipt of funds from England, conversion to United States currency, and then payment to me, with transfer of documentation—all of which meant considerable red tape.

Meanwhile, we were enjoying life at the marina, watching boats come and go and making friends with other cruising people. One day we spied *Euphoria* in the harbor and had a reunion with the Rabows. Their story of crossing the bank was quite different from ours. Making little progress into a heavy head sea, they had decided to anchor near Russell at nightfall rather than plug on through the dark. When the sun set and they could not see Russell, they were sure that they had dragged anchor away from it, and they spent a miserable night pounding so hard that they remained in the cockpit the whole time, feeling that they were being blown back along their hard-won course. At dawn, they were amazed that the spindly beacon was right where it had been the afternoon before.

It then took them half the next day to slam their way under power the fifteen miles to Northwest Light, fighting the short, steep chop of the bank. They thought it would be a relief to get out onto the deep water of the Tongue of the Ocean, but found only mountainous seas there, breaking steeply. They finally crept under the lee of Chub Cay in the Berry Islands for another bad night at anchor and waited three days for a crossing to Nassau, still in rough conditions.

A small schooner we met at East Bay had broken loose from her anchor while near Russell under similar circumstances and had been blown so far across the bank that she took a whole day to fight her way back to Russell after some trouble getting her bearings. A husband and wife in a bugeye ketch had taken seven hours to power from Russell to Northwest in a head sea, and they too had holed up at Chub Cay for a few days before they could face the rest of the passage to Nassau. Russell had evidently been out of operation for several weeks, to no one's surprise. After hearing these tales, I realized how lucky we had been with our mere few hours of anxiety over trying to find the light.

While we sat at East Bay waiting for the financial red tape to unwind and swapping sea stories, we became aware for the first time of some of the nuances of retirement. We had never been immobilized in one place this long on any previous cruise, as they had all been short ones in time snatched from duties in New York. Until this cruise, we had been on the move and loaded with projects, but here we sat, with time to kill, and each morning as I planned how to fill the idle days, I was reminded of the wry advice I had heard someone give another retiree: "Don't go to the bank and the post office on the same day."

We did have projects, though. The trailboard knocked loose by Gulf Stream seas had to be fixed, in almost a replica of the work done on the other trailboard in Miami, so I spent some time tracking down a Mr. Butler, who had been recommended as the best workman in Nassau for boat carpentry and fiber glass repairs. I finally found him in another marina—he evidently freelanced in all the facilities in Nassau. When, after a day or two, he got around to *Brunelle,* he did an excellent job, comparable to the Miami one and at almost exactly the same price.

I had an introduction to the squash racquets club in Nassau, and a few brisk games there helped to pass the days. It was great fun to challenge a variety of players, from the club champion to a novice. We used the English ball, which makes for a very different game from the American one, and the activity at the courts was a world apart from the life at East Bay.

The comings and goings of cruising yachts were a constant entertainment at East Bay. All of the sailors had stories to tell and notes to compare, and there was a great deal of visiting back and forth along the piers. The real social center for the ladies was at the laundry machines at the gas dock. There was one washer and one dryer, operated by special tokens, and there was a steady flow of traffic at them, with lots of chatter while waiting for someone's load to finish. The water hose also fostered a lot of visiting. There were several outlets for hoses but only enough pressure for one boat at a time to use water, and everyone kept a sharp watch to grab their turn. There was great conster-

Our favorite name for a Bahamian workboat

nation one time when the professional captain of a boat spent most of the day using the hose to work on his teak, until a delegation of angry owners and wives gave him the message.

East Bay is right next to Potter's Cay, which is where all the native sloops now congregate, unloading fish, conch, and inter-island freight (our favorite name for one was *Big Belly Tina*), and the activity there is constant and noisy from the first glimmer of dawn far into the night. When two Bahamians meet on the street or on the piers of Potter's Cay, the conversation, which may be concerned with anything from the weather to the health of someone's wife, is carried on in deafening decibels. The conversationalists may be perhaps a foot or two apart, but they shout at each other as though they were on opposite sides of the harbor, and a friendly chat about the weather sounds like the last confrontation before a declaration of war. Since all this begins at the crack of dawn at Potter's Cay, our days started early, and an added

81

Native boats being worked on at Potter's Cay

touch was the aroma of conch, strongly fishy, and the smells of cooking wafting on the breeze from the native food stand on the Cay. If you wanted local atmosphere, this was the place to be.

Jane is a very relaxed person, and this spell of inaction did not bother her at all. She is content to sit and read by the hour, and she is also perpetually involved with knitting or needlepoint. There is never a question of her becoming bored, and this self-sufficiency is a wonderful trait in a cruising companion.

The quiet time in Nassau also gave us a better chance for a husband-and-wife relationship. After all the crash landings in the Keys and rough Gulf Stream passages, we were gradually finding out about some of those questions raised at the start of our adventure. Naturally our cabin was an important part of our life, and we had by now adjusted to the special features of dealing with our folding bunk. I usually made it up at dinner time so that there wouldn't be any problem when sleep hit us hard later in the evening. For a while I was forever becoming wedged and entangled in the manipulation of the cushions. It was almost as frustrating a routine as the famous act by W. C. Fields with an uncooperative pool cue, and mornings were equally as embroiled as I tried to put the thing back together while Jane cooked breakfast.

Practice made it easier, though, and I finally figured out where to put the backrest (later to become part of the mattress) while upending the mattress to flip the leaf that had to fold out and be part of the support for the two-piece mattress—simultaneously keeping sheets and pillows out of the way but handy enough to be within reach when their time came. All this was something like assembling an express wagon at midnight on Christmas Eve with the instructions missing, and I am now quite proud of my prowess.

Sleeping in it took some adjusting, too. We always sleep with Jane on my right (if we don't, I can't sleep a wink), which meant that she was wedged against the bulkhead and had to crawl across me for nocturnal visits to the head. Sometimes I would stay asleep and she could make it across me without any problem, but other times I would wake up and try to sit up to make her passage easier, thus meeting her in mid-air in an unintentional wrestling match. Any other wrestling in the bunk had to take the navigation table, low over the foot of the bunk, into account, but all of this worked out day by day after the table received a few sharp kicks. Soon we were pretty well settled in to our home afloat (one set of questions more or less answered).

After a while, with a weekend approaching and no sign of *Tanagra*'s sale being consummated, we decided to head for the Exumas in hopes that we might finish our business when the financial centers opened the next week. We had a brisk, close reach for the thirty-plus miles to Highborne Cay in a fresh northeaster, once again enjoying the magic moment when the little lump of its highest hill looms on the horizon; we found that it has become the crossroads of the northern Exumas. In previous years, it had been a quiet little place with few boats, but now there is a long pier that fills with boats each afternoon, plus an overflow anchored in the tiny harbor and outside in the roadstead.

We were able to berth alongside, and we discovered that several boats seemed to have taken up semi-permanent residence so that there

The marina at Highborne Cay

was a back-fence sort of neighborliness, with children trading between boats and a great mixing of adults at happy hour—all very pleasant and sociable, but far from the isolation we had always associated with being in the Exumas.

And speaking of happy hour, we discovered in some dismay that our refrigerator seemed to be on the blink. The compressor works off the main engine, so the engine has to be run an hour a day to keep the holding plates charged. There are no services at Highborne, but someone mentioned that Jerry Hefty, who had run the charter ketch *Lelani* for years and had retired ashore at Highborne, knew a lot about refrigeration. I found him visiting another boat, and we renewed an acquaintance of years ago as I told him my problem—no indirect approach this time.

He soon determined that the current was blocked between the thermostat at the holding plates and the compressor, so that it was not calling for the compressor to start. He devised a manual control via a wire from the compressor that could be attached to a live terminal on a solenoid switch with an alligator clamp. We had to attach and detach it to start and stop the compressor, and it worked fine as long as we remembered it. Helpful neighbors again; my favorite repair service.

Norman's Cay, next to Highborne, used to be a favorite stop, but new owners, amid dark rumors of drug traffic, have barred all visitors, so we sailed on by on a quiet morning to Shroud Cay, where we did find the Exuman isolation we expected. We spent a lazy afternoon there doing our form of "sissy snorkeling," in which we drift along in our Avon inflatable dinghy and sightsee the life on the coral heads through a glass bottom bucket. Sometimes I do regular snorkeling, although, as I have said, I have never been very good under water. Jane cannot be persuaded that she is enjoying herself while snorkeling, and this form of underwater viewing is an acceptable substitute. It works when the water is shallow enough, and Shroud Cay has a fine collection of small heads in shallow water all along the shore. It is now a national park, and, with its arc of dazzling white beach, scrubby tangle of semi-tropical vegetation, and surrounding waters of every pale hue imaginable, it wraps up the Exuman experience in one neat package. The anchorage is protected from east, north, and south, but wide open to the west, and usually has a slight surge. At sunset we sat in the cockpit and watched the big red ball dip toward the empty sheen of the bank, an experience that heightens an awareness of endless space. And to a sailor, behind the peace and beauty of the scene there is also an awareness of that open bearing, and the lurking thought that this is no place to be if the wind should come in northwest.

It didn't, and our run back to Nassau the next morning was over a mirror-flat bank, with the bottom as clear and close as I have ever seen it. Never has that illusion of being headed uphill into shallow water been stronger, and I was subconsciously waiting for the crunch of keel on sand most of the time, even though I knew it wasn't going to happen. Nassau's high rises and the big stand of casuarinas on Rose Island popped up on schedule, and just as we went by Porgee Rock at the eastern entrance to the harbor, a fresh westerly came in on the nose,

Tanagra *(left) and* Brunelle *(center) at East Bay Marina*

and I thought of the Shroud Cay anchorage.

Bud had good news on finances, and the transfer of *Tanagra* was completed in the next two days. Soon afterward when *Tanagra* pulled away from the marina and disappeared around the point of Potter's Cay on her first charter, I felt like the father of a teenage daughter who has just gone out the door on her first date. She had been good to us and we wished her well.

We were becoming quite used to marina living, enjoying the lazy life at East Bay while it lasted. Some nights we ate aboard, others we visited Bridge Inn or the Pilot House for something fancy, and occasionally, when we were especially lazy, I would walk across to the shopping center and bring back a supper of chicken and cole slaw from a Kentucky Fried Chicken shop. One night I happened to notice that

A strong easterly blowing against an Exuman beach

they also served cracked conch and decided to try some in place of the
chicken. It turned out to be a delicious Bahamian dish, though it might
have surprised Colonel Sanders.

With our business finally wrapped up, we were free to move about
again, and, with friends aboard week by week, we made two cruises to
Eleuthera and one more to the Exumas. The latter was in a windy week,
and we took something of a beating crossing the bank and thrashing
our way down the Exumas as far as Sampson Cay. On our way back
from Sampson, we made the twenty-eight miles to Shroud Cay in
exactly four hours under reefed main and staysail, which averaged a
bit above the hull speed for a twenty-nine-foot waterline and was
a real express-train sail in the lee of the low islands. At Shroud, the
easterly, which was well over thirty knots, played a frantic tune in
the rigging, but we were snug under the lovely white beach. The next
day's sail back to Nassau in a moderating breeze was another swift
passage.

On our first trip to Eleuthera we had arranged to pick up our New Jersey neighbors, Hazel and Dave Freeman, at the Current Club on the northwest tip of Eleuthera. We had not been in there since 1962, when our boat was a twenty-four-foot Amphibi-Ette with two-foot-four draft. But the *Yachtsman's Guide* said that the controlling draft was three feet in the side channel from Current Cut into the Club. This looked like it might be a problem, but a phone call from Nassau to the Current Club before we took off gave assurance that there was plenty of water and that there was a boat with five-foot draft based there. Once again we were in a frontal cycle as we took off from Nassau and headed northeast up the cays between Nassau and Eleuthera in a warm, puffy southwester, with clouds gathering more thickly as we reeled off the miles. If we couldn't make it into the Club, there were two anchorages nearby on Current Island that we could use, effecting our pickup by powerboat from the Club, but we thought we would give the channel a try first.

We arrived off the channel at last twilight on the last two hours of a rising tide, and I tried to find the best water at the channel entrance without benefit of eyeballing, which was ineffective in the gathering gloom. Poking cautiously, we nudged onto sand twice and backed off, but we were able to make VHF contact with people from the club on one of the boats at their pier, and they promised to send a guide out. Soon a small powerboat was alongside, and we gratefully followed it up the winding channel along the shore. We had been too far out from the beach in our efforts to find the entrance, as it was right along the land, too close for comfort for a stranger. The tide was ripping by the pier and it took the entire population of the Current Club, guests and management alike, to sweat us into the end of it in what was by now complete darkness. On the other side, the horizon was wide open, but we were assured that a bar there gave protection from southerlies.

Dinner ashore was pleasantly informal, and during the night, the expected front whistled through on schedule. Again, a stand of casuarinas was along the shore to windward of us, and the frontal gusts moaned and sighed as they swished through the tall trees. It wasn't an especially virulent front, but it did mean a day in port while the northwester moderated. It was an eerie experience to gaze to the south across the wide open expanse of water, watching the gusts of wind skitter away to leeward, but the off-white paleness of the water, milky under the wind's agitation, told how shallow it was. The bar actually dried out a bit in spots at low tide.

Although it was to windward, we decided the next day to head through Current Cut, with its racing tidal flow, for Spanish Wells, an unusual settlement on an island off the northwest tip of Eleuthera. Jane always makes the cabin secure for sea, and she is so conscientious at it that I never give it a thought, but this time, when we hit the first steep sea on the open bank outside Current Cut, there was a loud crash from below as our bow rose and dipped. I had always made sure that the controversial table was down and locked in place with its leg securely on the cabin sole whenever we went to sea, as I didn't trust the longer hook that had been our solution to folding it up against the bulkhead back in Tampa Bay. However, I had never made a point about this having to be done, and I had forgotten it this time. The noise had come from the table, with its weighty extra leaf, crashing to the deck while ripping out the whole piano hinge that held the bottom of it to the bulkhead.

Aside from that, we had a good beat to windward across the lime-green waters, with the seas gradually calming as we neared Spanish Wells, and we were well snugged down at Sawyer's Marina soon after lunch. Spanish Wells is unique. There is no place else like it in the Bahamas or anywhere else, and a visit there is a rare experience. The harbor is a long, narrow cut between two small islands, reached by a tortuously twisting channel that winds through the flats for a few miles and is marked by tiny stakes that are sometimes submerged and often just plain disappear. The houses, in every shade from dazzling white through soft pastels to glaring purples and oranges, line the harbor front to starboard, with a bustle of native workboats berthed along the long quay that follows most of the shoreline. Sawyer's is well up the harbor, one of the neatest and best tended marinas I have ever been in, featuring a large shed that houses two enormous, glossy power yachts with hailing ports in Texas and Oklahoma.

Spanish Wells got its name when galleons of Spain used to stop there to take on water on their long voyages home from the Caribbean. The wells have long since disappeared, but the name remains. It was settled during the American Revolution by Royalists from the colonies, who fled to it in loyalty to George III when the Yankee rebels began to win their struggle. The same families have lived there ever since, with a tremendous amount of inbreeding, and a handful of family names, like Pinder, Sawyer, Higgs, and Sweeting, covers the majority of the population. No blacks have ever settled in Spanish Wells, and for years none who worked there could remain after sundown. Things are not that rigid now, but it remains an all-white enclave—and the residents have a distinctive look.

Generations of inbreeding have produced a type that is gaunt, with prominent nose and chin, sandy complexion, blond or reddish-blond hair, and a host of freckles. The island men, who all wear broad-brimmed straw hats, look so much alike that you are sure you are talking to the same man again when you are first greeted by the dockmaster, then someone selling bread, and another man offering to act as a guide. While this might be imagined to have fostered a backward society, the people of Spanish Wells are industrious and enterprising, and, through an economy largely based on lobstering, have developed the most prosperous community in the Bahamas. The houses are freshly painted, and many are new, with neat lawns and gardens; almost everyone has a new car in the driveway, even though the island is less than two miles long; and enormous TV antennas, high enough to bring in Florida broadcasts, tower over almost every house. The teenage population tears around the quiet streets on motorbikes.

It is a very religious community, with churches in evidence all through the town, and on many nights of the week the sound of hymn singing soars over the water. Liquor is not sold by the bottle, although a couple of the restaurants serve drinks, but the markets are otherwise well stocked.

Spanish Wells craftsmen are noted for their work in many fields, especially marine repairs, and they are unbelievably conscientious about

One of the new houses on Spanish Wells

doing good work. I have always remembered the way an engine mechanic answered me once when I checked with him about when he
could do some work on *Tanagra.* "Right after now," was his answer,
as he picked up his tool box and headed for the boat.

I had hoped that this would be a good place to have the table
repaired, but my first efforts to find a carpenter were not successful.
The man recommended as the best was hard at work on a major project
on a lobster boat and was very apologetic about not being able to help
me. "If I said I would, I would only let you down," he said. "I have
to finish the work on this boat, because she's due to go back to work."

He thought a while and then said that his uncle, Dot Higgs, just
might be able to help me. "He's mostly retired, getting kind of old now,
but he takes on work when he finds the time."

I wound my way through back lanes to Higgs's little house and
found him cooking up an enormous fish chowder.

"Live by myself," he said. "Have to do my own cooking."

He was a diminutive, stocky man in his late seventies or early eighties, with the Spanish Wells look to his eyes, mouth, and freckles, though his own cooking seemed to have kept him from the gauntness of most of his fellow townsmen. He agreed to come down the next morning, and there he was at breakfast time, tool kit in hand. He spent a couple of hours drilling and gluing, with a bit of help from Dave Freeman and me when needed, while we discussed the affairs of the world. He eventually had the table firmly back on its hinges.

"What do I owe you?" I asked as he started packing his tools. Looking up shyly, he said, "Would three dollars be too much?"

It was all I could do to contain myself, as I gave him double that and thanked him very much. We should break down in Spanish Wells more often, we all agreed.

We liked Spanish Wells so much that we came back again the next week with a new crew, Al and Genevieve Gagnebin. When you have a limited time to cruise and don't want to be held in port by weather, Nassau is an excellent base. Rose Island, just a few miles away, is a great day anchorage, and no matter what direction the wind is from, there is a downwind target for cruising. Andros and the Berry Islands are to the west and northwest, Eleuthera stretches from northeast of Nassau to due east, and the Exumas are southeast. They are the preferred area, but the wind is often in the southeast in good weather; if you don't feel like a slug to windward, you can take off on a broad reach for the Spanish Wells area in the lee of the cays that string out between Nassau and Current Cut.

Once again there was a front approaching when the Gagnebins arrived, about the twelfth front of the new year since our nasty one at the christening party, and we decided to reach toward Spanish Wells in the day-before southerly and sit out the expected frontal day in its fascinating surroundings. This worked out as expected, starting with a great sail over the deep-blue waters of Northeast Providence Channel, reaching at close to seven knots with the low, rocky cays sliding astern, thin pencil lines on the horizon to starboard, and the wrecked freighter on a reef at the entrance to the bank off Spanish Wells popping up

Brunelle *underway off Nassau*

ahead as the first landmark in that area. It was a beautiful day at sea, also one of the few I remember with two ladies doing needlepoint in the cockpit. While the rollicking blue waves hissed their whitecaps at us and slid by under the hull, Jane and Gen were peacefully plying their needles through their patterns and perfectly happy in their work. Jane seemed quite surprised when I made some small remark about the incongruity of it, at least in my eyes. I was definitely not complaining, but somehow it didn't look very salty.

As expected, the next day was a frontal lay-day, and we poked

Jane at her needlepoint

around the town, especially taken by the neatness and sometimes-gaudy decoration of the many new houses. On the north shore, the norther sent a froth of small breakers across the reefs that stretch far out from the beach, but *Brunelle* rode easily in the complete protection of Sawyer's.

Next to us was a Whitby 42 from Montreal, with her owner and his wife and the owner's brother and sister-in-law on board. We had gotten to know her professional captain at East Bay while he was waiting for them to arrive, and they had then given him time off and had taken the boat out by themselves. He had asked me to keep an eye on them if we happened to meet, since they were new owners and this was their first venture alone, so I introduced myself to them. The owner was Jean-Louis, a jolly, robust man with a crinkly-eyed smile, and his wife, Claudine—boyishly slim, with her dark hair cropped to match. Their English was a bit uncertain, though better than my French, but Al Gagnebin, who is the retired chairman of International Nickel and of Swiss descent, had grown up speaking French at home; he moved in with relish as interpreter, rolling his "r's" and tossing idioms around with abandon.

Jean-Louis and Claudine lit up like candles when they heard him, and the two crews were soon deep in happy hour. It seems that they were terrified by the shallow-water navigation on the banks. Claudine was the navigator, and she rolled her eyes and sighed as she admitted this.

"The water ees so skinny," she cried in her delightful accent. "I do not trust where we are going when I see the bottom all the time."

They had been confused by the poor markings of the winding approach to Spanish Wells and had run aground on their way in, and they had been there several days getting up their courage, as they were very reluctant to leave. Jean-Louis explained that they couldn't stay in Spanish Wells forever, because he only had a two-week break and had to go back to his practice as an orthodontist.

"I cannot stay away too long," he said. "I must go back to my patients and tighten up all those leetle screws on their braces." He gave a very French shrug, with a wide grin, as though apologizing that anyone could be in such a ridiculous dilemma.

Claudine and I spent some time going over the charts and the *Guide,* but the worried frown never left her face as I pointed out the routes out of Spanish Wells.

"We're going to Hatchet Bay tomorrow," I said. "If you'd like, you can follow us down there."

"Oh could we?" she cried in obvious delight. "Would you mind? I would feel so very much better if that could be so."

And so, on the bright morrow, with the clearing northwester on our quarter, we led them out the harbor and across the bank to Current Cut, and the Whitby 42 was never more than one hundred yards off our stern for the next three days. We had some wonderfully dégagé conversations on VHF, and each night the rendezvous turned into a fine party, trading equally between the boats. Via Hatchet Bay and West Bottom Harbor on Rose Island, we led them safely back to Nassau so that the children of Montreal could have beautiful straight teeth.

10. Onward and Southward

This was the end of our marking time in the Bahamas. Back in Nassau, we had one final day for poking around, and it was well used in one of our favorite junkets—a sail to Rose Island. This ten-mile-long splinter of land stretching northeastward just outside the eastern entrance to Nassau Harbor is privately owned and sparsely settled. Bottom Harbor on its south side is a good anchorage in all but strong southerlies, but its best feature is a gorgeous beach on the north side of its western tip, backed by two magnificent stands of casuarinas.

Beaches are public in the Bahamas, and this one is a favorite for day trips. Even on a Sunday, when dozens of local boats come out for picnics, it doesn't seem crowded; it is as pretty a spot as anywhere in the Out Islands. I had touted it to the Gagnebins as a lovely place to explore, so we eyeballed our way carefully through the many, but highly visible fringing reefs to anchor close to the beach in water so clear over white sand that every grain could be seen, with the anchor and rode as visible as if they had been in air.

Al and Gen took the dinghy to explore ashore, and, as they wandered along the beach, I was horrified to see a horde of people emerge from the casuarinas and take over the beach, so that a section of it would have made Coney Island on the Fourth of July seem deserted. The Gagnebins walked right in among them and were swallowed up in the crowd, and I couldn't imagine what was going on. I had never seen the place one tenth as crowded.

When Al and Gen got back and I started to apologize, they laughed and said, not in the least, they had had a fine time. It seems that this was a Club Med picnic (Club Med has a place on Paradise Island), and they had enjoyed mingling with the crowd and making friends. Al has a lively interest in people, and an especially Gallic

The anchorage at Rose Island

preoccupation with young ladies in bathing suits; he enjoyed himself thoroughly. They were even invited to join the chow line at lunch— "No one checks up or knows the difference," they were told—but they hadn't mixed in that far. Everyone was having a fine time, they reported.

It was time to leave *Brunelle* for a few weeks and tend to things at home. It was now early March, and such realities of life as the income tax loomed over us. Jane also had a paper to give at a literary club she belongs to (her attendance record had not been very good that winter). She had been reading Matthew Arnold all through the islands, and now she had to write the paper and present it. Also, there were squash tournaments for me to play in, but, most pressing of all, that old problem of uncooperative teeth had cropped up, and I needed emergency attention for an abcess. When we arrived home, I went right from the airport to the dentist, but at least the abcess had waited until we were ready to go home to act up—not in the middle of the Great Bahama Bank or some such isolated place.

Friends tended to *Brunelle* and delivered her to George Town, Exuma, during March, and we went back to her on Easter to continue our passage southward. George Town was the limit of my previous cruising in the Bahamas, and from there for the eight hundred miles to the Virgins, it would all be new territory for us. In my usual approach to such a venture, my feelings were a mixture of excitement and apprehension. I had heard and read tales of the difficulties of this so-called "Thorny Path," and my wakeful night hours were filled with visions of thirty-knot trade winds on the nose for weeks on end, unmarked reefs, and Dominican Republic officials in hob-nailed boots tromping over the boat and shouting at me in Spanish. I did look forward, though, with some pleasure to such places as Long Island and the farther Out Islands of the Bahamas, and the Turks and Caicos Group. Somehow, this British colony that lies on an isolated stretch of the Atlantic between the Bahamas and Hispaniola had always seemed as remote and outlandish a place as I could imagine; it was a challenge to be headed there.

On our flight south, between National Airlines and Bahamasair, a small bag was lost. It contained a newly bought Hewlett-Packard computer and a specially programmed navigation system, put together for me by Mort Rogoff, who was writing a book on the subject of computer navigating and wanted me to try it out. We wouldn't need celestial here, but I thought I would be using it later on in the lower Caribbean. I had not done any celestial since subchaser days in 1944, and Rogoff's system would have been a good way to get back in practice. The bag also contained the log and notes from the first two months of the cruise. It never turned up, and I eventually received the standard four-hundred-dollar compensation. It is extremely frustrating when irreplacable material is lost, and "nobody knows from nothing" no matter to whom you talk at the airlines.

John Yeoman had brought *Brunelle* down from Staniel Cay and had her waiting at the Exuma Services Dock. He met us at the charter plane that had flown us from Nassau. There was an interesting moment when a young lady who had been aboard for a week and was taking the plane back passed a young lady who had come down with us to be aboard for the next week. John, who had not been able to prevent this little confrontation, drifted behind a baggage cart and pretended to be studying the airport windsock during the encounter.

The girl with us was Ellis Taussig (everyone thinks her name is Alice or Ellen), who had never been on anything bigger than a Sunfish. Dark and petite, with a lively curiosity, she learned fast and was a good shipmate. John had taken *Tanagra* on several ferrying trips over the years and had the additional background of commanding a river gunboat in Viet Nam. Slender and wiry, he is a quick and helpful hand on a boat, with a pixie sense of humor that enlivens life aboard.

Easter Monday was hot and airless, with Elizabeth Harbor at George Town a plate of glass under the bright sun. We left early and powered toward the eastern entrance, with our wake arrowing a vee across the unruffled surface. In Nassau, we had been able to get Miami VHF weather, but here we were too far for that and had to depend on commercial radio (ZNS, Nassau) for what information we could glean, which was meager. The Coast Guard broadcasts on Single Sideband are all but useless, as they talk in vast generalities about ocean areas of thousands of square miles. The breeze was supposed to come in southeast, but all we saw was a gentle northerly, and we finally gave it a chance at the sails in late morning, mainly for the joy of turning off the engine. We were headed for Cape Santa Maria on Long Island, a run of less than thirty miles from George Town, so we could turn the engine on later and still make it before dark.

In checking our two guidebooks, Harry Kline's *Yachtsman's Guide* and the hard-cover *Cruising Guide to the Bahamas and Caribbean* by Stone and Hart, there was disagreement between them on entering Calabash Bay at Cape Santa Maria. We came in via Kline and went out the next morning via Stone and Hart and felt that the latter offered an easier route to negotiate as it is more direct to the anchorage off Cape Santa Maria Club, which was surgy even on a calm night. The Club is a small resort with units strung along a fine stretch of beach.

During the small hours, I heard the wind in the rigging setting up a little tune. It was the end of the calm, and it would be some time before we found ourselves in another one. The breeze was from 060 degrees and piping up nicely when we powered out the Stone and Hart exit and north around Cape Santa Maria, giving it the recommended wide berth. In an hour we set main and jib and squared away for a reach down the outside of Long Island. Featureless cliffs stretched for miles into the distance as we reacted to the deep-water feel of Exuma Sound and began to make knots. I was convinced the breeze was going to head us by going southeast, and I started out by holding offshore a bit from the direct course of 160 degrees (I refer to magnetic courses at all times). But as the day wore on, the breeze held steady in the same direction, and we coasted along on a delightful reach, averaging six knots for the forty-two miles to Clarence Town.

Long before the shoreline tells you anything significant, Clarence Town can be picked out by a pair of remarkable landmarks. Two enormous white churches on high land above the harbor stand out from afar, gleaming brilliantly in the sunlight. One is Catholic; the other, Anglican. Both were built by the same priest, who started as an Anglican and had a large, imposing edifice erected for his flock, doing much of the work himself. Then he converted to Catholicism, and his new flock had to have an equally magnificent building. Now they provide a slightly incongruous and highly visible addition to the rather featureless landscape, the only such phenomenon in all the Out Islands.

There were several cruising boats at the one big town dock in Clarence Town's small harbor, where yachts may tie up free on the north side, leaving the south side open for commercial craft and the mail boat. Water, however, was quite expensive, as the minimum charge was eight dollars no matter how much you actually needed.

The dockmaster was a cheerful, stocky Bahamian named Henry Major, who was helpful and hospitable in getting us settled, and, in our short stay in Clarence Town, we found that the Major family is a major factor indeed on the local scene. Henry controls the pier, and his wife, an efficient, forceful, deep-voiced woman, controls almost everything else. She manages the supermarket, which was surprisingly well-stocked for such an isolated place, and was very helpful in advising us on where

The town dock at Clarence Town

to find such items as bread and fruit.

I wanted to keep going, but Jane made a strong point over stocking up on fruit, bread, and vegetables before we set out. It had been Easter Monday when we left George Town, a holiday throughout the islands, and we were low on fresh stuff, so I relented, and we toured Clarence Town in the morning. Supplies were not ready right away because of the holiday preceding, but bread was a-baking at Captain Jim's Bread Box, and a well-dressed and beautifully spoken woman on the pier promised us fruit and vegetables in a few hours.

While we were waiting for these to materialize, we wandered the hilly streets of Clarence Town, whose houses were set far apart amid open fields, with fish nets drying on racks, and youngsters and livestock tumbling about in the yards. Hibiscus and dusty oleanders lined the roads and rioted through the yards, and as we climbed higher toward the great church buildings, magnificent vistas opened up across the whitecapped blue of Exuma Sound beyond the harbor. The churches exuded a musty, seedy grandeur that was at once proud and pathetic, but they were obviously in use and an important part of the community.

The commissioner's office was high on an open hillside, and we stopped there to inquire about checking out of the Bahamas, since Clarence Town was evidently the last port of entry we would hit. The guide books said Mayaguana was one, but checking with northbound crews at the pier, we found that they had been unable to clear in there, as the service had been abandoned. Mayaguana, they said, was a forlorn, forgotten outpost of the outermost Out Islands. The commissioner was a genial, rotund man, excessively polite and pleasant, who said yes, he could check us out, but he had no forms for the purpose and would just have to endorse the transire we had picked up in Bimini in January, clearing us to the Turks and Caicos. He mentioned that things had not quite settled down after Easter weekend. "Easter is, after all," he said, "the queen of religious festivals."

When we got back to *Brunelle,* the mail boat had just arrived, and the pier was an incredible bustle of activity in the bright, hot sun. Everybody in Clarence Town must have been there, greeting arriving friends, seeing someone off, or collecting incoming freight. And who was in charge of checking the freight out to consignees? Why Mrs. Major, of course. With a clip board in front of her, she knelt among piles of goods that had been off-loaded, and the citizenry lined up in front of her. One by one she checked them off as they collected their packages, while children ran hide-and-seek routes through the piles of gear, dogs barked, and passengers on the boat waved and whistled. In half an hour, the boat had pulled away and chugged out of the harbor, the freight had been cleared from the pier, and the yachts were left in peace and quiet.

At the time our bread was to be ready, we walked back to Captain Jim's, a tiny shack down a back alley redolent of baking aromas, and the ancient woman in charge threw in a bonus of limes and bananas as we paid for the warm, fresh-smelling bread. Back at the pier, the elegant vegetable lady arrived with cabbage, eggplant, celery, and tomatoes; we were well stocked. Celery is practically a fetish with Jane

Mrs. Major dispensing freight

for preparing lunches. We don't ask, "What's for lunch?" We simply say, "What are we having with our celery today?" She chops it up fine and then mixes it into a salad of chicken, tuna, shrimp, or salmon, all very healthy and very tasty too. When no celery is available, she loses heart over making lunch, and we are practically on our own.

By 1500 the breeze was still fresh from 060°. I had been expecting it to swing into the southeast, which would be on the nose, and would then hope for it to go around to the south in the cycle we had seen so many times during the winter. This would mean a reach for us past Crooked and Acklin's Islands to Mayaguana on our way to Caicos, and that had been behind my reasoning in lingering at Clarence Town. But I had the itch to be off, and the wind was still favorable, with a very steady feel to it, since it had been in exactly the same direction for over thirty hours. No one had any valid arguments or excuses for staying in port, even in the face of a night passage, so we collected ourselves and

The freight boat leaves

headed for sea at 1520, with Henry Major bidding us a cheery farewell.

Our course was 115° for the north end of Crooked Island, which meant a close reach, and we set main, jib, and staysail and took off over the blue, whitecapped seas. As the afternoon wore on, the breeze gained weight, and we doused the staysail, which seemed enough of a change. *Brunelle* moved on in the gathering twilight with a quick motion in the short, steep seas, but dry and comfortable. Jane managed a stew for dinner, and by 1930 we had sighted the powerful beam of Bird Cay Light on Crooked Island. A freighter came close enough a bit later to have to alter course astern of us as we watched her closely, and we charged on into the night, passing the light at 2230 and changing course to 120° for the northeast point of Acklin's. We were standing four-and-four watches, and when I came up at 0345, I found we had been set inside the point of Acklin's, where there is quite a jumble of reefs. We tacked out around it and made sure we were clearing a nasty little rock called Northeast Breaker before altering course to 135° to go west of the Plana Cays. These are sandy, uninhabited islands stretching for nine miles east and west, and they looked like the end of the earth in their loneliness as we swept past them under the rising sun. The *Guide* said there was a comfortable lee midway off the western cay, but it looked mighty surgy to me, and we were happy to reach on to Mayaguana.

I had not expected to make such good time, and our present rate of progress would put us off Providenciales in the Caicos during the night. One look at the *Guide* was enough to confirm that the intricate entry could only be made in daylight, so we decided to break the passage when we got to Mayaguana, waiting until we could make an early-morning approach to the Caicos.

The breeze had not varied a degree since we left Cape Santa Maria, and it gave us a fast close reach on the 120° course from Plana Cays to Mayaguana. Since the freighter that passed us off Crooked Island, we had not seen a vessel or plane of any description. We were alone without even a bird or a flying fish on a rough, windswept ocean, plated with rippling gold in the morning sun, and Mayaguana's low profile peeked over the horizon at 1055. It was so low, and we were going so well, that we were under its lee by 1145, and we rolled up the jib and jogged along under mainsail for a comfortable lunch hour.

Stone and Hart recommended a good temporary anchorage off Start Point, a third of the way along the south shore, and this had more appeal than fighting our way into reef-strewn Abraham Bay, the only real harbor on Mayaguana. Start Point was only a few hundred yards off the direct course for Providenciales, with a good, shallow-water anchorage near a fuel pier that looked big and impressive but seemed deserted. Stone and Hart offered, "There is a good dinghy beach here," and I wondered why anyone would want to land a dinghy in this forsaken spot until I remembered that Jerry Hart always cruises with a dog on board and needs good walking-ashore places.

It was a lazy afternoon of napping and reading, and under the lee it even appeared as though the wind had moderated. We had a good chicken dinner at anchor and then got underway on the fifty-seven-mile passage at 2030, in what seemed like light air. This illusion soon vanished, however, as we worked out from under Mayaguana, and by the time Jane and I went off watch at midnight we were plunging across Caicos Passage in short, steep seas, black and glittering under the waning Easter moon, as whitecaps rushed out of the night at us. This was our first rough night at sea, and sleep below was difficult. I turned in on the sole of the main cabin on the mattress of the upper bunk, and Jane was on the lower one, but it was too bouncy and noisy to sleep. It was like being inside a great drum, as *Brunelle* charged across the waves and occasionally fell off a big one, and I was also lying next to a water tank which is under the lower bunk. It sloshed and gurgled right in my ear to add to the cacophony of a sailboat pressing hard through seas. The best I could manage in the way of sleep was half-awake dreams and hallucinations.

John and Ellis had the portable radio with them in the cockpit to sustain them through the mid-watch, and occasional snatches of music drifting down added to the sense of confusion and unreality. Jane had none of these problems and sawed wood peacefully just above me. (No conjugal couch this!)

By the time we were due on watch, the breeze was up to about thirty. Ellis, to whom this was all a new experience, had been asking John whether this was rough or normal, and he had been saying it was all perfectly routine until I came up and decided that we should reef the main and replace the jib with the staysail. Ellis began to get the message then. We hardly seemed to slow down under reduced sail, and it was a testing passage that *Brunelle* passed well. We had made good time, and were mostly dry on deck, although there was naturally some spray flying now and then.

To add to the excitement, this was also another case of a nonworking light. The chart and *Guide* showed a lighthouse on North West Point, the outer end of Provo, as that island is universally called. Reefs extend fairly far off the point, and it would not be a good place to charge into in the dark. If we had been faster than I estimated, and farther south, this could be a problem, and it was a nagging uncertainty of our watch until first light of dawn showed the point right where it should be, well off the starboard bow. We learned later that the light had not been working for two years. At least the *Guide* said "(unrel)" next to it.

Landfall on Provo is a tough one, with landmarks on the low shoreline difficult to identify, and we jogged outside the line of breakers on the reef that runs all along the west side of the Caicos trying to pick out objects. Seas were running very high with the wind even stronger at 060°, and the reef was a welter of white, throwing a curtain of mist between us and the rising sun, whose light was hard and harsh on our salt-caked, windblown faces. Instructions in the *Guide* said to call Turtle Cove Marina on VHF 16 and ask for a pilot, and I waited until after 0730, figuring someone might be up by then. A powerboat in the marina answered and someone said that Peg Withey, who runs the marina with her husband, Doc, would be with us soon. When she came on the air, we managed to establish where we were by describing houses on the beach. We had gone too far to the northeast and were off Leeward Cut rather than Sellar's Cut, where the marina was.

Peg said an outboard would be out to guide us in and for us to head back along the reef. Soon we saw a small white speck of a boat coming out from the reef through what looked like solid breakers, catching the sunlight when she bounced—literally leaving the water as she soared over the wave crests, standing almost on end, only to plunge out of sight in the troughs. As soon as we came within visual signalling distance, she turned around, and the lone figure at the wheel waved for us to follow.

We were headed for what looked like unbroken breakers, surfing on the waves as they crested in the shallowing water, but eventually a small patch of blue opened in the solid white of the surf. Waves were humping up against an ebbing tide and breaking in the channel, and I thought that we could easily broach. We were under power with the main up (this was no place to have an engine failure) for maximum control, and, though it looked fearsome, *Brunelle* behaved like a lady, answering the helm well as she reared on the big seas sweeping under us. At last we were past a tiny white marker at the edge of the cut and were turning to starboard in the wake of the outboard into suddenly

It's a long way in from the reef to Sellar's Pond

calm water. To windward, the great rollers were spending their fury in a welter of foaming surf and spray, while between us and the long curve of beach on the island, the pale greens and powdery blues of inshore waters smiled in the sun in a pattern with large, dark green-and-brown patches of coral.

With a great sigh, I settled down to following the guide boat through the intricate snake's path of a channel into the marina.

11. Provo

"Big Stud from Boggy Creek——" the words of the song went.

A man in blue denims, cowboy boots, and a ten-gallon hat strummed his guitar and sang of Big Stud's adventures, his gravelly voice carrying over the sound of the trade wind rustling the palm trees around the Third Turtle Inn at Providenciales. People from the Inn, the town, and the boats in the marina sat in scattered groups at tables in an open-air court listening to the evening's entertainment on our first night in Provo. I don't know quite what I expected from this remote, inaccessible patch of sand and scrub set on the rim of a fifty-mile-wide bank on the edge of nowhere, but it definitely had not been country and western music.

The singer was Tommy Coleman, whose lined, weatherbeaten face and drawling accent seemed right off the plains of West Texas, but he billed himself as the "resident hippie of Parrot Cay" in his patter between songs, and he had evidently lived in the Caicos for many years. He and a female companion were the only inhabitants of a small sandy island at the outer end of the Caicos Cays that strung along inside the reef we had negotiated that morning from Provo to the next large island, North Caicos. Once a week Tommy "came to town," riding a Boston Whaler the ten miles in from his hideaway to sing songs and drink whiskey with the group at the Third Turtle, and he was one of the hits of an informal but highly entertaining evening. Anyone who wanted to could sing or tell a joke, and before it was over, I had even been dragooned onto the floor to tell a story.

The Turks and Caicos have always been out of the mainstream of life in the Bahamas and Caribbean. Physically part of the Bahamas chain—the very farthest outpost—they have been political orphans through the years, being shunted between Bahamian, Jamaican, and

British rule, which is what they are under now, as a colony. They have had little economic importance except for some salt flats and a few struggling plantations in colonial days, and the natives have scratched out a hard existence fishing and gathering conch, which abound on the Caicos Bank as prolificly as anywhere in the world.

Now, in the air age, airstrips have opened the islands up to more visitors in the past few years than they have known through all the centuries, and there is considerable development in resorts and in land sales. It is still off the beaten track by water, but more boats are coming through, and there are several marinas. The Third Turtle, with its central building at the harbor's edge and the other units on a bluff above this, is owned by a young member of the duPont family, and, with a certain set that travels by private plane, it has become an "in" place, though not widely publicized. In an informal and casual way, it is as sophisticated a spot as any of the better-known resorts of the Bahamas and Lesser Antilles. Excellent bonefishing is one of the main attractions.

We had followed the guide boat in from Sellar's Cut on the tortuous route through coral heads via a privately marked channel to a narrow, man-made cut into half-mile-round Sellar's Pond. This had been landlocked until dredging opened it, and there is now a channel around its perimeter leading to the marina's long bulkheads and the Inn on the south side. There is also room for a few boats at anchor; it is one of the most secure harbors anywhere in the islands. Our guide was Thurber Withey, college-age son of Peg and Doc, and he led us to a berth at the quay near his family's big Chris-Craft, *Dar-Bee,* that they live on and which serves as the marina office. Peg, a round-faced, smiling woman met us with a pleasant welcome as we came alongside, and from the first moment on we were made to feel that we were a part of the scene.

The Witheys are Great Lakes sailors who tired of the short boating season there and headed south, and they seem to have established themselves well, as they also run a liquor-importing business.

We had heard tales of difficulty with customs and immigration here, but an hour after our arrival a polite, soft-spoken man came

Dar-Bee *(foreground) and* Brunelle *at Third Turtle Marina*

aboard and checked us in with a minimum of fuss. He seemed especially happy to see us since his name was also Robinson. The only "price" we had to pay was to buy a program for the Annual Caicos Regatta for one dollar.

We were still licking off salt and puttering around drowsily, though Jane did find the energy to houseclean the refrigerator, when an attractive blonde hailed us from the quay and invited us to a cocktail party at the Inn that night. She was Ann Honsacker, who, with her husband, Brian, managed the Inn. They were from Dallas— Texas is big in the Caicos—and had pulled up stakes and followed "the dream" in a Gulfstar 41. Brian had been an assistant district attorney in Dallas, a proper young lawyer in a three-piece suit, but had switched to denim cutoffs and a cowboy hat, barefoot and happy. They had been heading farther south for the Caribbean, but circumstances had developed that ended with them managing the Inn, and

Brian and Ann Honsacker

they make it a lively and friendly place.

The party was a mix of duPont friends, local people, boat people, and guests at the Inn, including some Europeans, and everyone crowded into the tight little bar, swapping sea stories and "where-are-you-froms." John and Ellis found some of their generation, and it was a jolly affair, leading into dinner and the country-and-western show. Brian was as big a part of it as Tommy Coleman, as he did well with the guitar and has a fine sense of rhythm, putting his songs across with an ingenuous, "little boy" charm, head tilted back and a smile on his face. In addition to country and western, he was a big hit with the "MTA" song. The only thing I could possibly find to complain about was the absence of Mount Gay Rum, the sailor's drink found almost everywhere in the islands. Haitian Babancourt was a good alternative, though a bit heavier.

We were glad we had left Clarence Town when we did, because the wind, still in the same groove of 060 degrees, was even stronger, with some overcast and a few spits of rain. The Coast Guard weather broadcast on SSB talked of a high-level trough out of a stationary high in the Atlantic north of us that was funneling the northeaster our way. We were snug and happy since we had four days to wait for our next crew anyway, but John and Ellis were hoping for better beachcombing weather. They walked around the harbor to the untouched miles of white sand on the outside but almost got blown back off it.

The only other unpleasantness was a taxi ripoff. All four of us took one to the supermarket, just a couple of miles away, and the fare was twenty dollars because the driver charged by the person—five dollars per head. That made the already expensive marketing even steeper, and from then on we bummed rides, or one person went at a time.

Another inn, called Erebus, sits on a bluff overlooking the harbor, and we climbed its steep path for dinner on two of the nights and found the food—lobster one night and conch the next time—better than the Third Turtle. Only problem there was in trying to get martinis before dinner. The young lady bartender used sweet vermouth the first time, a large dollop, but was very amenable to trying again.

The Third Turtle Bar was still the social center, and we ended up there every night. The weather had kept Tommy Coleman from leaving for Parrot Cay, so we had more country and western music, with one especially big affair as an "end of season" cookout. This didn't seem to affect the festivities the next night, and I asked whether that was

Brunelle *holed up at the Third Turtle*

a "start-of-the-next-season" party.

The Turtle's owner had flown down a husband-and-wife singing team from Fort Lauderdale, a young couple with fine voices and a real musical sense, who were good on folk songs and ballads and provided a gentle counterpoint to Tommy's antics. One nightly feature of whatever music that was going on was a young man with a fiddle who managed to inject himself into almost every act, scraping away and bouncing up and down like Old Zip Coon. He didn't happen to be very good, but he sure got "A" for eagerness, and everyone tolerated him until he tried to string along with the professional singers, who put up with him for a number or two, then smiled wanly and took a break. We wondered who this poor man's Isaac Stern was and were told he was a pilot for Southeast Airlines, the link with the outside world for Turks and Caicos. John and Ellis were due to fly out the next day, and we told them that they had better get off the plane if they heard a fiddle scraping up in the cockpit. With the happy-idiot grin he put on his face while sawing away and bouncing up and down, he looked like someone who would have trouble in a self-service elevator, much less in the cockpit of an airliner.

The day they left, he was still at the Third Turtle, so we hoped they had a safe flight. While waiting for Jim Lillie, our next crew, to arrive courtesy of Southeast Airlines, we spent a day sightseeing with Peg Withey over the dusty-white coral roads of Provo. There is considerable development in private houses, well scattered over the rolling hills. Houses along the bluff running west from Sellar's Pond have a magnificent view to the north across the pale waters inside the reef to the tumbled line of white and its curtain of fine spray at the edge of the open sea's deep blue. To the northeast, the gentle curve of Provo's long beach stretched out toward the next harbor, known as Leeward Going Through, where there is another marina.

We stopped at one of the largest and most impressive private houses atop the bluff, home of the Ericsons from Michigan, to meet Mrs. Bonnie Ericson, whom I would rank as the grande dame, albeit very friendly and informal, of Provo's winter colony. The Ericson yacht is a big Hatteras sportfisherman, largest one at the marina, and they follow the big game tournaments around the islands. In doing so, they had spent some time in the Dominican Republic, and Bonnie had offered to give me a letter to a man named Nadim Bezi in Samana, where we planned to stop. She said that he was the leading citizen there and very involved with all the activities, and that he would be an interesting person for us to meet. Since I viewed the Dominican Republic as one vast, dark question mark, any smoothing of the way was very welcome. We ended the trip with cocktails aboard *Dar-Bee* with Peg and Doc and their tiny terrier. I caught the dog's name as Harriet, but found later that Peg had explained to Jane that it was really Hairy-It.

We had a good visit comparing notes and reminiscing about distance racing on the Great Lakes, which seemed a long way from the Caicos. The Witheys allowed that they really didn't miss it very much.

Marina living has a wonderful small-town, back-fence kind of atmosphere and even after a day or two we felt very much a part of it. Soon we knew something about most of the boats in the harbor, and as usual, each boat had its story. There was one interesting setup, where all that was visible for the first few days we were there was an older man and youngish woman. Then one day it was evident that there was a third person aboard—an older, grayhaired woman. Seems this was a secretary and wife arrangement, with the wife's social awareness confined to a short period in the morning before they led her into the liquor locker, leaving them to their own devices (or whatever) for the rest of the day. The situation was complicated by frequent calls from the secretary's boy friend in the States pleading with her to come back. Most communication is by radio in the Caicos, although they do have overseas phone service, and whatever goes on becomes party-line public property.

One boat in South Bluff Harbor on the other side of Provo, a large tug anchored there almost permanently as home for a family with young children, was on the air via VHF constantly, relaying messages and weather information and reporting on all the local doings. The children had friends on another boat nearby, and it was something of a surprise to hear piping voices on the air with messages like "Can Judy come over to play this afternoon?" followed by "This is *Final Victory* out with *Susabelle* and standing by on Channel 16." One day the youngsters were on the air when a message came through for their father, and a little girl with a Shirley Temple voice took the transmission accurately and then signed off in her squeaky little tones with "Roger Dodger you old codger."

Jim Lillie arrived on April 24th on schedule, though a couple of hours late. I listened carefully for fiddle music from the cockpit of his Southeast Airlines plane as it sat on the ramp at the Provo Airport, but there was no sound beyond the whine of the turbo-jets. Since we were at the airport, we took the opportunity to check out of customs and immigration with Mr. Robinson in hopes that the 060° breeze was not perpetual at thirty knots plus, and again it was a gracious social occasion (he did not sell us another regatta program).

Jim was at the time a recent college graduate—Wesleyan—who had not made up his mind on a future career and was marking time. There was a possibility that he might go to law school, but he did not want to make any precipitous decisions. With a few months to think things over, he had come into the *Yachting* office in New York to find out about the possibilities of getting a crewing berth for a few months just about the same time the crew we had lined up for the passage onward from Provo had to back out because of a business conflict. I interviewed Jim about his sailing experience, which seemed solid enough since his family owned a Hinckley Pilot, found out that he didn't use pot or other illegal substances—I had no desire to tangle with customs officers in strange ports over this subject—and signed him on. I had qualms about a twenty-three-year-old confined to small quarters with people practically old enough to be his grandparents, but he showed a maturity and intellectual curiosity in the fairly brief chat I had with him that seemed to stamp him as a self-sufficient young man. He had spent a college year abroad and traveled all over Europe by himself with a knapsack on his back, and he looked like the kind of guy who could keep his own counsel without having to "make the scene" too often. Tall, red-headed, and very fair-skinned, with a strong build and a shy, self-effacing manner, he settled in quickly, familiarized himself with *Brunelle,* and showed obvious relish in the activities at the Third Turtle when we went over there that evening.

We were ready to leave, and I was getting a bit tired of a howling, moisture-laden breeze from 060°. It was the ninth day of this very persistent weather pattern. Not a boat had moved in or out of the marina since we had arrived, and our only hope was that the breeze moved about ten degrees to the eastward the next morning. Just maybe that high-level trough was breaking out of its rut. The Coast Guard told of a heavy storm in south Florida (it had poured sixteen inches of rain on Fort Lauderdale) moving northeastward into the North Atlantic and taking its fifty-knot winds out of the area, so perhaps there would

Jim Lillie

be a change. The only other weather information came from an 0700-broadcast each morning from a religious station at Cap Haitien in Haiti, ninety miles to the south. The announcer, with a good American accent and a fine radio-announcer-type voice, would read off a weather report received over his wires with all the understanding and emphasis of a Chinese coolie reciting a Shakespearean soliloquy, and it took a bit of interpreting to follow him intelligently. Both broadcasts always spoke of the whole Caribbean area in one lumped reference, and I never once heard a variation from the statement, "wind east fifteen to twenty knots; no significant weather features." After a while, I figured that this meant there were no hurricanes in the area, and it would be news in April if there happened to be one.

That night, with the wind still howling, there was a great amount of chatter on VHF from South Bluff about sea conditions there, with the boats at anchor making heavy weather of it, climaxed by the big tug breaking a four hundred-pound kedge in two and going adrift. Safe in the snug confines of Sellar's Pond, it was an odd experience to hear all the excitement and concern and not be able to do anything about it—a little like viewing a TV show.

Overnight, there was rain, and the wind clocked down to southeast, which was the first real change in many a day. The radio broadcasts said that the storm system that had been causing the unusual conditions was on the move northeastward off the Georgia coast, and things were looking up. Despite the charms of the Third Turtle, we were getting itchy, and it was time to be on our way. After all, we were supposed to be circumnavigating the Caribbean, not just marina-sitting in Provo.

We settled our fuel and dockage with Peg via an Amex card, gave Hairy-It's ears a last tickle, and prepared to get underway. Brian volunteered to pilot us out the maze of reefs, and Ann and friends followed in a powerboat to pick him off at the cut in the reef. This time we took a short cut that eliminated a big zigzag in the normal route. This was a narrow pass, only about twice our beam in width, through a hole in the biggest reef. It was called the English Channel, and in my concentration on things local it took me a few minutes to wake up to why this had a familiar ring. The breeze was strong from the land, knocking down the seas in Sellar's Cut. The motorboat eased alongside to pick up Brian, and, amid a flurry of waves and farewell cries, we met the first surge of the Caicos Passage in the cut and powered on to open water to round up and set the main.

This was to be one of the two longest passages of the whole trip, 175 miles to Puerto Plata, Dominican Republic—the other would be the Mona Passage between Hispaniola and Puerto Rico—and it was one of the major worry boxes that had been lurking in my mind since we first decided to embark on the project. Normally, it would be all to windward. The way the wind was blowing at the moment, that would certainly be the case, and I knew from navy duty and from reading a great many articles, published and unpublished, at *Yachting*'s office that this could be a very rugged stretch. There had been a thirty-one-foot Bertram at Turtle Cove that had been driven back to Cuba, and then to Haiti, in trying to make Provo from Long Island, and I had a great respect for the stretch of water that lay ahead of us.

First, we had to go westward around North West Point and its dormant lighthouse. On the way, surging along on a direct run, we passed a boat headed into Sellar's Cut from South Bluff, and she was rearing and plunging over the head seas even under the lee of Provo. I had visions of what the trade-wind seas would be like out beyond the Caicos Bank from watching her motion, and that old ambivalence, that "what the hell am I doing here?" feeling, began to build.

Ah well. No problems at the moment, so press onward, which we did, clearing North West Point and setting the jib for a reach south-westward past Sand Bore Channel, entrance for the South Bluff an-chorage, to West Caicos, where I planned to anchor for the night. Once the site of plantations, and more recently of failed construction projects, West Caicos (six miles long and low and featureless along its barren western shore) is uninhabited and about as lonely a looking spot as I have ever seen. The *Guide* touted an anchorage midway down the island, but I couldn't pick out any reason for one spot being any better than any other. It was all of one piece—forlorn and featureless except for a couple of abandoned houses and a long stretch of crumbling stone wall paralleling the shore.

We finally chose a spot opposite an abandoned dragline machine and anchored in sixteen feet close under the beach. There was some-thing of a surge, but not too heavy, and its ebb and flow on the rocky shoreline was a nervous counterpoint to *Brunelle*'s slow rocking. The sky was still overcast, but the breeze had dropped off noticeably. The VHF was alive with chatter between Brian, the tug *Final Victory*, still full of her anchor dragging adventures of the previous night, and assorted boats at South Bluff and Sellar's Pond. I joined in to tell them where we were, and when I mentioned that we were anchored off an "abandoned dragline" the skipper of *Final Victory* came on vehemently to say that it was not abandoned. It was his, and he had left it there after vainly trying to establish a marina, but he would be back some day. The chit-chat went on for over an hour, but it subsided at supper time, and we settled down to chicken for dinner and thoughts of the next day.

Before turning in, I sat in the cockpit and contemplated the weather, feeling the surge under us and the faint whisper of the dying southeaster, and watching a spasmodic display of lightning on the empty horizon fifty miles to the westward over Great Inagua. Its fitful illumination of towering thunderheads fitted the uncertainty of my mood as I watched the nervous interplay of light and dark and wondered what the morrow would bring.

12.   Landfall

The morrow brought a surprise. The wind was around to southwest, an almost unheard of phenomenon in this part of the world. Through the uneasy night, I had listened to the rustle and swish of surge on the rocky shore of West Caicos and had a half-awake illusion as the night wore on that it was getting louder. As it turned out, this was no illusion. When I came on deck at first light to find our bow pointing at the great empty spaces in the west, the stern was just off the surf line, with a few yards to spare. We were not in any danger, but it was an uneasy spot. The waves from the southwest were piddling ripples, and the anchor was holding well, but the boulders and coral heads along the beach were startlingly clear and close in the limpid waters off the stern, and I decided to leave right away.

Before breakfast, we up-anchored and were powering south along the featureless shoreline by 0730. We also made sail to get as much as possible out of the southwester. It was fitful and weak and faded with the rising sun. From then on we powered along at 2000 RPMs with the sails up as a steadying influence, occasionally catching vagrant puffs and filling but not much help otherwise. Booby birds and terns swooped low over the heave of sea and for a while we were convoyed by a school of small porpoises, the first we had seen since Florida waters. They were swift and playful and they raced across our bow and criss-crossed our wake, occasionally leaping alongside as though seeking applause.

I had not really been confident that the southwester would last and give us a favorable breeze, but from the moment of its demise onward, I fully expected the trade wind to start filling in on the nose. It was a weird experience to power on hour after hour over an oilily calm sea in waters where I had been expecting a trade wind bashing us on the nose. West Caicos dropped astern at 0845, and a powerboat that had come up astern of us as we cleared it headed eastward across the bank to South Caicos, leaving the empty sea to us. French Cay, a lonely little piece of land on the outer fringe of the bank was a smudge to port for a while and later we could see a tiny dot that was White Cay, our last sight of the Caicos. True and magnetic courses had been so close for all our time in the Bahamas that I had not thought about Variation in months, and I carelessly neglected to apply it as we set our course from the tip of West Caicos for Puerto Plata, 150 miles away. We were now back in an area with some Variation (about 6 degrees) and my error soon became evident when we came up on light-colored bank waters, something that was not supposed to happen.

This woke me up, and, somewhat abashed, I altered course from 135° to 142° to compensate. For some time after that, the bank was a pale green line on the horizon, and cumulus clouds, gathering in the heat of the day, formed a pattern to the north—an arc that was a perfect "map" of the lay of the islands rimming the Caicos Bank, to a last pile of white over Grand Turk off to the east. It was a graphic illustration of how sailors of ancient times could navigate by nature's signs. (Better than I had just done with the compass!)

The calm persisted all day as we droned on into emptiness. We had set up a watch system in which Jim and I took two-hour wheel tricks, and Jane stood the 10–12 in the morning and at night, giving Jim and me four hours off at a stretch twice a day. This would not work too well on a long passage, but for an over-nighter it seemed to serve the purpose. For a while, we had a gentle northeaster that kept the sails full, but never with enough promise to let us think of killing the engine. Sunset was lost in a bank of clouds astern, and the night settled in quickly as a very black one. We were in the dark of the moon now, so there would be nothing to look forward to in that department, and low, damp clouds blacked out the stars. Now and then a bright planet would glow moistly in a quick break between them, but inky blackness was the rule for the long hours. The dampness was penetrating enough to make a foul-weather jacket a must, and the chief sport of the night was in trying to stay awake at the wheel—alone with the rush of water under the stern light just behind you, and the binnacle light almost too bright in the blackness as a focal point.

I persisted in being unable to believe that no wind had come up, expecting it at any minute all night, but the only observable weather was a far-distant flicker of lightning over Haiti off our starboard quarter and one squall that bounced lightning between black, heavy-hanging clouds off our port bow for a while but did not materialize in any wind or rain. To keep myself awake on watch and make the minutes, some of the slowest ever in passing, move more quickly, I sometimes think up lists of things I have done, like the number of countries I have visited (transit lounges don't count), the states of the United States I have slept in, places I have played squash, or the number of cruises Jane and I have taken—and where. This is a generally inane practice whose only justification is as a time passer, but there has been some more lasting benefit from it, as the list of cruises gave me an idea for a book—eventually published as *Cruising: The Boats and the Places*. Would that all my idle thoughts could be as productive.

Heading to the east, as we were, we were moving into an earlier time zone. With our clock still on Eastern time, daylight began to suffuse the blackness as early as 0430—a wonderful moment at the end of a long night and one that seems to speed the clock and bring rescue from a feeling of imprisonment in timelessness. As soon as gray seeped over the scene, we began to pick out a darker bulk to starboard. There had been no lights or other signs of civilization, but this formless bulk gradually began to take shape as a headland and was identified as Cabo Isabela. It was the first sight of Hispaniola, the favorite island of Columbus, and appeared as little more than a growing awareness of solidity. Soon a new, higher darkness loomed over the bow. Strips of red, and then gold, were showing through the murk in the east, and gradually we could make out a high, double peak directly ahead that was Isabela de Torres, the 2,600-foot mountain that rises directly behind Puerto Plata. It was a faint, bluish gray at first, and mists lay low along the shore to starboard and formed skirts on the mountain's hips. In the growing light, gray washed away and the blue deepened to a shade of purple.

So here it was, a purple island in the West Indies directly over the

Long swells broke against the rocky shore

bow at sunrise, one of the major landfalls of our whole adventure, dramatic and impressive as it gradually emerged in the strengthening visibility. The sun had been hidden in clouds, showing only streaks of color, but now it began to break through, radiating out in isolated shafts of gold playing across the face of the mountain.

As we rolled closer over huge, long-shouldered swells that seemed to sense the nearness of land and broke high in the rocky shore, the mists burned off in the coves along the coast. The whole face of Isabela de Torres took on a hazy, diffused, golden glow. On top of the higher of its two peaks was a thin pencil of white, a statue of Christ with arms outstretched, standing out brilliantly in the slant of sun.

In all the years we had been coming to the West Indies by plane

126

The statue of Christ atop Isabela de Torres

to cruise between the islands, and on my subchaser duty in the Caribbean, there had been no landfalls quite like this one, and to make it in our own boat after the long string of passages down the Bahamas was one of the thrills of a lifetime of sailing. The fact that we had made it under power over a windless but restlessly heaving sea, took away some of the excitement, as I normally do not favor long passages under power, but the relief of avoiding the expected heavy head winds overcame the lack of the aesthetics that a sailing landfall would have brought. After our ten unbroken days of twenty to thirty knots from

060°, I still could not believe a hiatus in the trade winds of over twenty-four hours.

In the hours before dawn, two sets of running lights had crept along our port side at a good distance, evidently on a course from South Caicos to Puerto Plata, which is the shortest possible run (about ninety miles) from the Caicos. We could see two powerboats making their way into the harbor ahead of us. In broadening daylight, Isabela de Torres stood lushly green over the harbor, backed by ranges of mountains receding to cumulus-capped ones in the blue distance inland; big, long rollers sweeping in from Africa dashed their spray high on the cliffs and rocks of the foreshore.

A wrecked cargo ship was a prominent landmark at the entrance to Puerto Plata, and we could see some men crawling around on the bridge as we rounded it and headed between the channel buoys into the harbor. An old Spanish fort guarded the entrance on a point to port, and the town stretched along the inner shore of the harbor in a dazzle of morning sun. It was 0745, and we set clocks ahead an hour to Atlantic Time.

We had progressed into Harry Kline's second book, *Yachtsman's Guide to the Antilles,* and, following its directions, without a flag flying, turned to port around the point, where we could see several yachts moored stern-to a quay next to a big commercial pier. The powerboats that preceded us were backing and filling into berths amid the boats that were already there, and a few more yachts were anchored out.

When the powerboats were secure, a man on the quay waved us into a spot next to one of them, and we proceeded with our first "Med moor" in *Brunelle.* This method saves space in crowded harbors, since boats back into the quay after dropping an anchor well out. It is a necessary fact of life in many harbors, but I have never liked it because a cross wind puts the wrong strain and load on the anchor. It is also a nuisance to keep the dock lines correctly rigged if there is much rise and fall of tide.

Playing it safe, we dropped the anchor so far out that I almost ran us out of rode backing in, and Jim paid out with questioning looks over his shoulder as we neared the stopper end. There was enough line, though, and Jane and I tossed stern lines to the quay, a rough affair of heavy timbers armed with mean looking spikes and enclosed by a barbed wire fence, where a gaggle of "helpers" milled on the quay making suggestions, shouting, and running in various directions with our lines. Usually no one does anything right in a situation like this, and my meager Spanish could not possibly accomplish anything by adding to the shouting, so I just let them yell and tug and run back and forth until things finally settled down and we were somehow secured to Hispaniola. Scratch one major worry box; just a fizzled firecracker this time.

13.   Méringue Country

Amid the milling throng of helpers, all of whom immediately began trying to sell us fruit, fuel, taxi rides, Coca Cola, beer, and maybe their sisters for all I could tell, one pencil-thin man in khakis and an outsize military hat gradually could be understood as speaking English and making sense. He also had a badge on, and it turned out that he was the official customs guard for the yacht pier. He said that the port officials were on one of the newly arrived powerboats and would be boarding us very soon. The eager would-be vendors gradually drifted away, convinced by our repeated "nada" answers, and the customs man then led a small procession of officials over to us. With some difficulty they climbed down from the quay through our pushpit gate, since *Brunelle* was heaving up and down on a considerable surge. (We discovered as time went on that it was ever-present. I would hate to be there in a norther.)

Chief of the delegation was the be-medalled Commandante del Puerto, a navy officer with side arm and dressed in crisp military khakis. He was all smiles and graciousness as he shook hands and welcomed us to Puerto Plata. The customs man acted as interpreter, and we were given clearance very quickly after a cursory look through the cabin. I thought it politic to show them a copy of *Yachting* and explain my connection and that I would be writing articles and a book about our cruise. This was greeted with great smiles and expressions of impressed delight. The interpreter, who flashed a wide, gold-toothed smile, was José Fernandez, who said he had learned English while living in Queens, in New York, where there is a large colony of Dominicanos.

Timing their jumps carefully to the upswing of our surge, the commandante's party made it back up to the quay one by one, and José said that as soon as the immigration officials arrived we would be fully

The yacht dock at Puerto Plata

cleared. They came in another flurry of timed leaps, three of them, all in casual civilian clothes. Only one did any talking, and that in English; he, too, had lived in Queens. The forms were filled out somewhat laboriously, and then we were asked for two beers, "Unopened, por favor." I brought them up, and the man opened his attaché case and deposited the forms and the two beers there, and I could see that it was completely full of bottles. On checking later, we found that he had extracted a bottle of whisky from every boat he had visited except us. I don't know if it was an insult or not only to be asked for two beers.

José proved very helpful and a real friend. He seemed to be on duty almost perpetually, and we wondered when he ever saw his family. The yacht pier was completely under control of customs, with a guarded gate, and only authorized locals were allowed on it. The mob who had taken our stern lines consisted of vendors who were allowed to work the piers, and they were not a nuisance after the first spasm of activity when we arrived. Every time we went off the pier, anything we carried had to be inspected, and José made a big joke of poking into Jane's ditty bag each time we went through the gate. It was also a joke of ridiculous proportions when we took our laundry ashore later on, as this too had to be cleared. José escorted us from the yacht pier across a parking lot to the main customs office on the adjacent commercial pier, where we had to dump our complete collection of dirty linen at the feet of a froglike official, who was as surly and unresponsive as José was helpful. He poked a well-polished boot toe at a couple of dirty towels, wrinkled his nose, and waved us away imperiously without having said a word.

After we had been cleared that first morning and had replaced the yellow quarantine flag with the courtesy flag for the Dominican Republic, we decided to take a look at the town, a small city of about thirty-five thousand people, which is on a gentle incline of foothills across wide, empty fields along the waterfront. As soon as we stepped through the customs gate onto the street outside in a hot glare of mid-morning sun, the inevitable urchins attached themselves to us and gave us the usual spiel of how much they would help us and how friendly they would be to us, in that peculiar mixture of bravado and timidity so characteristic of Hispanic youths. They were Pablo and Francisco, they said, as they shook hands manfully, turning their large, liquid, dark eyes up to us; we had them as unavoidable escorts as we crossed the waterfront boulevard and started up the streets of the town.

It was a completely typical Latin-American city, with sleepy, narrow streets and the redolence of open sewers in the gutters, fried cooking, garlic, horses and mules, dust, and sweating humanity. The houses, of wood, with balconies overhanging the street, or of cracking plaster stained with moisture, looked as though they had been there since the second voyage of Columbus (and maybe they have, as this is an old settlement). The first house we came to with signs of life, in a strategic location near the waterfront, had an open balcony one level up from the street, garlanded with pretty, over-made-up girls, smiling gaily at our little procession. Obviously I was not a good prospect with Jane at my side, but Jim received some wider smiles, giggles, and small waves.

Pablo and Francisco guided us solicitously along with the first stop at a currency exchange. I had said we wanted to go to the office of Cafemba Tours, a travel agency run by an American, Mike Ronan. Harry Kline told us to look him up when I had telephoned Harry about our plans before leaving the States. Mike is an ex-Peace Corps member who had married locally and settled there to start his own tour and travel business, and the boys led us to the Cafemba office just off the main square. Here there was the usual array of cathedral (with bells), city hall, and hotel, all facing on the plaza, where there were trees, benches, statues, crosswalks, a bandstand, and a promenade around the perimeter, which was used in the traditional nightly parade of young people—boys in one direction, girls in the other as they giggle and ogle and make signs about meeting later. Taxis lined the curbs while the drivers lolled on benches, playing gambling games, laughing, and whistling at girls. Méringue music blared from shops on the side streets, pigeons wheeled and fluttered through the trees or strutted across the walks, vendors sold ice cream or pastries from little carts, and barbers plied their trade with customers sitting on the benches. Puerto Plata's life concentrated here, and the rest of the streets were almost deserted in the midday sun.

Mike, wiry and energetic, with a long, lean face and a bristling bar of a Jerry Colonna moustache, is a rapid-fire talker in a husky voice. He was enthusiastically hospitable and offered to help in any way he could, as Harry Kline had predicted, since Mike is a sailor himself. We made plans for getting together later and taking a tour car for some sightseeing the following day.

Pablo and Francisco had been waiting outside the office, noses pressed to the glass, and they picked us up as soon as we came out. We said we wanted to go to lunch and tried to ease them on their way, but they insisted on staying with us and tried to steer us to the Palacio Hotel. On the way down the street, we noticed another hotel, the Castillo, that had a Visa sign on the door. When traveling, I always try to use charge cards to conserve cash, and we decided to go in there. The boys were horrified.

"No! No!" they cried. "No go Castillo. Bad place. No good!"

I tried to find out why it was no good, but they just kept saying this over and over. I figured they had a tie-in with the other place, but this one looked all right, so I gave them some coins, and they reluctantly parted company, acting as though we were going to our doom.

The hotel was an old-fashioned, high-ceilinged wooden building with balconies on the second floor. Its lobby was open to the street, and a large dining room, with fans thunking slowly overhead and potted palms standing in the corners, gave off the lobby. It was plain but neat, with clean tablecloths, and the native style "criolla" lunch for three dollars a head was hearty and quite good—soup, rice and meat, and fried plantain. When I tried to use my Visa card, the young woman cashier showed some confusion over taking it, and we finally understood that she was not allowed to accept cards unless the boss was there, and he would not be back until supper. Would I please leave the card until he came?

This seemed a bit odd, but I finally agreed, amid many reassurances that "everything okay." The bar was right next to the desk, and a Dominicano sipping a beer there leaned over to me and said, "Is okay man. No ripoff." Probably had lived in Queens.

Life at the yacht pier was colorful and interesting, and we soon entered into the community spirit of it. The powerboat next to us was *Boobie Hatch,* one of the two boats whose lights we had seen during the night. She was an ex-navy launch converted to a sportfisherman by her owner, Don, and his wife, Olive, Floridians in their forties who had chucked jobs there when the boat was finished and were heading for the Virgins to go into fishing charters. Don was a casual, blue-collar type who liked his beer and liked to relax and shoot the breeze; most of the executive decisions seemed to come from the female half of the partnership, who had the type of figure that goes with executive decisions. Whenever she wanted something done, she would yell "Don" at the top of her voice, and he hopped to it quickly. They were friendly and helpful and we enjoyed comparing notes with them.

On the other side was a big charter ketch on her way north for the summer. The compact, sunburned skipper, a man in his fifties, had two young male crew members aboard, plus a lithe and lissome girl from one of the islands, who made a most decorous sight lounging in the cockpit in a bikini. We went aboard for drinks, and he made noises about just having one drink because he intended to get underway before sunset. This brought a frown to the dark, handsome face of the girl, who obviously was not ready for sea, and she pouted prettily and worked on him not to sail via kisses, and then a second scotch. As he took it, I could see by the light in his eye that he was a goner, and her spirits picked up dramatically. They eventually had dinner ashore, and he climaxed the evening by falling in when they came back to the boat at a late hour. When they did sail the next morning, it was in an excess of sobriety.

During the afternoon, there was a fire aboard the wreck at the harbor entrance, and we wondered whether the men we had seen climbing over it that morning had anything to do with it. We were told that salvagers were at work with cutting torches, and perhaps something had gotten out of control.

Farther down the pier, two medium-aged auxiliaries that had seen better days were side by side and cruising in company. One of them had two men and a woman and the other had a couple. The men had long hair and various hirsute adornments, and the girls had that unkempt look that goes with dirty cutoffs and old sweatshirts. They were in their mid-twenties and were just "taking off" with no set plan in mind. The couple with the extra man was married, but the girl on the other boat had just joined in the Bahamas, looking for a ride to the islands, with no romance involved. Jim soon made friends with them, and, despite their scruffy appearance, they were perfectly pleasant, ordinary young people, intent on having a good time and worried about nautical responsibilities and the ramifications of operating on a shoestring.

A trawler at the quay was on a delivery voyage, and the professional skipper admitted with something like glee that he had been aground in every harbor he had hit so far and that he had virtually plowed his way across the Caicos Bank. A big Hatteras next to him had several fuel drums strapped in her cockpit to get her through the long gaps between fuel stops. We had seen her coming into the harbor entrance between great wings of white, and the next day, when she charged off to the eastward to keep schedule, she was just a moving cloud of spray on the heaving blue of the sea.

The trade had come back the afternoon of our arrival, blowing at about sixteen knots directly along the coast, and I decided to give it a few days before we thought about moving on. Not that the charms of Puerto Plata were that irresistible, and I have never been particularly taken by Latin-American life, but there was no hurry. There were a few things to see in the area, as well as the continuous side show of life at the yacht pier. One suggested method for negotiating the rugged north coast of Hispaniola is to travel at night, sticking close to the shore. Very often, especially in spring and summer, the trade dies with the sun and a counter breeze comes down from the mountains in the cool of the evening. When the time came, we would give it a try.

It is not a coast to be trifled with, and it has a deserved reputation as one of the ruggedest stretches of water in the West Indies. That first afternoon, as we were settling in at the pier and getting to know our neighbors, we had a first-hand account of just how much this coast should be respected. We had just had a little excitement of our own, when one of our propane tanks suddenly began to hiss and exude gas. Our two propane tanks are located under the helmsman's seat, with an overboard vent through the transom, and one of them had just been filled at Provo. With the sun directly overhead in Latitude 20° in late April, the heat was evidently too much. I didn't know the tanks had a safety release of pressure, and it was a nervous few moments until we realized that everything was okay.

Up on the pier, a slender, bearded man had been walking from boat to boat, and, as he stopped by our transom, the skipper of the charter ketch called over, "Listen to this guy's story, Bill. It's really something."

It was indeed a strange one as he told it to me, seated in our cockpit. He was thin to the point of emaciation, with a sad, semi-down-at-the-heel air, and his manner was almost dazed as he unfolded his tale in that diffident English drawl often associated with the academic world.

"I've lost my boat," was his opening remark, and I thought he meant it had been stolen and that he was looking for information from anyone who had seen it.

"It was my own fault," he went on. "I made a navigational error that put her on the beach——" he hesitated and then added apologetically "but I really was not myself. I'd had dengue fever. Now I'm trying to sell the gear I salvaged to raise some cash."

He was a single-hander, and the boat was a forty-two-foot schooner with a hull based on the Seabird type made famous by Thomas Fleming Day and later by Harry Pidgeon. Day's *Seabird* crossed the Atlantic early in the century, and Pidgeon circumnavigated in the homebuilt *Islander* in the twenties and thirties when that was still an unusual feat. Jeremy, the single-hander, had done most of the rig and interior of his boat himself. He started from the eastern Med, where he had been working as an engineer, and went through Gibraltar and down the African coast to Gambia, then cruised farther up the Gambia River than any yacht had ever gone before. Crossing to Brazil, he spent a year on the coast living and working with Indian boatbuilders and then made his way from there to the Caribbean.

His usual system on passages was to put the yacht on automatic pilot and turn in. (Later on I met someone who had cruised in company with him, who said that he even did this in confined waters like the Grenadines, and always went without running lights at night.) Knowing how poorly I sleep on night passages even when there is a full watch on deck, I was somewhat amazed at his methods, but I know that I would never make a single-hander under any circumstances, and each to his own.

In coming through the Caribbean, he picked up a case of dengue fever, the mosquito-transmitted disease which really knocks a victim out for several days with high fever, chills, ague, and a comalike lethargy. I have known people who have had it, and I am sure the debilitation would be very hard on a single-hander. Jeremy had recovered somewhat, but was still below par when he put into the little harbor of Escondido on the north coast of the Dominican Republic just inside Cabo Cabron, eighty miles east of Puerto Plata. This is one of the several bold capes that stand out on this barren, inhospitable coast. Navigation along it is a question of going from headland to headland, as several big capes are the only break in the miles and miles of cliffs and reefs.

He left Escondido at sunset, heading for Puerto Plata, and his first course had to be northwest to clear the next big cape, Cabo Francis Viejo, before he could alter course to due west. When he thought that he had gone far enough out to the northwest, he came left to west, set the autopilot, and turned in.

The next thing he was aware of was the dreaded sound of keel grating on the bottom, and by the time he arrived on deck, the schooner was well up the surf line on the beach. It was a lee shore, and every wave sent her higher onto the sand. Somehow, she had made her way through a narrow pass in the fringing reef, where huge breakers dashed on the coral, spending their fury after an unimpeded scend from the far reaches of the Atlantic. Instead of breaking apart on a reef, she had ended up on a bed of sand. When he had set the autopilot several hours before, he did not have enough offing. Instead of clearing Cabo Francis Viejo, he was a good mile inside it.

She was absolutely high and dry. He had no way of getting her off by himself, so he concentrated on salvaging gear. A few natives showed up out of the bush on this wild and seemingly deserted stretch of coast, and he was able to find a truck to rent. Loading it with all the loose gear he could manhandle off the boat, he set off for Samana, the nearest naval base, fifty miles to the east, to see if he could get help in salvaging the schooner.

He was gone three days, and his mission was fruitless, as there was no equipment at Samana that would be of any help, so he drove back to the scene of the stranding. When he got there, he found that his boat did not exist any more. In his absence, the natives had taken crowbars and axes and completely dismantled the hull, chopping it to pieces plank by plank for whatever lumber and hardware they could scavenge. Not one piece of her was left intact, and before he left the area, a man came up to him and tried to sell him one of his own winches. She was as much of a total loss as if she had hit the outer reef when she first came in from sea, but Jeremy at least had most of his equipment, and he drove on to Puerto Plata to see what he could do about selling it and raising cash. The boat had held everything he owned in the world, and, naturally, in the manner of wayfarers of this sort, nothing was insured.

He had planned to pick up a lady friend in Haiti to continue with him into the Pacific, and she had now joined him in Puerto Plata. They had a small apartment in town, where the gear was stored, and we promised to come see what we might need. (When we did go a few days later, Jane bought two books and a colander, and I bought a hand-held anemometer of French make. It consisted of four cups rotating on a spindle that activated a needle to give wind speed in *noeuds*. When we got a chance to test it after going to sea, I was not too surprised to find that it was not accurate.)

The vendors who had swarmed over us when we first arrived worked the quay at a slower pace thereafter, but one rather distinguished looking man was particularly persistent in coming back. With aquiline features and a rich mane of iron-gray hair, he looked as though he should be in a cutaway and striped pants, with an ambassador's ribbon across his chest, but he was in old work clothes and all he was interested in was in selling us some fruit, vegetables, liquor, soft drinks, or almost anything else we might want. Jane wanted to wait until we could examine what the town had to offer, but I thought it would be much simpler to order through him, and I ended up by asking him to bring us two dozen bananas, tomatoes, and what I thought would be limes. He kept talking about *limones*, and I said no, we did not want lemons. We looked in the Spanish phrase book we had and there was something called *limas* for limes. I insisted that this was what we wanted, after much arguing and gesticulating in attempts to describe a lime with the hands. When the order arrived, the bananas were all about twenty minutes away from being inedible. Far from being "lightly flecked with brown" as the Chiquita Banana commercials recommend, they were heavily streaked with black, and we figured they had been culled from somebody's reject bin at a market in town. The tomatoes were not ripe, and *Limas* turned out to be green, orange-sized fruit with a bitter, grapefruitlike pulp inside, almost juiceless, and what we had wanted after all was *limones*. Thus ended my career as a bargainer with native vendors.

We had already picked up the key word to all transactions in Puerto Plata. Whatever we asked, whatever we hoped to accomplish, the answer was always a smiling *"no probleme,"* and from then on this was the watchword for the entire cruise. Whenever I asked Jim to do anything, he would grin and say *"no probleme,"* and the fact that whatever Dominican *probleme* we happened to be involved in was seldom solved by our optimistic friends took nothing away from its charm as a slogan for happy cruising.

No matter what other plans we might have had for eating the first night, my Visa card was calling us back to the Castillo, and we returned there for dinner. The atmosphere was considerably more festive than at lunch time, with a juke box blaring American rock, and dinner was not too expensive, though there was far too much garlic on the sea bass for my taste (but not Jane's).

There was *no probleme* with my card, which was accepted for lunch and dinner under the aegis of the owner, who had returned. He was a suave, smooth-talking American of uncertain vintage—perhaps mid-thirties—with carefully groomed hair, a gold chain around his neck, and a satiny silver shirt with a neckline that plunged to a small corporation that should not have been bared to the public. We had a long chat with him and found that he was from Long Island, but his career had taken him into such diverse ventures as women's dresses in Hong Kong and pinball machines in Spain. He had happened to be in Puerto Plata during the recent period of political uncertainty when the Balaguer government was falling. The local owner of the Castillo had fears for his personal safety and for his future as a hotel owner. Recognizing a good opportunity, the world traveler from Long Island bought the hotel for cash out of pocket in what might be called a distress sale. (At least I had my Visa card back.)

The next day, Mike Ronan sent two of his tour guides, agreeable young men named Geraldo and Fernando, to show us the local sights. In the course of the day, we mentioned that we had been at the Castillo, and we noticed an immediate freezing up in their attitude. By gentle probing, I gathered that the new owner had caused considerable resentment in town by taking over the hotel, and there were veiled but fairly pointed references as to what went on upstairs. Evidently a respected local institution had gone the way of all flesh, in various forms of traffic, and I harked back to the attitude of Pablo and Francisco. There was nothing definite in all of this, but there was a strong undercurrent of emotion, and we did not dwell on the subject for long.

The feature of our day with Geraldo and Fernando was a trip up the funicular to the top of Isabela de Torres. It was Sunday, and the place was swarming. Whole busloads had come across the mountains from Santo Domingo, the capital on the south coast, for a day's outing, and we had to wait forty-five minutes in a long line that wound a serpentine course through barriers in the huge *sala de espero* (which means waiting room, but I thought my translation as "room of hope" was more poetic). The crowd, 99 percent native, with almost no tourists, was in a gala mood, which carried on with us when we finally made the cable car ride packed in with giggling Dominicanos. The view of the harbor and sea was magnificent, but while we had been standing in line, we could see the almost daily phenomenon of clouds closing over the peak in mid-morning, and before the lurching ride got us to the top, we disappeared into a soft, woolly mist that blotted out everything, amid loud cries of distress from the passengers.

As we stepped from the cable car at the summit into a five-acre park of beautifully landscaped gardens, a méringue band was scratching away enthusiastically on the walk way, with a tin cup set up in front for donations. Almost everybody did a little méringue step as they passed the musicians. This is the national dance of the Dominican Republic, and I once had a Dominicano lady teach me how to do it by saying, "Just imagine you are barefoot in a chicken yard: scrape, slide, scrape; scrape, slide scrape———." It now serves me very well as an all-purpose step no matter what Latin or Calypso music is playing.

A méringue step on top of the mountain

The clouds eddied around the peak, thickening and clearing as the trade wind blew through them, and the statue of Christ, mammoth at close quarters, loomed through the mist, now shrouded and faint, now startlingly clear, a great, brooding, dramatic presence. The statue is atop a fort built by Trujillo in the last years of his regime when he feared a Cuban invasion, a juxtaposition whose irony probably escapes most of the local visitors. Since the fall of the Balaguer government a couple of years previous to our visit, the Dominican Republic had enjoyed its first true democracy with the election of the government of President Guzman, and there was certainly a marked contrast to the atmosphere I had felt on two previous visits. The first was when Trujillo

142

was in power in 1956, with armed soldiers or police on every street corner in what was then called Ciudad Trujillo; the second was in 1964, when the civil war that erupted a year later was brewing. There was a shooting in our hotel lobby, and tensions were high. Certainly the crowds wandering through the gardens of Isabela de Torres seemed happy and carefree and in a holiday mood.

Through breaks in the swirling clouds, we could occasionally look out over the dense green of jungle below us to the distant inland peaks of this very mountainous island, and the clouds being torn away from Isabela de Torres by the trade wind made swiftly changing patterns as they scudded across the jungle.

We thought we had hired the car and guides for the day, but it turned out that we were guests of Mike Ronan, and Geraldo and Fernando seemed to relax and take it as something of a holiday, saying that we were a welcome change from the usual cruise ship passengers. "They always ask the same questions," Geraldo said, "and they are not really interested in our country. They just want to know if we have television and supermarkets, and a guide really doesn't have to know much of anything to answer them." He had worked on cruise ships, and American tourists held few surprises for him.

After the funicular, they showed us some of the new developments for tourism in the surrounding area. An enormous airport was under construction several miles east of town, set amid mile after mile of fields of rippling sugar cane, and near it were several real estate developments with condos, a golf course by Robert Trent Jones, clubs, and hotels. Puerto Plata itself has one modern hotel on the Malecon, the broad boulevard that runs from nowhere to nowhere along the sea front in an attempt at grandeur that is in sharp contrast to the jumbled city streets one block inland.

We took our guides to lunch at an enormous open-sided restaurant called *El Sombrero* (because its roof was literally shaped like one) overlooking the beach several miles west of Puerto Plata in the midst of one of the new real estate developments, and we had a fine time sampling local dishes. I had *arroz con pollo* (chicken and rice), Jane had *lambi* (minced conch), and Jim tried *laetta pastellas* (tacolike meat pies). Jane was able to get a proper dry martini, not always easy in such circumstances, and I found the local premium rum, Bermudez Anejo, to be very good. (Visa card accepted.)

As we looked out at the ocean, the trade wind was driving white horses across the deep blue of the Atlantic. A ketch going west was scudding along at hull speed, and a powerboat heading east for Puerto Plata was pounding hard and sending great wings of spray flying. I was just as glad we were sightseers for a while.

We wanted to bring Geraldo and Fernando back to *Brunelle* for a drink afterwards, as they seemed quite interested in her, but José, acting as though he was sending his brother to jail, could not let them onto the pier without a special pass from the commandante. This did not surprise the boys, and they shrugged and quietly drove away.

14. *Supplies and Red Tape*

Though I was ready to move on at any time, the trade continued to blow, and there were a few things to be done, like provisioning and arranging for fuel. Monday would be the day for shopping, since Tuesday was May Day, a labor holiday, and everything would be closed. Monday was also the day for laundry, which we took by taxi to a laundromat in town after we got through with that ridiculous episode in the customs office.

Shopping meant several stops. There was a *supermercado* within walking distance of the boat, and most things we wanted in the way of staples and packaged stuff were there, but the butcher was in another part of town, and shopping by pantomime for unidentified meat was something of an adventure. We could, however, order *pollo* and be understood. Jim tried manfully to work from our book of Spanish phrases, with only partial success. He could never seem to find the right page at the right time, as the pages had begun to fall out and were not in order any more.

The biggest adventure was the fruit and vegetable market. In most West Indian towns, this is usually a collection of stalls in a square in the center of town: sometimes under a tin roof, sometimes in the open, but in either case ramshackle and dilapidated. Puerto Plata has gone modern, and its market is on the outskirts of town under a big, open-sided concrete dome, with satellite buildings. Inside, there is the same oderiferous shambles as in the old-fashioned markets, with women tending individual stalls vying noisily for your trade in a profusion of piled fruit and vegetables that varied considerably in appeal and freshness.

Jane has become fairly experienced in native markets over the years, and she gets along fine with the salesladies, who always take delight in finding what she wants. Avocados, limes (real ones), bananas, cristofine (a form of squash), and sapodilla were the haul this time. Then came the problem of getting it all back to the boat, a long walk. Jim was great at toting loads when we shopped, but this seemed too far even with the stuff split three ways for carrying. There were no taxis in sight, but just as we started on the long trek in the sun, a horse and carriage appeared and we grabbed it, clip-clopping back to the harbor in leisurely splendor for two dollars. The route took us through a part of town we had not seen before, with even meaner streets, garbage and litter everywhere, a strong smell from the open gutters, and crowds of people just hanging around without any seeming purpose. There was a sense of threat in their idleness and in the long stares that followed us in our slow pace, but nothing happened.

Monday was cruise ship day in Puerto Plata, and two big white ships, *Song of Norway* and *Boheme*, had shouldered into the harbor at breakfast time. *Song of Norway*, a large, handsome vessel, just about filled the whole harbor while she was turning around and backing into a big pier on the south shore. *Boheme* came in at the pier next to us, and the town was transformed for the next few hours. Passengers were everywhere, and there were almost as many local kids, begging and selling all sorts of garish curious. Pushing through the tourist throngs, you were accosted every few feet by someone selling something, and it was a relief to get back to the boat after all our errands. The porch of the brothel was deserted on this day, as the girls were all inside, busy taking care of sailors from the cruise ships.

The yacht population had changed some, as it did every day, with constant comings and goings, most of them northbound at this time of year. One new arrival was a forty-foot motorsailer flying the Dutch flag, but with *Vigor*, Miami, Florida, on her transom. She was owned by a young Dutch couple, Karl and Luise, who had pulled up stakes at home and were seeing the world with their nine-year-old son. Karl was a shipwright, and money for their adventure had come from remodeling an old tugboat into a unique yacht and selling her. Their "cutting loose" was total. They had sold everything and headed for the United States, where they had never been before. In their early thirties, they

The Song of Norway *almost filled the harbor*

were trim and active. He had a short beard and glasses and the look of a lean, muscular professor, and she was lithe, olive-skinned, with black hair and big dark eyes that she accentuated with heavy makeup even when she was in old clothes and puttering around the boat. Their son, who had picked up the knickname Joe while traveling in the States and delighted in it, was a completely engaging lad, handsome, sturdy, and outgoing, with curly blond hair and a perpetual smile.

They had traveled all through the States for several months before ending up in Florida and buying their motorsailer. Although Karl was experienced at working on boats, he knew nothing about sailing, and *Vigor* was not a very successful vessel for them. She had a motorboat hull, with broad, flat run aft, which meant poor sailing qualities, and she had not been put together too well. She came from a small yard in South Florida that I had not heard of. Evidently, the price had been right, but Karl had spent a great deal of time trying to make her hold together, and they had had a rough time bouncing to windward through the Bahamas and across from Caicos.

147

The Dutch family from Vigor

They were fascinated by *Brunelle* and her layout and went over her enviously when we invited them aboard. When we returned the visit to *Vigor,* we found that they had made the best of her that they could, as she was set up in very homelike fashion. Joe's cabin was a typical boy's room with banners and pictures of planes and space ships, but she was poorly laid out, cramped, and not too comfortable.

Joe was all over the quay making friends with everybody, and

148

Joe and Jim horsing on the yacht pier

within a day he was running with a bunch of local kids in the fields near the pier. He came back in the afternoon, covered from head to foot with mud from digging along the shore with his new friends, and Karl had to give him a thorough hosing off on the quay before he could be permitted aboard. For him to make the long jump from pier to surging boat, they had rigged a line on the mizzen boom, and he would swing aboard like Tarzan.

The hose was a community affair on the quay, and there was no charge for water or dockage, but fuel was another problem. There was

149

no pump, and fuel had to be brought down in drums and hand-pumped into the boats. With fuel guzzlers like the big Hatteras, this was a tedious, all-day job, and I was worried about how we could handle it. We needed more fuel before we could head out along the coast.

May Day was a washout for anything like fueling. The town was shut tight, and labor rallies were held at the town square in the morning. Jim went up to have a look and reported that an apathetic group of men, with no women in evidence, listened to canned speeches over loudspeakers, complete with recorded music and applause, and then quietly drifted away, with no show of enthusiasm whatsoever. Afterwards everybody went to the beach.

Our last two dinners ashore were split between the Palacio and a restaurant called Portofino outside of town that Mike Ronan took us to. The Palacio was cheap, with chops, two hamburgers, five drinks, and three beers coming to fifteen dollars, and the bar seemed to be the unofficial hangout for yachtsmen. Pablo and Francisco had probably been right to steer us there. It wasn't exactly your "right burgee" crowd, though; rather an odd international mix of adventurers.

A chess game was in progress in the dimly lit bar between Jeremy and a man named Willi from a sloop that was anchored out in the harbor. His background was a mixture of Swiss, German, and Boer; he had a fascinating accent that blended all three influences, and he did not bother to hide the racist and political opinions that went with them. His cruising companion was an ex-Peace Corps woman from Long Island, who had joined up with Willi in Africa for his passage across to the Caribbean. She was an outspokenly liberal woman's libber, who made an equally definite show of her opinions; the thought of them as shipmates was intriguing.

Before going to the Portofino, Mike took us and the Dutch family to his house in town, a typically Latin-American setup with a plain front on the street, giving right on the sidewalk, and an airy, comfortable interior with high ceilings, elaborate woodwork, fine old furniture, and tile floors. A garden in back, completely hidden from the street, was a riot of flowers and grape arbors. His wife, Patricia, had spent a long day at a family party for her aunt's sixtieth birthday and was a bit over-partied when we arrived, but she gallantly regrouped her forces and went on with us to the restaurant, which was an unpretentious place with bare tables on a veranda next to an overgrown garden, with enormous trees hanging low around it. It was jammed with locals noisily ending the May Day festivities, and our fare was native, *patchugas* (chicken wrapped in cheese batter) and minced conch again, this time spelled *lamby* rather than *lambi* on the menu.

Patricia was fascinated with the details of our living aboard *Brunelle* and of the Dutch family's vagabond lifestyle, as the thought of such adventures seemed completely foreign to a Latin-American young lady of genteel upbringing. She asked many questions of Jane and Luise about housekeeping and cooking on board, and was amazed at the thought of living that way.

With the holiday over, it was time to think about fueling and perhaps getting underway. The trade had been blowing briskly ever since our arrival, and I was hoping that it might soon begin to languish. Mike Ronan, helpful as ever, said that he owned a service station and I could get diesel there (this was at the start of the fuel shortage of the summer of 1979, which was already being felt in the Dominican Republic). I would have to scrounge a drum from somewhere, and *Boobie Hatch* came through on that. She carried extra drums and had already fueled, and Don was able to lend me an empty fifteen-gallon one. He had had a real hassle getting fuel down to his boat via taxi cab, ending up in an argument that brought the entire crew of pier habitués into a great gesticulating, waving confab. José's calm reason eventually prevailed, but Don was in a state of collapse after the experience and wished me luck with my problem.

Mike and I rolled the drum to his pickup truck, and he drove me to his service station. As we turned in the drive, the attendant could be seen sitting disconsolately on the steps of the station's office, head in hands. Mike honked the horn, and the man looked up, spread his hands wide and shrugged. *"Nada,"* he called.

"Not even diesel?" Mike asked, and got another shake of the head.

"All gone," and his head went back in his hands.

"Wow," Mike said. "I guess we're out until the next tanker

arrives. Well, let's try another station. I think I know where there is some."

Fortunately he was right, and we wrestled the full drum back along the quay and transferred it via our hand pump. We still had almost half a tank after the run from Caicos, so I figured we were set for the one hundred-mile run to Samana, even if it was all under power.

I had been eying the weather all morning, and the trade had not begun to blow by noon. There were gentle zephyrs from the land, but the ocean outside the harbor was flat. If the trade held off a bit longer, it would probably not come in at all, and we should have a nightime calm for pushing on to Samana. Again the thought of a power passage was not thrilling, but neither was the expected prospect of beating around Cabo Francis Viejo and Cabo Cabron for a couple of days in normal conditions.

To be ready, I decided to obtain clearance from the commandante so that we could leave at any time. Even though port officials are now the soul of hospitality, and yachts are made most welcome and handled with polite efficiency in sharp contrast to the Trujillo days and the turbulent period after it, there are still restrictions about moving along the coast, perhaps a hangover from former times. You must enter and clear each Dominican port, and the next port must be designated in your clearance, with no other stops permitted. I knew, though, that many boats had put into places like Escondido, where there was no customs office, and I was curious about the realities of the situation. I asked Mike what he knew about it; he said he would ask the commandante, an old friend.

The commandante, in full regalia as before, was, if possible, more effusively friendly than on our clearing in, and formalities in his office were carried on amid smiles and pleasantries, with much banging of rubber stamps by his clerk, until Mike asked him about the regulations covering stops in intermediate ports. The result was a fifteen-minute discourse in rapid-fire Spanish, with many gestures for emphasis, and I began to think I had started some sort of international incident as the commandante went on and on with intense feeling. When he finally ended, though, he had another big smile for me, and we shook hands with great warmth.

Mike's version of the fifteen-minute lecture was simply that it was only possible to give clearance to one port at a time, but, should it become necessary because of weather conditions to put into another port, there would be *"no probleme"* as long as your papers were in order. We were cleared for Samana, and I was fully intending to make it nonstop unless we ran into trouble.

By 1430 there was still no sign of a trade wind, so we thanked Mike profusely for all his help and hospitality, slipped a bottle of Scotch in a paper bag to José, whose gold tooth flashed in delight, and bid fond farewells to the Dutch family and *Boobie Hatch.* She would be leaving soon after us, and *Vigor* was also heading east and would probably run into us again.

In the hot, breezeless sunshine, Jim wrestled in the long scope of rope and a mucky anchor finally cleared the bottom and settled into the bow chock. We powered out on the glassy heave of sea beyond the sea buoys and turned east for the first landmark, Cabo Macoris, at 1500, headed into the worry box labeled "north coast of Hispaniola."

15. *A Forgotten Corner*

≈≈≈≈≈≈≈≈≈≈≈≈≈≈≈≈≈≈≈≈≈≈≈≈≈≈≈≈≈≈≈≈≈≈≈≈

I had vivid memories of this coastline from a flight in 1943 in a Sikorsky amphibian, a former Pan Am Clipper, with high wing, great round ports for windows, and a stately rate of progress that made for wonderful sightseeing. It was a navy plane from San Juan to Guantanamo, and the pilot had taken us straight along this virtually harborless stretch of northeastern Hispaniola on a day of booming trades. I remembered well the sight of big, blue Atlantic combers dashing against the cliffs and headlands in explosions of spray, pulsating contrasts in white to the deep blue of the sea and the dark rocks and cliffs. Navy friends who had brought subchasers to windward along here said that sea conditions were as rugged as any they had met.

None of that was seen on this placid afternoon, with the beach on Cabo Macoris shining in the slanting light and Isabela de Torres hulking up as a black silhouette on the lowering sunpath in the west, gradually misting and fading. When the sun was gone, it was a long, dark night with little to see, as we followed the same watch system. There was a lighthouse on Francis Viejo credited with eighteen miles visibility, but it was merely a weak flicker when less than ten miles off. A few lights showed around it, but after we cleared it and were farther offshore in the bight between Francis Viejo, scene of Jeremy's disaster, and Cabron, there was nothing to see at all. Again a foul-weather jacket was needed against the penetrating dampness, with some spits of rain. I wondered whether the shore lights belonged to the people who had scavenged Jeremy's schooner.

The swells were long and smooth-backed, and we rolled some as we hummed along at 2000 RPMs, but there was not so much as a wind ripple on the humping shoulders of the swells until a land breeze came down from the distant mountains at 0200 and we were able to sail for a change. This rare thrill only lasted an hour, and we were back under power for the rest of the passage. Jim saw one boat pass to seaward of us on our course shortly after midnight, and a pile of lights that looked like a passenger ship sped by westward bound on the port horizon at 0330, but otherwise we had the black, empty night to ourselves until Cabron's soaring bulk loomed out of the dawn twilight at 0530. We rounded it several miles off and headed to starboard for its twin, Cabo Samana, at the other side of the entrance to Bahia de Rincon, a deep indentation that might offer some shelter in certain winds.

At 0715 we cleared Cabo Samana and started into the mouth of Bahia de Samana. The shoreline to starboard was a rich green in the rising sun, dotted with a few houses and signs of cultivation, but the bay is so wide that the south shore, over ten miles away, was a blue line of mountains, indistinct in the morning haze. This is probably one of the least known areas of the Antilles, a great bay that could, in the phrase of the description by Columbus of Graham Harbor at San Salvador, "hold all the ships in Christendom." It slashes for thirty miles westward into the eastern end of Hispaniola and looks as though it could be home to a major port, while Santo Domingo, on the south coast of Hispaniola, third largest city (after Havana and San Juan) in the West Indies, is on the tiny Ozawa River and has almost no port at all.

What probably kept Samana from being developed is a maze of reefs that almost spans the mouth of the bay. The only possible entry is close along the north shore, where we were following a line of buoys; vessels probing into the center of it in the days before charts either retired prudently or were wrecked. It was a haven for pirates, who hid among the reefs between forays, but civilization passed it by for centuries. Only a few Indians lived there, and in mid-nineteenth century, a ship carrying runaway slaves from the States ventured into the bay and was wrecked. The ship's company moved ashore and established a self-sufficient colony that remained cut off from the rest of the world for fifty years. Speaking English, and carrying names like Green and Jones, they lived in isolation, undisturbed until the automobile roads of the twentieth century finally penetrated their hideaway.

Las Flechas, the Bay of Arrows

Columbus came to Samana on his first voyage, and it was the first place in which he encountered difficulty with the Indians. The normally docile Arawaks were more warlike here, as they were closer to the fierce Caribs of the eastern islands than the other Arawaks on Hispaniola and Cuba, and they had learned to defend themselves against Carib raids. When *Nina* and *Pinta* arrived in mid-January 1493 on their way home to Spain, natives armed with bows and arrows lined the beach of a small cove a few miles inside the mouth of the bay on the north shore. They were Ciguayo Indians, a branch of the Tainos, Arawaks who lived on the eastern end of Hispaniola, and the cove has ever since been known as *Las Flechas* (arrows) to commemorate the incident. After some volleys of arrows were sent off, real bloodshed was avoided by judicious trading, but this was a foretaste of the conflict that was eventually to wipe out all Indians in the Caribbean.

Columbus had already lost *Santa Maria* on a reef near what is now

Cap Haitien, Haiti; he had established a settlement at Navidad in the same area—that was destroyed by the Indians several months after its founding—and had stopped at Puerto Plata and named it for the silver cloud atop Isabela de Torres. Now he was anxious to head home to tell of his discoveries. On Wednesday January 18, 1493, the two caravels sailed from Samana on the long, arduous voyage home. They had not yet learned how to play the trades and Gulf Stream, of course, and it was a rugged trip. He was back again on his return voyage in November of that year, but Samana did not figure in his plans for colonization, and it slept undisturbed through the centuries.

According to Samuel Eliot Morison, the historian who wrote prolifically and brilliantly on Columbus in several books, the admiral had been very impressed with Cabo Samana, which he described as "beautiful and high and round, all of rock, like Cape St. Vincent in Portugal." Columbus named it Cabo del Enamorado after some "lover's leap" he knew about in Spain, but this was one of his place names that did not stick.

Bahia de Samana today is primitive enough to bring thoughts of early explorations graphically to life. It is not hard to imagine what these bays and cliffs looked like when first seen by the white man, as there is little basic change today in making the same landfalls.

As we moved by Las Flechas, identified for us through Harry Kline's *Guide,* we could begin to see evidences of civilization that had not been there in the time of Columbus. The town of Samana came into view ahead, marked by one large, white sprawling building on a point enclosing the harbor; houses were closer together along the shore; fishing boats could be seen in the little coves and dotted across the bay; and we passed a marine railway with a workboat on it. Buoys marked the way into a single quay to starboard, where a few yachts could be seen. One of them was *Boobie Hatch,* and a few more boats were anchored out. The flat, breathless calm continued, and the boats and houses were reflected in the still waters of the harbor.

There was a startling sight off the beach of a small island to port while we were making our final approach to the quay. Close in against the shore, the superstructure of a Hatteras motor yacht of about sixty

A startling sight as we entered Samana

feet could be seen sticking out of the water, with the hull completely submerged, and from its condition, it could not have been there very long. From *Santa Maria* to Jeremy's schooner to Hatteras motor yachts, this coast could obviously claim its victims.

Once again there was that rewarding feeling of another worry box turning into a fizzled firecracker. The coast of Hispaniola had been one of the main features of my 0400 waking nightmares after my air view of it and the tales of other sailors. Richard Baum, whose book *By the Wind* written in the 1950s contained a delightful account of single-handed cruising in these waters, had had a particularly rough time going *west* here, which should have been the direction for a sleighride, when he was hit by a cold-front northwester. Francis Viejo had been his particular *bête noir,* and here we were, safely past all those symbols of frustration. I had to admit that the sailing had not been that magnificent, but we had made it with ease and comfort. There was still the Mona Passage, of course. On a percentage basis, after our calm passages since the Caicos, I figured we were due for a change.

Mooring here was again by the stern-to method, and it was like old home week to nestle up alongside *Boobie Hatch* once more. It was she Jim had seen passing us during the night, and she had beaten us in by a couple of hours. The docking crew here was not as large or as helter-skelter as the one at Puerto Plata, but there was still an impression that most of the town was there to supervise our arrival. There was the same type of security as at Puerto Plata, with a customs guard in charge of the pier, helped by navy enlisted men here, but there was no fence; the quay that served as a landing for motor launches also carried on a continuous ferry service to the other side of the bay. There was a never-ending ebb-and-flow of passengers to whom we were an object of some curiosity, and the privacy was about equal to that in the monkey house at the Central Park Zoo. Despite this, there was a good watch kept on the yachts at all times, and we never worried about security when we left *Brunelle.*

We had to be cleared in of course, and this too was in a lower key than the ceremonial, uniformed pomp in Puerto Plata. As soon as the lines were secure, we were boarded by port officials consisting of a young man in casual clothes and a Marlboro cigarettes hat and two henchmen, who did not say a word. The leader was slow and reserved but perfectly polite as we went through the various forms, and his English was good. His only "price" was a cold beer, opened this time and consumed in the cockpit.

It was breathlessly hot, with the sun beating down from directly overhead on its way north to its June 21 limit at the Tropic of Cancer, and we sweltered through lunch hour and the taking on of diesel fuel. There was a long hose from a pump at the land end of the pier, and we topped off at twenty-eight gallons, with two more still in the hose that we had no way of taking aboard, even though I was paying for

The busy quay at Samana

them. How I wished later that I had put them in some sort of jug. We had used forty-three gallons in fifty-one hours.

We were barely settled in, and still feeling like aliens in a strange land, when a young lady appeared at our transom and asked, "Excuse me, sir. Are you the captain? Are you going to Puerto Rico?"

I allowed that I was and we were, and she said, "I must speak to you on a matter of the greatest importance. May I come aboard, please?"

I said that I thought we could discuss whatever it was as we were, but her eyes filled with liquid and her lips trembled a bit.

"Oh no, sir. I must talk to you in private. Please. It is very important." She was dark and slender, with olive skin, large eyes, and pleasant looks, but you would not describe her as a beauty. She had a Latin accent, but not a heavy one.

After a few more demurrals on my part, she finally talked her way aboard, as Jane and Jim watched us warily.

"I am a woman alone," she said, softly but emotionally, "and I am trapped here. I must get to United States territory, but I do not have a visa. Will you please take me to Puerto Rico?"

Out of the corner of my eye, I could catch Jane's reaction to this one. Even if mine had not been the same, I knew that there was no way this young lady could come aboard for the Mona Passage trip.

"I'm sorry," I said. "I am writing up our cruise—sort of an official trip. If anything went wrong it would be very difficult for me, and I couldn't take the chance."

"Oh, but there is no problem, sir." She did not give it the "*no probleme*" accent, but I could see Jim suppressing a smirk at his favorite phrase. "I can guarantee you that I can get ashore with no difficulty long before anybody would know. Please, I beg of you; I must get there. You do not know what it is like to be a woman alone and desperate."

I was beginning to feel like someone refusing to contribute to the Hundred Neediest Cases, but I also knew that there was no way we were going to get mixed up with this one, so I stuck to my story and my refusal, and finally, after several more heartfelt pleas and promises of "no trouble," she took her tearful departure.

She went from us to *Boobie Hatch,* as we all exchanged murmured remarks about how long she would last there, and it was not exactly a surprise when Olive had her back on the quay in about two minutes.

After this episode and a few more strange encounters, we began to appreciate in retrospect José and his barbed-wire fence at Puerto Plata. There it had only been a question of buying rotten bananas, but here we were visited by a religious fanatic, a woman who never stopped predicting the most dire events as she handed out tracts, a sad, tattered single-hander who looked as though he had been dragged through a knothole and wanted to talk boats for hours, and various ferry passengers who just wanted to stare at us. There was also a large resident population of dogs who stood on the quay and salivated. Basic security was still good though. No one was allowed on the boats, and we had to clear things like cameras and handbags when we were taking them ashore.

Secure alongside with Boobie Hatch *after the squall*

My dislike for Med moors was reinforced when the oppressive heat was broken by a quick, hard-hitting squall in mid-afternoon. We were facing south, and the squall, building deep purple over the bay beyond the harbor, swept in viciously from the east. Nobody's anchor held in the soft harbor mud against its sideways thrust, and we all had to clear the quay in a hurry, with rain slashing horizontally across us, to stand by in the harbor until things calmed down. The strong wind was just a frontal gust, and it was soon humidly calm again. By mutual agreement, we all tied up alongside, as there was enough room at the moment to do this, and no one said us nay.

The town of Samana is a strange phenomenon. A few years previously, a decision had been made to clean it up and modernize it as a tourist center, and the entire town, to a house, had been razed. Evidently it used to be a typical, small Latin-American town of ramshackle huts, balconied wooden buildings lining dusty streets, and the usual running gutters, running dogs, chickens, pigs, and urchins. Now it was entirely of concrete block construction, with rows of modern-looking shops and bungalows lining the wide boulevard that ran along the harbor. Across the harbor, a big modern hotel, the white building that was the first landmark as we headed in, covered the top of a point in a magnificent location, and from the point, a long footbridge led to a casino on the little island that had the wrecked Hatteras next to it. All the buildings were new, but they were already assuming a rundown look, with cracks in the concrete and water stains on the walls, and there was a sad air of plans unfulfilled and dreams denied, or at least deferred, hanging over everything.

I had my letter from Bonnie Ericson at Caicos to Nadim Bezi. When I found that he lived in a bungalow not far from the quay, I went to deliver it and to see what would happen. He had an office off a waiting room in a wing of his house, and half the population of Samana seemed to be sitting there waiting to see him. I felt as though I were going to the dentist's (but I hadn't had any tooth trouble this time— knock wood). Finally he disposed of the visits of several people and asked me in to his office.

He was a swarthy, heavy-set man with a beaked nose, bright black eyes, a trim moustache, a head of thick black hair, and a flashing, gold-toothed smile. He was dressed in a plain white T-shirt, khaki pants, and heavy work shoes. I gave him the letter, and we immediately established that he spoke no English and my Spanish was not so hot, but he did gather who the letter was from. Holding it, he called loudly for his wife, who came from another part of the house and was able to translate it for him, but she did not remain as interpreter, so I was a bit uncertain, after he and I conversed in Spanish for a while, exactly what he had said he would do. I was pretty sure that he had said he would take us for a tour the next day, but I wouldn't have bet on it.

I could have, though, because it happens that I had understood him correctly. At 0930 the next morning, on a calm and humid day with clouds gathering over the inland mountains, a red pickup truck appeared at the quay, where Bezi, incidentally, had the fuel concession, and this was to be our vehicle for a sightseeing tour. Jane sat in regal

Ready to go sightseeing at Samana

splendor in the cab, with Bezi and the driver, neither of whom spoke English, a sign-language setup, since Jane's Spanish is even more sketchy than mine. Jim and I rode in the back, with a young man as interpreter. He was a true blue-black, not the coffee-colored mix so often seen in Latin-American lands, with a wide, white smile. His English was fine, and his name was Green, a descendant of the wreck refugees from over one hundred years ago. I asked him his first name.

"Well, my grandfather calls me Turkey, so everybody else does too," he said with a broad grin.

While Jane and her companions, in the isolation of the cab, communicated with gestures and "si, si" every so often, he gave us a running account in colloquial English of what we were seeing. The roads were very good, and first we headed east through rich fields of sugar cane and vegetables, backed by foothills of higher mountains. We took a look at the Bay of Arrows, and Bezi also stopped several times to chat with field workers. Turkey told us that most of the land being worked was owned by Bezi. The road ended at Rincon Bay, which we had passed at sea the previous morning. A long stretch of white beach, backed by rows of coconut palms, looked out at the twin capes, Cabron and Samana, guarding its entrance, and Bezi showed me a spot behind reefs to the left of the beach that he said was a good anchorage, although the mouth of the bay was open to the usual direction of the trades.

Turkey said something about soldiers and mines in connection with the beach, at least the way I heard it. Bezi had already said that this beach was one of the main tourist attractions of the area, where passengers from the once-a-week cruise ship were taken for a day's outing, and I conjured up a mental image of bevies of tourists in bathing suits being blown sky high as they stepped onto the sand. Jane saw my confusion and laughed at me.

"He said that soldiers 'mind' the beach," she said, pointing to a guard hut down the way a bit.

Bezi sent Turkey up a nearby tree for some coconuts, and he slashed their tops off and offered them to us for drinking. Jane has broad, catholic tastes in food and drink, but the one thing she can't stand is coconut. Nevertheless, she accepted the offering graciously and daintily sipped at it without showing how she really felt.

As we sat on the sand and drank from our coconuts, I gathered some of Bezi's background in the rather disjointed communication we could manage in Spanglish, with help from Turkey. His father and mother came from Syria and had been visiting in the Dominican Republic when World War I broke out. They couldn't go home, so they settled in and began acquiring land. He was born in the Dominican Republic and considers himself a Dominicano despite his Syrian background. In addition to owning much of the workable land in the Samana region, he has instigated the program to develop the area for tourism. Rebuilding the town was a start, followed by construction of an airport for feeder planes, the hotel and casino, and an enormous concrete pier for cruise ships that sticks out into the bay a few miles west of Samana.

The plan was to create all the facilities before attracting tourists, and then to enter into a promotion program. The problem developed that no one now wants to work the fields. They prefer to sit back and wait for the tourist boom. At the time we were there the program was just getting started, and the results had been slow. One cruise ship, *Carnivale*, from Miami, was coming in on Tuesdays, but that was about it for the moment. Later we went to the pier, which had a huge customs building and waiting room, and the modern, attractive Hotel Cayacoa on its cliff across the harbor; they were eerily empty. We did not hit a Tuesday in our Samana stop, but I understand that the contrast between the weeklong torpor of the other days and the sudden invasion once a week makes an amusing scene.

The only vessel at the pier was an old United States Coast Guard buoy tender named *Hickory* (built in 1933), now owned by a private diving and salvage company from the States under contract to the government of the Dominican Republic to investigate the wrecks on the reefs of Bahia de Samana. She was an incredible bucket of rust and deterioration, but she was somehow still able to operate. In talking to crew members later when they came to ogle *Brunelle*, we found that there was an untold number of wrecks, dating back as much as 250 years, on the reefs. *Hickory* had also been out on the Silver Bank, eighty miles offshore, where there are many more wrecks, including the much-publicized *Concepcion.* Her major feature was a huge cylinder with a fanlike propeller in it poised over her stern—so ungainly that it looked as though it would upend her sternwards. This could be lowered over a wreck site and was used to blow silt away before divers went to work. As expected in the close-mouthed world of treasure hunting, no one would say much about the success or failure of the project, but they sure could have used some paint.

As a contrast to Samana, we were taken to Sanchez, about twenty miles to the west at the head of the bay. This was a typical country town without a vestige of tourism, and its sights and smells, its narrow, dusty streets, wooden houses with balconies leaning out, open-front shops, hordes of people gathered on corners and milling around the stores, skittering animals, and shining mounds of coffee beans awaiting sorting

The treasure ship Hickory

in sheds, all were reminders of how Samana must have looked before the "resurrection."

On the way back to Samana from Sanchez, the clouds that had been building all day came down from the mountains as a series of rain squalls, and the back of the truck was like the bridge of a ship driving into a storm. We were doing forty miles per hour, and as the rain stung us like bullets we huddled behind the cab for protection, with water

streaming down our faces. Not exactly sightseeing deluxe, but a fascinating day. In addition to the tip he shyly asked for, I gave Turkey a
Brunelle T-shirt as a thank you, which he could not accept in front of
the customs man, who moreover, did not allow him on board.

Life at the quay was continuously interesting, both in the comings
and goings of the unbelievably crowded ferry launches and in the mix
of yachts and world voyagers. There was a very odd story connected
with the arrival of an American cabin cruiser. We had seen her making
painfully slow progress up the channel from the sea *in reverse* before
she finally came to a halt a couple of hundred yards out and had to be
towed to the quay.

It seems that her transmission had packed in soon after she had
left South Caicos; she intended to run through to the Virgin Islands
nonstop, with extra fuel in drums on board. Her reverse gear still
worked, however, and she had taken five days to make it into Samana
under reverse gear only, with her fuel running out just short of the quay.
A hard story to believe, but it evidently checked out.

Salvage crews were working on the wrecked Hatteras out by the
island, leaving from the quay each morning with a huge collection of
masks and tanks. The report was that a local yard had paid twenty
thousand dollars for the wreck to the insurance company that had
declared her a total loss. She had been on a delivery voyage with two
professionals as crew when she "just started to sink," according to the
third-hand report we had of their story, but there was a suspicion
running around that a navigational error and a reef might have had
something to do with it. She should have been quite a prize for the
salvagers.

The lady-in-distress trying to get to Puerto Rico was still making
the rounds. For a while she had taken up with a young Dutch single-
hander in a small trimaran, but he was heading west, the wrong direction for her, and she was soon on the prowl again. The Dutchman, thin,
blond, and bearded, had sailed across from Europe and was headed up
the east coast of America, where he planned to go through the canals
to the Great Lakes and then come down the Mississippi to salt water
again, a unique way to see the country. It was a lifelong dream, he said,

to visit America, and this was the only way he could afford it. He had cruised in company with Jeremy for a bit and filled us in on his rather casual methods.

An attractive French couple on a modern sloop at the quay, a typical European design with reverse sheer and contoured decks, was also on the way to the east coast, so we gave them the *Inland Waterway Guide* to help them along. We traded cocktail visits, and they served us Martinique rum with that special, heavy "cane" smell that wafts up from it, so different from the more refined rums from Barbados, Antigua, the Virgins, and Puerto Rico. On *Brunelle* we were still sticking to Mount Gay, as ever, which I learned to drink in Bermuda in 1937 and have been partial to ever since.

They wore minimum bathing suits on their tanned, lithe bodies and seemed very efficient and well-organized in their life aboard. Pointing to a small ketch anchored out in the harbor, they told us it belonged to a woman from South Africa who had two small children aboard. Her husband had taken off from Cape Town in a boat with another woman, and the outraged wife and mother had taken up pursuit in the little ketch. (Could it be Willi, we wondered?) What would happen if and when she caught up with him, one could only conjecture, but a fly on the bulkhead might have an interesting time.

Another ketch anchored out was a run-down looking Atkin design from Connecticut. A tow-headed youngster brought an adult couple to the quay from her in a dinghy and hung on next to us while they wandered into town. Soon he was chatting with us, asking about *Brunelle* and where we had been and comparing notes. He had been aboard the ketch for six of his thirteen years, back and forth between Florida and the islands, and Samana was as far east as they had ever come. They had spent seven weeks in Puerto Plata earlier in the winter waiting for a break in the trades and had now been in Samana for several weeks. The crew was his father, his younger brother, and "Dad's girl friend." They had expected to haul out on Samana's slipway but found that their draft was too much. The boat, slightly hogged and with fittings weeping rust down her peeling sides, dated to 1939 and was obviously in need of a boat yard's ministrations. The lad admitted wistfully that he was tired of cruising and wanted to be in a regular school with other kids. Could be that seven weeks in Puerto Plata had something to do with this sentiment and I was reminded of my old plan to take off with our kids in their teens. Perhaps it had been better to wait twenty years.

We had stocked up in Samana's jumbled little market near the quay and had sampled the one restaurant nearby, where we had chicken, cooked native style with vegetables and spices, at a cost of nine dollars for three of us. We had fuel and we had had the benefit of a Bezi tour, and we were ready to move on from this forgotten, out-of-the-way and fascinating enclave. It was time to think of the Mona Passage. Actually, I had been thinking of it for many months, but we were now due for the frontal confrontation.

16. Mona Passage

~~~~~~

There is a little gem of an island off *Las Flechas* that Columbus described glowingly in his journal. It is called Cayo Levantado, and we had seen several boats anchored there on our way to Samana. I thought it would make a good stop for girding our loins for Mona on the way out of Bahia de Samana but was told that it was a restricted anchorage and that I would need permission when getting my clearance.

The customs and immigration office was across the boulevard in one of the concrete block buildings, and my friend with the Marlboro hat gave us clearance, with special permission to anchor at Levantado. *"No probleme,"* he said as we bid adios.

The morning calm lay heavily over the harbor, with rain clouds hovering around the hills, as we topped off with water and washed the dust of the Samana quay off *Brunelle:* no charge for this or dockage. Once again we said goodbye to *Boobie Hatch,* with promises to meet again, since they would probably pass us en route, and powered the two miles to Levantado down the channel, silk smooth in the morning glare. The island still looks as it must have when Columbus saw it, except that a small hotel has been tucked away on a cove on the south side. It can just barely be seen from the water and was not open at the moment, so Levantado could pass for a deserted "South Seas isle." Except, of course, for the fact that this was Saturday, and several families were having picnics on the palm-covered western point, girdled by a lovely white beach. Their outboards were drawn up on the sand.

In trying to anchor, we found there was quite a current, and the first attempt resulted in slow dragging. Pulling the anchor up to

Brunelle *off Cayo Levantado*

try again, we found it snagged on a large "tree" of coral. The second attempt was more successful, and Jim went over in the Avon to scrub reminders of Puerto Plata and Samana off the boottop, where oil stains had collected. After his labors, he took off to explore the beach while Jane and I relaxed over cocktails and breathed in the lovely scent of flowers drifting out to us from the island. About noon, a light breeze from the east rippled in, and the Dutch single-hander tacked past us in his tri, heading out to the capes, where it would be a fair breeze for him. With it, local fishing boats began to sweep in from the southern reaches of the bay, where they had evidently been working the reefs that fill it. They are small log canoes, with low, slender hulls, very low-aspect sloop rigs, and tremendously long booms extending far out over the sterns. There were two or three in crew, and they were smiling and waving happily as they swooped by us on their way home for a weekend.

Jim reported a friendly, holiday-minded group on the island, including some interesting bikinis, when he came back for lunch. My plan was to relax here until first light in the morning before taking off. We did not want to arrive in Puerto Rico on a Sunday because of overtime charges and the general nuisance of clearing in. It was 180 miles to San Juan, the longest single passage of the whole route from Tampa, but there were alternatives. If we were being slammed too hard on the nose, we could head southeast into the Mona Passage to Mayaguez, a port of entry—a passage of about 120 miles. There was possible shelter at Aguadilla at the northwest tip of Puerto Rico or at Arecibo, thirty miles along the north coast, although they were not entry ports. There was also Mona Island, a flat, rocky outcropping with a lighthouse in the middle of Mona Passage at its southern end, where the *Guide* reported a small harbor.

After all I had read about it, and considering those ominous notations on the charts about "confused seas in this area," and "vessels are recommended to avoid this area," I had no real desire to go through

173

Jim went ashore to explore

Mona Passage. We hoped for a straight run across the top of it to San Juan. It would be at the limit of our fuel capacity if we had to power all the way. Unless it got too rough, however, I intended to do this, because 180 miles to windward under sail would be too long a passage for the way we were set up.

After dinner, the breeze increased, rather than dropping off with the sun, and the new moon shone on a confusion of small choppy waves as the wind worked against the current; *Brunelle* rode uneasily, slewing sideways under the opposing influences, rolling and bouncing a bit. I tried sleep without success, and the motion felt suspicious. Checking bearings, I realized we were slowly dragging anchor. When we tried to bring the anchor in, it was snagged, evidently on another hunk of coral, but we finally broke it loose with the engine. Cayo Levantado, however picturesque, was an uneasy anchorage, and finding a good spot to anchor—out of the current and free of coral—seemed impossible in the

Native fishing boat heading for home

dark, so we said, "What the hell, let's get going." Since there would not have been much sleep there, we figured we might as well be on our way.

At 2300, we cleared Balandra Head and its little winking lighthouse at the entrance to the channel between Levantado and the main island and headed just south of east—well off the low, featureless coast that stretches out to Cape Engano, the eastern tip of Hispaniola. There was one harbor along here, Punta Macao, and we later heard of boats stopping there for fuel, but it was just a dim collection of lights in the misty distance as we plowed into a moderate trade and the moon slid down astern into clouds over Cabo Samana.

The last lights we saw were at 0530, just as dawn began to define the horizon over the bow, and it was then a long day of slug-slug, bounce-bounce on an empty ocean. There was a treadmill effect

175

in the unending march of bright blue waves and white crests as they slid under us and hissed off to leeward through our quickly erased wake, and the Westerbeke purred along at 2000 RPMs. Perhaps a few turns more would have meant better progress, but also a harder bounce and higher noise level. It was a lovely day if you were headed anywhere but east. There were no ships and no planes all day, but flying fish skittered away from us, and birds skimmed the waves as they circled. Brown boobies I recognized, and there were delicate white gulls with long, forked tails, and darting black birds with a white V on their wings. (Obviously, ornithology is not one of my fortes.)

The sun's path was from dead ahead to directly over us at noon and right down our wake in the afternoon, and as it wheeled across us, I began to develop an aberration—we were stuck there forever in one spot on the ocean, with the waves sliding past us, endlessly condemned to bobbing up and down in an empty world. Could there be teeming cities, dusty Puerto Platas, airports, marinas, suburban houses, and snowy mountains in the same world? Nothing else could possibly exist but this small, plunging hull, these onrushing waves, and the glitter of sun on the sea, crinkling your skin and dazzling your eyes; nothing but us and the booby birds. (And how glad I was there was no lady-in-distress hitchhiker.)

Jane did her needlepoint as usual, and she takes a stubborn pride in producing full meals on time when we are on offshore passages, no matter what the bounce and heave. I, too, had to stick to the bartending routine of a cold beer at 1100, cocktails when the sun passed the yardarm, and again before dinner, to support her in her efforts. We had a regular breakfast with eggs and bacon, one of her celery-and-shrimp concoctions for lunch, and a fine dinner of chicken and cristofine as darkness took over and the gibbous moon became a friendly sentinel.

This was one time when estimates of speed were difficult, as I had not had experience with a power run in these conditions. It was obvious we were not making the six knots we had averaged from Caicos to

Puerto Plata and on to Samana, and I was hoping that four and a half might be it. This should have given us the sight of a glimmer of something from Puerto Rico by mid-evening, but it wasn't until Jane was ending her wheel trick just before midnight that we picked up the loom of light from Ramey Field, an air base at the northwest tip of Puerto Rico.

After some big rollers off Hispaniola at dawn the previous morning, the waves had been about the same all day, and I figured the breeze at about twelve to fifteen. Now both were moderating as more and more lights showed, and Borinquen Light and the Ramey aero beacon could be identified. The night seemed even longer than the day in the slow change of bearing of these markers, and I began to wonder about the fuel holding out. By 0930 we were off Arecibo, and I decided to duck in there in hopes of finding diesel. We had averaged 4.2 knots for thirty-five hours and had about forty miles to go to get into San Juan. I thought we could just make it, but it would be better to get fuel if we could.

There was a long quay with few signs of life at Arecibo, a small commercial harbor, and the two auxiliaries with the "long hairs" aboard we had met in Puerto Plata were anchored there. From them we found that you had to take a taxi several miles to a service station in town, using your own container to pick up fuel. Rather than get into all of that, we turned around and headed east again.

While Hispaniola had evoked a constant sense of history and of the explorations of Columbus and those who followed him, the low green coast of Puerto Rico, with mountains far inland, did little to arouse similar reactions. It is built up and cultivated, and a feeling for the past is lacking.

All day we plugged eastward in the same kind of breeze as the day before, passing villages, resorts, and small towns. We had gone by the enormous sprawl of hotels along the beach at Dorado, with Point Salinas and its prominent white radar domes coming up and San Juan a distant blur ahead, when the engine coughed, and I knew we had had it with the fuel. I killed the engine immediately in

177

a vain hope that it would not need bleeding to get it started again, and Jim and I quickly made sail. I thought ruefully of those two gallons I had paid for that we had left sitting in the long hose at Samana. They probably would just have gotten us to port, but it was really no hardship to be sailing. The wind was directly along the coast, with no favored tack, and we went to it under main and roller-furler.

It was fine sailing and great fun, but the forward progress on course was only about three knots, and it confirmed to me that sailing all the way from Samana would have been a bit too much. In our younger days it would have been a cinch, but those long nightime hours seem to stretch much longer and blacker as the years go on. I still had a small feeling of guilt about having done so much powering. It just didn't seem very salty, but, here we were, and at least we were entering San Juan under sail.

The old Spanish fortress of El Morro on the eastern side of the channel loomed high above us as we took our last tack in from offshore to pick up the sea buoy, and we reached into the harbor, with big-city sounds, sights, and smells all around us and the wind growing puffy and erratic when we moved under the land. Astern, a huge white ship was following us up the channel, but we were still ahead of her as we cleared by El Morro and headed for Club Nautico, which is tucked away at the end of a narrow channel that extends inland, eastward from the main harbor. Our pursuer was *Festivale*, one of the larger cruise ships, and she made a fine sight while she towered above us and moved on by to the cruise docks, where several other ships were berthed: Lots of waving from passengers lining the rail.

We had a quick-tacking drill up the channel to Club Nautico, with Jim and Jane working as a good team on the winches and jib sheets, and twilight deepend around us. There were freighters and fishing boats lining the bulkheaded shore, plus one big cruise ship, the *Guglielmo Marconi*, barges, tug boats, and the usual clutter of a commercial harbor, and we swooped up to them and tacked away at the

Big city sounds and sights surrounded us

last minute in two-hundred-yard legs.

I had not been to Club Nautico since 1958, but I knew where it was, and the *Guide* said there were no obstructions in the channel. A few boats were anchored out, and the club marina piers were to port at the head of the channel. We doused the jib, and I sailed around under main to case the joint for a powerless landing—quarters were a bit confined, and I did not want any repetition of our arrival at Lower Matecumbe.

The only open place was at the fuel dock, next to a big black schooner called *Escapade*. She was moored stern-to, and the approach to the open space alongside her was dead to windward, so we headed up off her bow and slid in along her side with dying momentum, nudging up to the bulkhead with the last of our carry, and one of *Escapade*'s crew took our lines. We were forty-five hours from Samana, and there on the pier stood Don and Olive from *Boobie Hatch* welcoming us to Puerto Rico.

17 *Adios*

~~~~~~

The lady-in-distress was so right about *no probleme* on arrival in Puerto Rico. She could have been having breakfast in New York before we were checked in by customs and immigration. First of all, she could have hopped off in Arecibo, but San Juan would have been just as easy. After we tied up and Don and Olive said they would see us tomorrow to help us bleed the injectors if we had to have it done, I dutifully walked up the pier to the Club Nautico clubhouse where there was a telephone with a plaque next to it that gave several numbers to call for checking with customs. There was no dockmaster, incidentally; he had gone off duty at 1700.

I went down the list of numbers, one by one, without getting an answer, but finally somebody did say "Hello," and I asked how we could check in with customs.

"Oh, I am retired," the man said. "I do not work for customs any more."

"How come your number is still listed here?" I couldn't resist asking.

"Well, amigo, I just like to talk to people. It is lonely since I have retired and I enjoy talking to people on the telephone."

I choked back a smart-ass remark, and he told me one more number to try, but no one answered there either, so I gave up for the night. After two nights of watch standing, we were all a bit groggy and I just wanted to hit the sack. Jane had whipped up a cold supper that was all we needed, and we were soon fast asleep.

In the narrow confines of the Club Nautico marina, very little breeze made its way through the tall buildings hemming us in, and it was a sharp contrast to the two previous nights on the open sea. Perhaps it was the lack of moving air that gave me a night of strange, claustro-phobic nightmares in which I continually felt I was suffocating.

The morning was hot and humid with rain showers, as I went back to the telephone. Finally one of the numbers produced the information that someone would be down to see us soon. The man, complete with uniform and businesslike briefcase, arrived in about an hour and every-thing was *no probleme.* As he settled down in the cockpit and opened his briefcase, he looked around and said, "Nice boat. Nice boat. What is it? A sportfisherman?"

He was gone in five minutes without looking below, but I found out later that the customs men are not always so cursory. It must pay to be a middle-aged square, because the two boats with the young longhairs aboard whom we had seen in Puerto Plata and Arecibo had arrived and anchored out during the evening, and Jim heard later that they got a stem-to-stern going over for more than an hour the next morning, even unto inspecting their peanut butter jars.

When the dockmaster came on duty, he told us we would have to clear the fuel dock, and I said I would be happy to once we had fuel and could get the engine going. We then proceeded to take fifty-four gallons, at least by the pump's meter, in what CSY had told us was a forty-eight-gallon tank! Just one of life's little mysteries. After we got the fuel we couldn't start our engine. The dockmaster said there was no hurry about moving since Tuesday morning was never very busy at the fuel dock.

I was wondering what to do about bleeding the injectors: whether to go find Don and ask him if he could do it or try to locate a mechanic, when a man wandered over from a Columbia 43 in a nearby slip. He had heard that we had come from the west, and he wanted information about the Dominican Republic, since he was heading that way. He had been down island for a year and was on his way back to the States. We compared notes for a while, and I told him about good old José Fernandez, and the subject of our running out of fuel and our currently helpless condition came up.

His eyes lit up. "Injectors need bleeding?" he asked.

"I guess so." I said. "I've never run out before."

"I've had it happen a few times. Want me to see if I can get her going for you?"

"If you've got the time and the inclination, that would be great," was my humble answer, and he went right to work. I watched him and was sure that I could now do it if I had to, as he soon had her turning over, and, after a few coughs, purring away in fine style. Once again, Friendly Marine Service had come to my rescue. The dockmaster said we could do a Med moor and stay where we were next to *Escapade,* which made life simple.

San Juan meant stateside type supermarket shopping and telephone calls to home and office to check how daughter Martha was doing taking care of my finances. Nothing untoward had happened in either place during our isolation in the Caicos and Dominican Republic. Calls to the States went through in the flick of a dial, but a call to Fajardo at the eastern end of the island to make a slip reservation for our estimated arrival was like getting through to the moon and consumed about half an hour.

Club Nautico had changed radically from my visit of twenty-one years ago. Then it had been a busy, beautifully maintained club, with hundreds of members and an array of glossy yachts at the pier. Now it was really a commercial marina and restaurant, with very few members and a generally run-down air. The boats were mostly transients, and the yachts of former members had all moved to Fajardo as a base. Only an hour by road, it is on the protected waters of Vieques Sound. There is easy access to the islands and no longer a need to plug the thirty miles to windward in the open Atlantic to get to those waters from San Juan.

Don and Olive came aboard for a drink and reported that they had had a slow, bouncy trip over, but nothing untoward, and Don added a little postscript to the story of the cabin cruiser that had arrived in Samana in reverse. There appeared to be no repair service there capable of fixing the transmission, and the best bet would be to get her to San Juan somehow. Don made a business proposition to tow the helpless boat across for one thousand dollars, and the response he got was "Up yours. I hope your boat sinks."

San Juan was also a chance for dinners ashore and some sightseeing in Old San Juan and El Morro, interesting but highly hyped for tourists. Jim had been trying to get Tio Pepe sherry as an aperitif ever since Caicos with no luck in the gin mills of Puerto Plata and Samana, and he struck out again when we ate at Club Nautico. He finally made it the next night at the Swiss Chalet in the Condado section, where we were right back in a New York atmosphere in posh dine-and-dance surroundings. For a few hours here *Brunelle* and the lonely seas of the Mona Passage seemed a myth and a dream.

Puerto Rico was not our objective, even though it was an important milestone in that we had no more long passages, and cruising country was a few short days away. Two days in San Juan were plenty, and we were back to reality at 0630 as we slipped away from Club Nautico across a calm, misty harbor. El Morro was a dramatic silhouette against the early sun when we powered past it, and the trades hit us in the face as we rounded eastward and felt the first deep sea swells. On the backside of El Morro on the slopes below the historic buildings of Old San Juan, a jumbled *barrio* of shacks, many of them painted a startlingly bright blue, cascaded down to the water's edge in a filthy huddle, but it was at least a slum with a view.

Slums gave way to the Miami Beach look of the Condado section as we plowed on in a repetition of the passage from Samana, slugging into trade-wind seas. Again, sailing would have taken too long to make the thirty miles to Cabo San Juan at the northeast tip, and the tricky entrance to Vieques Sound, in daylight, but at least this was the last of this sort of thing. Magnificent towers of cumulus rose half way to the zenith over dark and brooding El Yunque, the broad shouldered, 3,484-foot mountain known as the Rainmaker on the eastern end of the island, and isolated showers broke away from the great blue-black curtain shrouding the slopes. They swept along the coast, ever coming closer, and by the time we reached the cape and its lighthouse high on a bluff, we were moving into a wall of rain that soon blotted out the sun and enveloped us. This was a time to celebrate, and a critical point: the last confrontation with the open Atlantic, and a turn to starboard into protected cruising waters.

Yachts and high rises at Isleta Marina

I had first seen Fajardo as a sleepy little fishing village in 1958 and had heard plans then for a hotel on the bluffs just inside the cape and a boatyard-marina-resort complex on a small island in Fajardo Harbor. There were no modern buildings and only one small harbor, Las Croabas, with a few little fishing boats and launches.

Now, through the streaks of rain, we could see El Conquistador Hotel sprawling across the bluff, high-rise buildings and a collection of fancy yachts at the little island, Isleta Marina, and all along the shore, great tall buildings towering over jam-packed marinas. I have seldom seen a more dramatic transformation.

We had booked at a three-hundred-boat marina in a dredged harbor that did not even exist in 1958, and, checking by radio, I was given a slip number. In a downpour that would have done Sadie Thompson proud, we eased through the narrow channel and finally found our slip at one of the dozen or so concrete piers, entered it, and tied up. No one was in sight, and there we sat, alone in acres and acres of concrete and fiberglass, for the rest of the day. No one from the marina came near us, and all the boats around us, mostly cabin cruisers and sportfishermen, were tightly enclosed in canvas curtains in mid-week loneliness. The rain was not merely heavy, separate drops; it was literally a solid cascade. We napped and read all afternoon, as alone and as isolated as if we had been halfway between the Caicos and Puerto Plata, but Jane did find some laundry machines in one of the sheds on the pier and managed to get that chore out of the way.

As it turned out, some adjunct of Howard Johnson's had taken over management of this great complex of marina, high rises, condos, and a shopping center. Considering our relaxed state and Jane's labors in Mona Passage, I said I would find some sort of food ashore to bring back for supper, as the rain continued to teem, and I came upon a Howard Johnson fast-food shop in the shopping center just off the marina. Perhaps even more bizarre than having Colonel Sanders Cracked Conch in Nassau, now, at the end of our dramatic (to us) conquest of the "Thorny Path," when we had finally turned the corner at Cabo San Juan and moved out of the trade-wind rollers of the Atlantic into confined waters and were in the islands at last, we had HoJo pizzas (for Jane and Jim) and fried chicken (for me). These were the purple islands?

The rain continued through the night and next morning, and we were at least sure that all the salt was off *Brunelle*. She and we were as clean as we could possibly be, as we took baths right on the pier, revelling in the warm, tropical downpour, and not even bothering to find the showers. Since we still had had no contact with marina personnel, I thought it would be a good idea to find the office and at least check in and perhaps pay a courtesy call on the marina manager. I would be writing up the cruise for *Yachting*, and it seemed a good idea to show the flag when possible.

Three times I went to the marina office, a walk of almost half a mile, and inquired for the manager. Each time, I was told he was busy, so I sent my business card in, with a note indicating our slip number, and felt I had "made my number," as the British would put it. I always

The big marina at Fajardo, with no signs of life

like to talk to people in the business when there is a chance, and helpful
information for columns and articles sometimes results. On the third
visit, I said I would like to pay my bill, since we planned to leave early
in the morning; the receptionist asked me to have a seat. I sat there
for half an hour with no results, and finally my patience failed. There
is something about obtuse lack of cooperation when I am trying to be
helpful that sets me off. I don't lose my temper often, but dealing with
the "mañana" attitude in this part of the world has a special effect. I
had kept my cool through the Dominican Republic and San Juan, but
this suddenly got to me.

"I don't usually have to wait this long when I am trying to pay
a bill," I exploded and stalked out of the office, feeling like an idiot.

Now what would I do? I did not want to run out on the bill, strong
as the temptation was, but I refused to cool my heels at the manager's
reception desk any longer. There was an office for the whole com-

plex—condos, marina, and real-estate sales, on the floor above, so I went in there and asked to see someone who could give me my marina bill. This caused complete consternation and the answer, "We do not handle that here, sir."

I explained that no one else seemed interested in taking my money, and after a confused flurry of action and telephone calls, I was handed my charges. There was a Visa sign in the window, so I presented my card. There followed a few minutes of more confusion, and I was then told, with the most expressive of shrugs, that they did not have the right machine. Finally, though, my Amex card made it *no probleme,* and, being made to realize that they had done me the greatest of favors in accommodating me this way, I was ushered out with condescending smiles.

Until the moment we departed the next morning, we had yet to see a dockmaster or anyone else with any authority connected with the marina, and I couldn't help but reflect, looking at the tremendous spread of concrete slips, electric and water outlets, garbage bins, gear lockers, and all the expensive appurtenances of a first-class marina, that the people who had put their money into it were being short-changed. If every transient had the same experience we had, they could have been missing quite a bit of revenue. Later, I commented on this in a column in *Yachting* and got a long, irate letter from the manager (an American) asking me who I was to claim such expertise in marina management. My answer was that it was too bad we hadn't been able to get together when I was there, since we might have had a constructive chat on the situation.

It was sunny and clear the next morning, with a pleasant trade riffling in from the east, and we were delighted to get away from this poor imitation of civilization and be on our way again. Now we could sail, with no more worry about plugging to windward under power, as the distances would all be short. We were headed for the island of Culebra, halfway between Puerto Rico and the Virgins, eighteen miles dead into the wind, and it was a delightful day of tacking across the bluish-green waters of Vieques Sound, mindful of the reefs that dot it, over a short chop that was quite different from the deep-sea rollers of the past few days. Astern, clouds built high over El Yunque, the long, hilly island of Vieques lined the southern horizon, and the succession of cays called La Cordillera stretching eastward from Cabo San Juan separated us from the Atlantic on the port hand.

Culebra is less than ten miles long, with a bevy of small satellite islands surrounding it, and it has had a checkered history. For many years, it was a bombing range for planes based at Roosevelt Roads, the big United States Navy base at the eastern tip of Puerto Rico, south of Fajardo. Culebra is politically a part of Puerto Rico, and a native population has hung on there through unpleasant years of constant explosions just over the hill from their back yards. They did not want to give up their houses and they continued to fish and farm, but they lived under the perpetual harrassment of the bombing barrage, and they were hardly ever visited by off-islanders because of this unusual situation. The best beach, Bahia Flamenco on the north coast, was the heart of the bombing range, and this was bitter cause for annoyance, as the natives huddled in their houses and cursed the explosions.

As time went on, an opposition movement gained strength, and, after years of hassling, protest, and legal actions, Culebrans finally won their case. The bombing ceased, and the whole island is now open. Vieques, twice as big, is still used for Navy and Marine exercises, and while we were in the area, there were protests there and at Roosevelt Roads, including sabotage, bombings, sniping, and interference with military exercises, by local people, particularly fisherman, who are excluded from working a good part of the coast of Vieques.

That night, while we rode at anchor on the gentle surge of the roadstead at Culebra's main town, Dewey, also known as Playa Sardina, we were reminded of all this by the sight of red flares floating over the east end of Vieques, off to the south, during some sort of night exercise.

Dewey has dual waterfronts. The roadstead on Vieques Sound is open and surgy, but is used regularly by yachts weekending from Puerto Rico, or on their way through to the Virgins. Across a small isthmus on which the town sits, the other waterfront faces Ensenada Honda, a long, narrow bay that slices for over three miles into the center of

Culebra and is one of the best natural harbors in the northern Carib-bean. Theodore Roosevelt wanted it as a base for the United States Navy, and a small station was established there, but the Puerto Rican base named for T. R. won out as the main one in the area. Ensenada Honda, which has many protected coves on both its shores, is a favorite hurricane hole for yachts from Puerto Rico and the Virgins.

We explored it the next day, after a walk around the quiet streets of Dewey, which was highly reminiscent of the side streets of Puerto Plata in sights, sounds, and smells. There is a small canal that runs through Dewey from one waterfront to the other, with a lagoon in the middle. Litter-filled and stagnant, it is just about deep enough for a rowboat, but, at the Ensenada Honda end, there is the incongruous sight of an enormous drawbridge over it, with big steel lift towers that are taller than anything else in town. It was a somnolent Sunday morning as I walked around, but Jim had gone ashore the previous evening after we arrived and had scored a miraculous shopping coup. Ever since Clarence Town, we had felt the need for a fly swatter, but we never could find one, even in the big-city supermarkets of San Juan. We had tried everywhere, but here, in a tiny catch-all market in Culebra, Jim finally came upon one. Sunday was Mother's Day, and he gave it to Jane, with appropriate ceremony, as her Mother's Day present.

Under sail, we looked into each of Ensenada Honda's many coves. Four Canadian yachts were anchored in company inside a fringe of reefs at Ensenada Dakity on the south side of the entrance, but the rest of the coves were empty. A few cottages dotted the shoreline, and the former naval station, no longer in commission, was on the north side. There was a sense of emptiness and isolation that was a fascinating contrast to teeming St. Thomas, which could be seen twenty miles away, outside the entrance. We finally chose a north-shore cove called Santiago for anchoring and dropped the hook in twelve feet in the complete solitude of its mangrove-lined privacy. After lunch, we explored ashore and found ruins of an old plantation on a hillside on the northwest side. There were extensive foundations and a massive cistern covered in tropical growth. The hillside was fairly open, between widely spaced trees, and we were startled, in this lonely, deserted setting, to hear movement in the underbrush. Suddenly, we came upon three horses grazing; they were as surprised to see us as we were to see them. They were skittish and wary and kept their distance, and they were the only signs of life that we met. As we rowed back to *Brunelle* on the still, black waters, schools of little fish spooked around us, skittering away in cascading showers of silver, and sea slugs spread over the bottom in the shallows.

As we relaxed over a dinner of curried shrimp, rain came and lasted through the night in intermittent showers. Squalls were all around us in the morning when we weighed anchor at 0630. There had been no difficulty coming into Ensenada Honda from the south around Dakity, but the eastern exit toward St. Thomas presented a confusing problem. We had Kline's *Guide,* a chart, and a book called *Westward from the Virgins,* which had a sketch chart in it, and each one showed a different buoyage system for the channel leading out to the eastward.

I thought I had it figured out visually, and we powered out into a dull, rainy morning, with the water a slaty gray. At what I thought was the proper place, I changed course to port a bit for Sail Rock—the aptly named crag off the western end of St. Thomas—and headed for its distinctive lump. All at once, there was a gentle thumping under the hull, and my first reaction was that we had hit some driftwood. The thumping increased, so I knocked the throttle back and looked over the side, and there, right under the hull, was a full garden of coral, with heads, fans, and mushroomy growths poking up toward the surface.

"Jesus, we're aground!" is what I think I said, as I stared at them in horror.

Fortunately, we had not run up on a shallow ledge and had just been bumping into small protuberances of something called Grampus Reef, so we backed carefully off and retraced our path to deep water at idling speed. Then I could see, as I checked the buoys again, that there was a nun farther out, not indicated on my various navigational aids, that we should have observed.

Trusting that we had no damage, and relieved that there was no propeller vibration, we went out to the nun and took our departure from it for Sail Rock after a rather shaky "Adios" to the Hispanic part of our outward passage.

18. Journey's Middle

~~~~~~~~~~~~~~~~~~~~~~~~~~~~~~~~~~~~~~~

In fitting fulfillment of the dream theme, the Virgin Islands—our objective for this leg of the cruise—should have been an alluring smudge of purple up ahead, a symbol of what we had been seeking throughout the long miles down from Tampa. Actually, they were an indistinct gray in the ring of rain squalls that hemmed us in on all sides.

The biggest squall was a towering black one off to the south, sweeping up from the area of St. Croix, with horizontal lightning forking through the tumble of clouds. The breeze was sucking into it, giving us a fresh northerly, cool and damp; we set sail once we were clear of that last elusive nun, and had a fast, close reach. Sail Rock, which gleams white on a sunny day and lives up to its name accurately, was just a dark lump in this weather, and we swooped by it in less than an hour. As we passed uninhabited Saba Island and closed with St. Thomas half an hour later, the rain moved in and killed the wind; we then powered through the western approach to Charlotte Amalie in a drenching downpour. I thought we had to check with customs, and we came alongside their bulkhead on the Charlotte Amalie waterfront, only to be told we were okay when coming from Puerto Rico.

Charlotte Amalie is not my favorite West Indies harbor, as it and the whole island of St. Thomas have become a cluttered mess, though there is a certain excitement in a harbor filled with yachts of every description. This time there was an extra bit of excitement. A large cruise liner, *Angelina Lauro*, was burned out, aground, and listing badly alongside the West Indies Docks, where most of the cruise ships in this port, the most frequently visited cruise port in the Caribbean, tie up. It was less than a month since she had caught fire there, but her rusted, ravaged hull and superstructure reminded me of some of the bombed-out wrecks I had seen in the Pacific in World War II. As she sat there,

The burned out hulk of Angelina Lauro *at Charlotte Amalie*

gaunt and conspicious as a specter at the feast, she was not exactly a good advertisement for the cruise-ship trade.

There are several marinas in Charlotte Amalie Harbor, and we headed for the big one called Sheraton Homeport, formerly Yacht Haven, at the far eastern end, threading our way through scores of anchored boats. The marina did not answer to our call on VHF as their ad in the *Guide* said they would, but we were able to raise *Cordonazo,* a charter yacht based there and run by our friends Charlie and Marty Peet (who have since sold her and opened a brokerage office there). Marty's warm voice came right back answering our call, and she had a slip all arranged for us by the time we arrived.

Except for the pleasure of seeing friends like the Peets and of having the chance to ogle a great number of boats in one place—a real floating boat show, since over one hundred professionally crewed boats base here—I can leave St. Thomas astern very quickly with no regrets.

Shopping in town on a cruise-ship day is like a free-for-all in a disco. The marina is so big that no one cares who is there; it is a mammoth, impersonal shambles that is sort of a nautical version of the Times Square subway station, everybody coming and going in a great rush. That it rained continuously did not help the atmosphere. Another high-level trough seemed to have moved into the area from a stationary weather system in the Atlantic north of the islands, and radio news told of floods in Haiti and Puerto Rico. This "never happens," of course.

While we were housecleaning the boat at the marina, where there were at least the advantages of shore power and water (at a price), the good old dinette table was hooked up out of the way. We had used it infrequently in the past few weeks, as we seldom ate below except in rainy weather, and, with only three of us aboard, we never needed its extra leaf, so it had not been much on my mind. Jane was vacuuming in the after cabin with the little portable vacuum we carry for the occasions when shore power is available, when suddenly there was a tremendous crash. I was in the cockpit, and I jumped below, wondering what on earth could have happened to her, but it was not Jane. The table had come unhooked all by itself, probably jarred by the wake from a passing boat, and Dot Higgs's handiwork lay in ruins on the cabin sole. Oh well; what can you expect from a committee design?

One enjoyable rendezvous was with fellow Cruising Club member Jim Moore and his wife, Carol, whose forty-five-foot Alden ketch *Tabaitha* was anchored out. Here we were, feeling pretty smug about making it all the way down from Tampa, but they had just completed a world circumnavigation and were on their last leg back to the east coast. With basically just the two of them, although joined for portions of the voyage by others, they had made a leisurely affair of it, taking several years. They had used our system of coming home from time to time to catch up with their family and with personal business, leaving the boat when they reached a place where she could be left under good supervision. She was a bit weatherworn but in generally good shape, and the Moores, perhaps ten years younger than we are, looked trim and healthy. One interesting comment from Jim was that they had run into their first windward work of the whole circumnavigation when

Tabaitha *after her circumnavigation*

they got into the Caribbean in the Windwards and had to beat northward against a northeaster.

"We'd forgotten what it was like to be on the wind," Jim said with
a grin. We at least could tell him about that.

The British Virgin Islands, starting a dozen miles east of Charlotte Amalie, were our real target, the goal of this phase of our cruise,

and, since two nights in the "big city" had been enough for us, we moved on through Current Hole and Pillsbury Sound—alternately sailing and powering while the wind played tricks in and out of rain squalls. We entered the BVI at Soper's Hole, West End, the appropriately named port at the tip of Tortola. The customs station is at the waterfront, and the bulkhead was empty, so we received our clearance ($5.80) in a matter of minutes and were on our way again under slowly brightening skies, flying the British red ensign as a courtesy flag.

I was aiming for a favorite spot, Little Harbour on Peter Island. Percy Chubb of the marine insurance family owns a marvelous house on the point that encloses this small cove. The view from this veranda is a breathtaking panorama of the entire sweep of Sir Francis Drake Channel from St. John's to Virgin Gorda, with Tortola three miles away across Drake Channel to the north. The harbor is small and quite deep, and anchoring can be a problem. Also, the breeze backwinds as it swoops over the hills from the east and "toilet bowls" around the harbor so that anchored boats ride every which way.

It is the nearest harbor to Road Town, where the bulk of more than three hundred boats in the BVI bareboat charter fleets base, and many of them head across to Little Harbour as their first stop after their morning briefing and provisioning session. The anchoring antics are then something to behold, as the nervous first dayers try to cope with Little Harbour's depths and swirling winds, and the varying angles of the boats, with sterns swinging around and touching in what had looked like clear spots, cause much consternation. Percy, who spends most of the winter in this retreat, says that the teatime entertainment is superb, and he thinks he has seen just about everything.

In the center of the harbor, he has had a special mooring put in for members of the Cruising Club; it is marked with a CCA burgee and the notation that it is private for members. It is a great convenience, and we have used it many times in Virgin Island cruises. This night, I felt it was too late to head into Road Town as the CSY marina, our ultimate objective, would be closed after 1700, and we planned to ride easily here and head across in the morning.

There was just one problem. Bareboaters, ignorant of harbor cour-

tesy and the unwritten rule that you treat an empty mooring as though
a boat were moored on it, often anchor close enough to block the
mooring, and sometimes they even pick it up. This makes for embarrassment, as you hate to act like a privileged snob and start talking
about club moorings, but it is also very annoying to run into thoughtless
or ignorant people and be denied use of a mooring that is your reason
for coming in there in the first place.

Sure enough, a thirty-foot bareboat was parked within a few feet
of the mooring. We came to a halt alongside, and the two youngish
couples on board looked at us nervously. We made a show of picking
up the mooring and then dropping it again, shaking our heads and
staring at them; they broke first in the war of nerves.

"Is something wrong?" one of the men called over weakly.

"Well," I answered, "we did come in here to use this mooring,
and you do have it blocked."

There was a long pause, with whispered discussions in the cockpit,
and then the man said, "Do you want us to move?"

"I'm awfully sorry," I said, "but I would appreciate it very much.
This mooring is why we came in here."

The females on the bareboat were obviously dead set against
moving, and if looks could take direct effect, I would have dropped
dead at the wheel and *Brunelle* would have sunk, but finally the men
shrugged and proceeded to shift their anchorage a couple of hundred
feet with ill-concealed resentment. Not too proud of my role as a Class
A Shit, I nevertheless was happy to be moored.

To smooth things over a bit, I rowed over to them with a bottle
of Cruzan Rum (about $1.75 in St. Thomas, so I wasn't being all that
extravagant) as a peace and thank-you offering, and then they had the
grace to act embarrassed. Suddenly the first man who had spoken burst
out in a breathless rush, "We didn't want to do anything wrong, but
you see nothing, absolutely nothing, has gone right on this cruise so far.
First the airline lost our luggage, and then the boat wasn't ready, and
last night it rained and we dragged anchor, and we tore a sail, and then
we found this nice place and finally got anchored right, and then
somebody comes along and tells us we have to move, and——"

He ran out of breath and his tumbled words slowed down, as he put his hands out in a gesture of helplessness.

"Well. I hope you're okay now and I do appreciate your moving," I said.

"You've cruised here before?" I was asked.

I allowed that I had, so we then ended up with an information session as they asked advice about good places to go, and I rowed back to *Brunelle* with smiles the order all around.

Our stupid swimming ladder was so unmanageable that we used the dinghy for getting out of the water onto the boat after swimming. This was the first place since Cayo Levantado where swimming over the side was possible, and I took a mask down to see whether Grampus Reef had left its mark on us. There were a few scratches, and the bottom of the keel was scraped clean of paint, but there was no damage and not even any gouges; I breathed a bit easier.

And so, there we were, the BVI at last, and we decided to cele-brate with caviar hors d'oeuvres and champagne. Jane chopped up the hard-boiled egg and onions; she had bought some sour cream in St. Thomas, so we had all the fixings. John Yeoman had stocked *Brunelle* with fairly fancy French champagne in the Exumas and had said one bottle was left at the bottom of the refrigerator, so I reached far down, grabbed the icy neck of a distinctively shaped bottle, wrapped it in a dish towel, popped the cork with a satisfactory explosion, and poured out the bubbly. It tasted fine, and the hors d'oeuvres were a great success, and it was not until I took the towel off the dead soldier that I realized that this was the $3.98 bottle I had originally bought in St. Pete as the cheapest thing I could find to break on the bow at the commissioning party. We all agreed that it had tasted pretty good, but maybe the surroundings had something to do with it.

The pressure was off now. Here it was May 17 and our plane reservations home were not until the twenty-fifth, since we had Memorial Day weekend commitments at home. We would check in with CSY, where the boat was to have some warranty work done before being hauled out for the summer at Tortola Yacht Services (TYS) boat yard in Road Town, and then sample Virgin Islands cruising for a few

First time for the Flasher since the Bahamas

leisurely days with no schedules to keep, no passages longer than ten miles, and absolutely no worry boxes at all.

Except for the fact that the trough persisted and it rained every day—not all day, but quite frequently, in a very un–Virgin Island fashion (while a professional camera crew was going nuts trying to make a promotional film for CSY)—it was a delightfully relaxed interlude.

We sailed a lot, and for the first time since the Bahamas, there was a chance to use the Flasher. When the sail had been shaken all the way out of the bag, I could feel that there was still something in there; it turned out to be a cloth doll of a little old man with a mild leer on his face and a tag identifying him as "The Flasher." He was dressed in a long trench coat, and when the skirts of the coat were pulled apart, it was revealed that he had all the equipment to qualify as a flasher. There was a note with it from Ellis Taussig and John Yeoman thanking us for a fine cruise and hoping that we would find this replacement crew a good shipmate.

We ate ashore at favorite spots like Bitter End and the Last Resort, where the owner, Tony Snell, puts on a marvelously entertaining evening of satiric songs in the best British comic tradition. Before a last night at Little Harbour, where we finished the ship's supply of caviar and the real bottle of French champagne (which didn't taste all that much better) in the eerie, all-pervading, coppery glow of an unusual sunset, we sailed out between Dead Chest and Salt Island to the seaward side of Norman Island before rounding it and doubling back to Little Harbour. Once we were south of these islands, it was the first time that *Brunelle* had actually been in the Caribbean. After we came back next fall, we expected to see a lot more of it.

19. *Reappraisal*

The CSY marina at Road Town is a busy spot, with the seventy-seven yachts in the charter fleet constantly coming and going on turnaround. The crew there is not set up to deal with private boats, but Jack Van Ost had promised, before we left Tampa, that we could get work done in Tortola, since we had gone out of the country so quickly. Simon Scott, the local manager, was most accommodating. The major jobs were to repair the refrigerator and to refinish the varnish on the cabin sole. Jerry Hefty's makeshift on the refrigerator had kept us going ever since February, although you had to remember to disconnect it when the engine was not running, or it would pull the batteries down very rapidly. The cabin sole had not been properly finished at the plant in the hurry of getting *Brunelle* to us on time, and it had begun to look scruffy in the first week. And then there was the table. . . .

After the work was finished at CSY, *Brunelle* was to be hauled out at Tortola Yacht Services, just across the harbor, where an enormous field is chock full of boats in dry storage—imagine such a thing in the tropics in the days of wooden boats. She would have her topsides waxed and her bottom painted and be ready for launching when we gave the word in the fall.

At CSY we got rid of the table leaf and were right back to the old two-and-a-half-person job. We acquired two important adjuncts to gracious living afloat: a cockpit table and a proper swimming ladder. These were stock items in the charter fleet but had not been available when we left Tampa. They made quite a difference, and we were very happy with them, but not so happy with another acquisition: cockroaches. This is a perpetual problem in tropical ports. We had avoided it up till now by being very careful in loading supplies and not bringing cardboard cartons below, but little visitors hopped aboard somehow

The busy CSY marina at Road Town

while she was sitting there unoccupied, and an unending war had started.

Our first inkling of this came when I telephoned Albie Stewart, head of TYS, in November and gave him our arrival date.

"She'll be all ready," was his cheerful report. "We've had bombs aboard, and I think we have the problem licked."

"Problem?" I moaned, thinking immediately of what Jane's reaction would be, and knowing exactly what he meant despite my question.

We had been in touch a couple of times over the summer about much more of a problem than coackroaches. For the first time in twenty years—natch, since we had a boat there for the first time—hurricanes had come directly through the Virgins. David and Frederic were their names, and they made an anxious time out of most of September as they swept in from beyond the Leewards. Fortunately, neither did damage to anything at the boat yard, but the charter operators had a wild time of it tucking their fleets away in various hurricane holes.

Meanwhile, we had the summer at home to think about our project and reappraise our plans. It seemed odd to have laid a boat up on Memorial Day and be putting her back in commission on Thanksgiving, but we did have our eighteen-foot Sanderling catboat, *Polly,* for puttering around in and racing, a perfect boat for home waters on the Shrewsbury.

How had those questions that had been raised at the start worked out in the doing? Had things gone as planned? Were there any surprises, pleasant or unpleasant? Could we continue as originally planned, or should we think that over? Had *Brunelle* lived up to expectations?

The basic questions all had happy answers. We were more than pleased with *Brunelle* in sailing performance, seaworthiness, construction strength, and comfort. If we were to start over again, there would not be many changes we would want to make. It would be nice to have the heads on opposite sides so that one could always be to leeward, important only on offshore passages. This was a plus we had had on *Tanagra.* The SSB radio had been of no use, and I was glad that I had not gone for any more electronics. Estimating speed for the Dominican Republic had not been difficult, and yarn telltales on the shrouds were as helpful as an electronic wind gauge in sailing her. A depth sounder, definitely yes, and the VHF and a portable RDF had been useful (just once for the latter, but we used it constantly as a receiver for weather and news). The nav station table in the after cabin had never been used for charts. It was a catch-all desk that soon looked like the W. C. Fields filing system, and it was a hazard to the feet in nocturnal marital relations (which had otherwise not been affected, as originally feared). And then there was that dinette table. . . .

Personal relations of all types had worked out extremely well. In thirty-seven years of marriage, Jane and I had never spent so much time together without interruption, something I hadn't given much thought to in advance and that might conceivably have developed into a problem, but the reverse was true. We probably talk less, read more, and do more crossword puzzles than many married couples, and I won't say that we didn't have any fights, because who could be together constantly without some disagreements, but they were minor and infrequent, and the steady companionship was an enriching experience, strengthening ties and deepening our dependence on each other. My impression is that she doesn't really enjoy the long passages but will not complain about them, but she very definitely enjoys the life aboard and the chance to see interesting places and people, as do I.

There were no problems with guests, all of whom were chosen because we know them well and know what to expect. Couples do not get along well unless the wives do, always an important consideration, and no matter how good the relationship, a week is about right for living together in the close quarters of a boat, though every rule has its exceptions.

It would have been hard to set up a guest schedule for the Caicos-Virgins section, and we were really fortunate that Jim Lillie worked out so well and that we could keep one crew for the whole time without worrying about making connections somewhere. He was remarkably self-sufficient in entertaining himself on board, mostly as a voracious reader, and in making friends and doing his own exploring when we were in port. As well as being a great help nautically—I almost forgot what it was like to work the anchor and halyards—he was a completely congenial companion. It would have been a real chore and strain to do the trip by ourselves, so this was a very happy solution, and we signed him up for the next winter. Once or twice in situations that we could not control, Jane and I have been shipmates with people who have abrasive personalities. It is a condition that completely colors the experience, and I have seen the same problem more often on ocean racers. Good shipmates make good cruising.

As to surprises, there were few unpleasant ones, unless you count the number of pots in Florida Bay. On the pleasant side, we had calms in areas where we had expected heavy wind on the nose. I still had an ambivalence over all the powering we had done, but the balance was still on the plus side. The lack of difficulty with port officials, red tape, and unfriendly natives was another welcome surprise, and I really never had expected to encounter any "black holes," pirates, or hijackers in the "Bermuda Triangle."

Our health had been excellent except for that one dental problem at the end of our stay in Nassau, and we had actually lost weight despite living fairly high on the hog most of the time. We drank more than we do at home, as the life kept us on a perpetual holiday schedule, entertaining different guests by the week. Without this, we no doubt would have lost some more weight, but things never went beyond pleasant socializing in this department, and it certainly added to the relaxed mood of most days. I think the only time I might have wanted to get drunk was after our crash landing at Lower Matecumbe, but sleep won out before booze after that one.

The big question, though, was whether to stick to our original idea of going all the way around the Caribbean. As a concept it was artistically neat and well-rounded and gave a focus of sorts to the whole project, but by the time we had reached Tortola, I had many doubts about it. Both in our own modus operandi and in situations over which we had no control, there were many factors that were all on the negative side. When they were added together, they far outweighed the supposed glamor of closing the circle, Florida to Florida.

Beyond our control was the political situation in Central America. While we were on our way down from Florida, a civil war had been raging in Nicaragua, and there were political assassinations in Guatemala. Although El Salvador was on the Pacific side, it too was in ferment, adding to the general instability of the whole area. As I have said, I find it difficult to adjust to the Latin-American way of doing things anyway, and these developments made that whole stretch of the Caribbean into a virtual no-man's land.

To get to the interesting areas of the Western Caribbean—the San Blas Islands off Panama, the Bay Islands of Honduras, and the reefs off Belize—would mean two nonstop passages of more than six hundred miles. Venezuela was okay and an attractive cruising area, but Colombia was off-limits on my Lloyds of London insurance policy because of the heavy drug traffic and proven piracy there. We would have to bypass it completely, heading offshore for six hundred miles to get to the San Blas. To break the eight hundred-mile passage from Panama to the Bay Islands there were only tiny Colombian islands off the Central American Coast, and then it would be several hundred more miles through the Yucatan Channel to get around Cuba and back to Florida.

By now, I knew that we were not capable of long passages by ourselves or with only one other in crew, and I did not want to become involved with arranging bigger crews for long offshore runs—especially if I were to end up having to pay some extra air fares in order to get people.

I had already been to the attractive areas: Venezuela, San Blas, Bay Islands, and Belize, and only the Rio Dulce of Guatemala would be a new one. I would love to explore the San Blas thoroughly, and there was more to the coast of Venezuela than we had seen, but these were not strong enough magnets to outweigh the negatives.

Also, it seemed foolish, once we were there, to hurry through the prime cruising areas of the Eastern Caribbean and end up back in the States fairly soon. Once we turned west along the Venezuelan coast, there would be no heading back, as it would be all downwind thereafter. No one in his right mind beats eastward into the trades in the open Caribbean.

All this added up to a decision to stay in the Eastern Caribbean indefinitely, and I set an alternative target of getting to Venezuela by the end of the next winter's cruising and leaving the boat there for the next summer—out of the hurricane belt and in a big new marina being opened by friends we had visited in 1975. Instead of a circumnavigation, it would be South America, Ho! as a new objective.

We had cruised the Virgins several times as well as the islands between Antigua and Grenada, but always on a quick schedule of a week or so, and I was looking forward to doing them at my own pace. Also, we had never cruised the islands between the Virgins and Antigua—Anguilla, St. Martin, St. Bart's, St. Kitts-Nevis, and Barbuda. This would give us the opportunity to explore there.

From Anguilla to Grenada, the next landfall can always be seen from the last island, and the trades make a perpetual reach out of most

'Where the islands loom purple on the horizon'

of the sailing. It is here that the dream—an island looming purple on the horizon as the boat slips across the cobalt of tropic seas with trade-wind clouds overhead—would become actual experience, an image come fully to life. This was what we had plowed through the long miles from Tampa for: the area of fulfillment. Once we were in it, why hurry on into uncertainty? It was mildly disappointing to abandon what had originally seemed like a good plan, but it was here, where the purple islands stretched away in landfall after landfall, that we would live out the dream.

20. *Idle Virgin Idyll*

Nowhere on earth has nature assembled a better arrangement for relaxed cruising under sail than in the Virgin Islands. Everything combines to make them the perfect cruising grounds. They are not at the ends of the earth, the weather is sunny, mild, and remarkably reliable, good harbors abound mile after mile, the water is beautiful, the navigation is simple, there are no open stretches of rough water, shore areas are colorful and interesting, the scenery is gorgeous, and the breeze is as consistent as the breeze can ever be. The distances are not great enough for the islands to appear as purple, but the sailing is great.

So what is the fly in this ointment? What's the catch? There must be something amiss amid all this perfection. No place could have all these advantages without some hidden drawback. The answer is that very little is amiss, and the only drawback is that the area is so good that it has become too popular. It is almost impossible to "get away from it all" in a quiet cove with no other boats in sight. When you cruise in the Virgins, you cruise in company with many other boats. To some purists, this is a disadvantage, and, with the number of boats now basing in the Virgins, the law of averages is bound to mix in some noisy incompetents who detract from the atmosphere of any harbor they are in and never know how to anchor properly.

Also, while some may think that it adds to the quaint charm, air connections into the British Virgins, where most of the charter boats base and where the best harbors are, leave something to be desired. If you enjoy flying in DC-3s that are almost never on schedule, and you consider it amusing to wait anywhere from a few hours to a few days for your luggage to catch up with you, then you will laugh gaily and call it local color. Most people find it a bit disconcerting.

For us, when we went back to *Brunelle* right after Thanksgiving,

Perfect cruising conditions in the Virgins

the Virgins meant our first chance since the Bahamas to revel in relaxation. There is no such thing as a schedule in cruising the Virgins. Everything is so close that you can get from anywhere to anywhere in one easy day, and the drill is to take it as it comes, making up your mind each morning on what to do for the rest of the day after looking at the sun, sniffing the breeze, and gauging the temper of your shipmates.

There were, however, a few things to set right when we first came aboard before life could be relaxing. We arrived at *Brunelle* from the airport after dark as she sat in the slip under the Travelift at Tortola

Yacht Service, a temporary berth we would have to vacate in the morning. She had been dropped in the water late that afternoon, and there was a forlorn feeling of neglect about her, with her headstay slack, the Bimini top scrunched up in the cockpit, and the cabins stuffy and dark. There was a ridiculous interlude while I tried to remember how to turn the lights on, and then we wished I had not, because corpses from the bug bombing were strewn all over the place. The newly varnished cabin sole gleamed in the lamplight, however, adding a richness to the interior. Naturally there was no food or ice aboard, so we fled across the road to Mariner's Inn at the Moorings for drinks and dinner and went right to bed when we came back, putting off reality until the morning.

An inventory of problems then produced the information that the refrigerator was not working, the water tasted unbelievably awful (we should have had the tanks drained), the tachometer was not functioning, the depth sounder was defunct, the roller furler was frozen and would not unfurl, and someone had mysteriously and wantonly cut the cord to the VHF mike. When a list like this confronts us, Jane usually quotes that old "sick" joke, "Aside from that, Mrs. Lincoln, how did you like the play?" Only we are so used to it by now that we both just cry "Mrs. Lincoln!" and this was a real A-Number-One Mrs. Lincoln.

We had the best part of two days before our first guests arrived, and it was a busy time as we moved to CSY and went to work. I set up the rig, which had been taken apart when the boat was on the launching lift, and I put the Bimini back up; CSY personnel rallied around and helped us with the other problems. Jane went at the cabins like a Dutch housewife, and by the afternoon of the second day, when we went shopping, we were in pretty good shape. Steve Marsh, the knowledgeable CSY rigger who put our roller furler back in commission, is an Antiguan who has worked on many of the better known charter yachts over the years and has been to the States. He is familiar with the top ocean racers, going back quite a few years, and we had a good session of boat talk and sea story swapping while we worked around the deck.

Advice on the refrigerator was to put hot water on the expansion valve as moisture in the system was freezing in there and blocking circulation, but this only worked temporarily. The system eventually had to be bled and recharged. We ran water through the tanks several times, loaded the tanks with Clorox until we might as well have been drinking out of a swimming pool, and added baking soda, but the terrible taste was a problem for weeks and we bought bottled water for drinking and making coffee and tea. We keep bags of cubes in the freezer for our drink-ice supply, as the system doesn't make cubes. The tachometer proved recalcitrant for several months, a few cockroaches were always with us thereafter, despite all efforts, and the mystery of the cut microphone wire, which was replaced, was never solved. The depth sounder, mounted on the after end of the cabin in the cockpit, had evidently been in the sun for several weeks, once the Bimini had been taken down as a hurricane precaution and its face had warped so much that its needle would not rotate. Fortunately the local electronics shop had a second-hand replacement, but this is the sort of instrument that should be mounted below on a movable arm that swings it into view in the hatch when needed.

Our first guests were Bermudian friends, Neville and Jean Conyers, and they arrived a bit dizzy from the great circle routing they had to take to get there: Bermuda–New York–San Juan–Tortola. It was no surprise at all that their luggage had been left behind (it came twenty-four hours later). Whenever we had the VHF on in the Virgins—which was fairly often, as it is a real "party line" of information—we would hear charter parties calling in from their boat to its base to check on missing luggage. We had gone through this several times ourselves, and the most memorable time of all was when we arrived at the check-in counter at San Juan to take our connection to Tortola and saw a mound of baggage stretched from right in front of the counter all the way across the one hundred-foot wide room. It was a jumble of well over fifty pieces, belonging to fourteen members of the Nippon Ocean Racing Club, who had come all the way from Tokyo to take out two bareboats. One look at that mess and I was absolutely sure that passengers and luggage were not going to get to the BVI together. While the two desperate looking young ladies on duty at the ticket counter grappled with the problem, the owners of the luggage were all over the place, clicking cameras like crazy, smiling at everyone, and giggling like little boys at a zoo. Nobody's luggage got on the plane we all flew in, with the cameras continuing to click out the windows for the entire flight, but at least the airline managed to get it to us on the same day, which is practically a record.

From the arrival of Neville and Jean, with a ten-day interlude to go home for Christmas, we cruised the British Virgins until early February. It was the most relaxed, easygoing, and rewarding time we have ever spent on a boat. This is not adventurous or challenging cruising; no sailing away over the horizon on cresting seas, and as I have said, you are always 'in company.' If you will relax and accept this, there can be fun and amusement in watching some of the antics; there are also many opportunities for visiting back and forth, comparing notes, and swapping sea stories. Almost all the boats are from the charter fleets, but there are some privately operated ones. Americans predominate, but there are Canadian and European boats too, and there are many Europeans (and even our Japanese friends) on the charter boats.

The choice of harbors seems almost unlimited, amazingly so in an area that stretches for less than forty miles. In the British Virgins (where we stayed, not wanting to bother with customs clearance in and out of the American Virgins) there are over thirty anchorages, counting Road Town—the main town and base—as one, though it has several different anchorages and marinas around its shores. We have our favorites, and we only went to about a dozen, including lunch stops. We made somewhat the same rounds week after week, since we wanted each new set of guests to see the places we liked best.

The only real adventure is in going north to Anegada, about twenty miles from Virgin Gorda. Bareboats are not allowed to go there, as the approach to it is heavily strewn with reefs. The island itself is flat and sandy and unspoiled, so I have been told. We could never seem to get ourselves organized for getting there in the lazy way we were running our cruising. *Mañana,* as they say in the Dominican Republic.

While in the Virgins, we based informally at the CSY marina at Baugher Bay on the east side of Road Town Harbour. With seventy-

You are always 'in company' in the Virgins

seven boats operating out of there, and a certain percentage of them always in process of being turned over between charters, it is a busy spot. We tried to duck in and out at the least busy times when we were changing crews or shopping. There are also moorings off the marina, where we would lie if the scene on shore looked too busy.

It is always fascinating to see the day start at o8oo at CSY—or any other bareboat base—with the sudden onslaught of maintenance

214

crews swarming down the piers to go to work on cleaning the boats, making any necessary repairs, and setting them up for the next charter. From peace and quiet, the atmosphere quickly switches to controlled pandemonium, as the hum of vacuum cleaners, the splash of hoses washing down decks, the rumble of handcarts, and the roar-splash-roar-splash of engines being run to charge batteries and refrigerators fill the air. Over it all is the blare of radio music, as that New York habit of carrying large portable radios around seems to have spread to the BVI. Sometimes it is rock-and-roll or disco, but every once in a while a Calypso number reminds you that you are not on West Forty-second Street.

There is a great deal of horseplay and kidding around among the workers, both male and female, without noticeable interruption to the work. The costume is jeans and T-shirts, bearing all sorts of slogans and messages; a peculiarity among the men is the wearing of woolen ski caps no matter what the weather. The talk is so broadly accented that a visitor couldn't possible understand it, but it is toned down to coherence when directed to whites.

We also spent some time across the harbor at Village Cay Marina, the most modern setup on Tortola. Concrete piers with slips that have electricity and water extend out from a shore complex of shops, restaurants, and a small hotel; "downtown" Road Town is just a few minutes away. The basin is behind a high manmade sea wall that protects Village Cay Harbor from the sweep of the main harbor, which is wide open from southeast to southwest.

Many private boats are based here permanently, and Tortola Yacht Charters operates out of here. On the other side of Village Cay Harbor is the Tortola Yacht Services yard and the large new installation of The Moorings, a major bareboat company, and there is a small marina at Treasure Isle Hotel on the north side. It is all very snug and secure, with the usual community atmosphere among the boats—a small "neighborhood" as it were, having many comings and goings.

The even tenor of life here was upset on one of our visits when a United States Navy missile patrol boat, *USS Pegasus*, a hydrofoil vessel of about 130 feet, came in on a state visit. The manager of

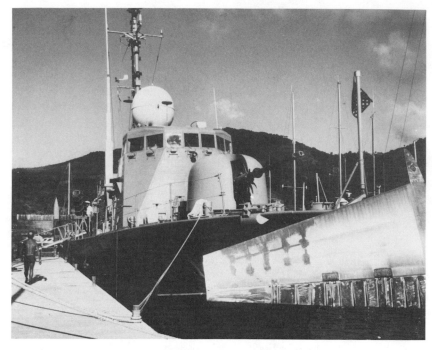

USS Pegasus *literally caused a stir at Village Cay Marina*

Village Cay, a soft-spoken and very polite Englishman named John Ackland, had not realized, when he said he would give the vessel a berth for two days of open-house visits, that she would have to keep her own generators going in order to maintain all her complicated electronic equipment. To his horror and the consternation of the regular customers, the whole area was enveloped in a whine like that of a jet plane taxiing down the runway. Someone asked the ship's crew why they couldn't plug in to shore power.

"We'd black out the whole island in thirty seconds if we did that," was the answer.

Ackland was also sensitive to the fact that Dr. Spock, the famous pediatrician and anti-war activist, was on his boat in the slip next to us, and the juxtaposition of his ketch and the howling war machine seemed almost too ironic. Dr. Spock, however, only seemed concerned with a deck leak under one of his stanchions.

A typical day of cruising in the BVI would find us, say, at Little Harbour, riding peacefully on the mooring after a visit with the Chubbs in their house on the hill, with its magnificent vistas, or a cocktail visit by them on *Brunelle*. After a night in which we perhaps have to close the hatches twice in brief rain showers, my first waking action is to switch the batteries and flick on the testing meter to make sure that they are properly charged. Then I turn on the switch for the electric bilge pump and listen for the pump to signal me with a hollow sucking noise that the sump under the main cabin sole is empty. Once a day is enough unless we have taken showers. While Jane is making breakfast, I wrestle the bunk back to its daytime condition. Sometimes, if I am unusually eager and everything feels right, I will take a quick plunge over the side, thankful that we now have a proper swimming ladder, which stays rigged in the transom gate while we are in a harbor. If the cockpit shows smudges from whatever went on the night before, I neaten it up a bit.

At 0800, there is a weather forecast on the St. Thomas commercial radio station, jointly sponsored by The Moorings and Tortola Yacht Service, and I try to catch that, even though it is so repetitious that the same tape could be played on it day after day. If I miss it, there are other reports from San Juan and St. Croix stations. We also try to pick up a news broadcast, usually from an American network via San Juan, even though it is amazing that nothing seems to happen to change the world if you go for several days without getting the news. It all sounds awfully familiar when you get back to it, but there was some extra interest at this period because the American hostages in Iran were at the top of the news.

We both usually have a novel working, and, in the absence of the *New York Times*, whose crossword puzzle is usually the start of the day for Jane and me, we have books of puzzles edited by Margaret Farrar, who started the whole thing in the *Times*. We both work one before switching gears for the rest of the day. I usually catch up at breakfast with the very informal log that I keep. It is a lovely, unhurried part of the day as I sit and write at the cockpit table. Jane only wants tomato juice, toast, and coffee for breakfast, but she makes me a poached egg and bacon with my toast, banana, and special breakfast drink—Rose Hips tea, which has lots of Vitamin C. She does the same for guests. It is a time for watching the sun break free from hills around the harbor, for looking at the cloud formations and guessing what they tell about the prospects for the day, and for gauging the breeze in relation to what sailing we want to do. There are very few days when the prospects are anything less than delightful. In our seven weeks of Virgin Island cruising, we had three days of wind over thirty, when it was more comfortable to be in port, and one or two when it rained for more than the brief one-cloud squalls that sweep in on the trades for a few minutes of sun-splashed showering. Rosie Curley, my assistant at *Yachting*, and Marcia Wiley, the managing editor, spent one week with us in which the weather never varied from perfection. Rosie's first remark of the day, as she poked her head out of the hatch and saw the bright sun and fresh breeze, turned into a running gag of "Well, just another god-damned lousy day!"

We never rushed a morning start in this kind of cruising. Break-fast clean-up was all finished and everyone had been to the head, put on their sunburn cream, and gathered their knitting, needlepoint, novel, can of beer, or whatever their entertainment was to be, before we faced up to getting underway. Some days, the morning went so lazily that it was time for snorkeling or a swim and cocktails before we had managed to think about getting started, and sailing would be deferred until after lunch.

Every few days, I would be conscientious enough to check the lube-oil level and the water in the batteries, but there was very little ship's work to be done except for the actual moving around. With our daily need for an hour of engine time to keep the refrigerator going, I tried to combine running the engine with weighing anchor and clearing the harbor, as we did not overly enjoy sitting in the cockpit in harbor while the engine was turning over.

If we managed to get organized by mid-morning and started sailing, as let's say we did on this hypothetical day, we would make sail outside the harbor, unless we had already logged enough engine time in which case we might sail right off the mooring. Although we have seen the opposite in the past on one or two occasions of west wind, it is almost certain that the wind will be between northeast and southeast. On many days it would be a pleasant twelve to sixteen. We did have one norther, and those few days of wind over thirty, to vary the pattern; otherwise, the weather could really be depended on.

From Little Harbour, it would be a good sail to the Baths at the southern tip of Virgin Gorda, a beat of about eight miles if the wind was due east. Sir Francis Drake Channel is protected water, and the chop just comes from wind waves except when you are directly opposite areas between the islands that are open to the Caribbean. There would be a parade of boats beating eastward from Road Town, and, despite the casual nature of our sailing, I could seldom resist an informal brush to see how *Brunelle* would do against other types. Actually this was not very conclusive, as our sails are well cut six-ounce cloth with proper roach on the leech of the main, and battens. They make an amazing difference in comparison with the nine-ounce roachless, battenless slabs used on many charter boats. We found that we would walk away from any charter boat under fifty feet except in reaching or running in winds strong enough for a longer waterline to make a difference. When our daughter Alice had a C & C 36 on charter, supposedly the hottest performance boat in the bareboat fleets, and with well-cut sails, it was gratifying to find that *Brunelle* gradually inched away from her on the wind in about eight to ten knots. We had not bought a racing machine, but it is always satisfying to sail well.

On the way to the Baths, Tortola is a high bulwark to the north, dappled with the moving shadows of trade-wind clouds, and Beef Island, where the airport is, extends from it with a steep bluff on its eastward end. To starboard, there is a string of lower islands between Peter and Virgin Gorda, starting with high-sided Dead Chest, a small, rocky finger that is supposed to be the source of the "fifteen men on a dead man's chest" pirate legend. Salt Island, next, is the scene of the wreck of the steamship *Rhone*, sunk in a hurricane in October 1867 and still an awesome sight for experienced Scuba divers. There is a tiny native settlement there. Cooper Island has a restaurant and beach club

Brushing with Alice's chartered C & C 36

that is a favorite spot for eating ashore, with a surgy, backwinded anchorage in its lee, and Ginger Island beyond it is rocky and deserted.

The wind comes off their gently contoured hills in uneven puffs as you continue eastward into the glittery path of the climbing sun, and between Ginger and the Baths there is a string of oddly tumbled rocks and crags. The biggest is two-hundred-foot-high Round Rock, with steep-faced sides and a frowsy topping of scrub. Then a topsy-turvy bunch of boulders aptly called Fallen Jerusalem, as they look like a city having suffered an earthquake, strings along reefs to the tip of Virgin Gorda. On Virgin Gorda, the Baths carry on the same odd formations, with great boulders—high as a three-story house—leaning against each other, creating caves and tidal pools in the dim spaces below them. Several stretches of perfect beach separate the piles of grim, pinkish-gray rocks, with palms bowing over them, and the sum total is a unique, strikingly dramatic stretch of shore, very different from the rest of the Virgins.

The water is deep right up to the beach, and there is almost always a surge, so this is only a lunch stop. On some days, the surge is too strong for dinghy landing, and then the anchorage is empty. A calm day will see forty to fifty boats gathered here by late morning, bobbing and rolling in the surge, while shore parties explore the fantastic rock formations and snorkel in reefs just off the beach. It is a gay, busy, scene, with yachts coming and going and dinghies in a steady parade to the beach—quite a contrast to our first visit in 1964, when only two other boats were anchored, and there was no road along the shore. Now guests from the hotels on Virgin Gorda come here for a picnic, joining the yachtsmen on the beach.

There are many good lunch stops in the Virgins, but this is the most interesting. We do not always stop for lunch, but it is easy to do so almost anywhere you might be, and snorkelers and Scuba devotees find plenty of places to explore. Hurricane David, however, had destroyed some of the better shallow water reefs, such as those off Marina Cay and at Saba Rock in Gorda Sound.

After one of Jane's celery-with concotions, it would be time for another sail. From the Baths, in the usual wind, it is a run across the

The Baths are a great place to stop for lunch and snorkeling

widest part of Drake Channel to Beef Island or Marina Cay, which means that we could use the Flasher—always fun to break out, especially amid charter boats that are not equipped with light sails. With everybody on the move by mid-afternoon, Drake Channel would be a panorama of sails in every direction, and the sailing would be great.

There are many good places for eating ashore, such as Cooper Island, the Bitter End or Biras Creek on Gorda Sound, Marina Cay, or, if you are feeling flush, Peter Island Y.C. Bitter End does a fantastically efficient job of processing over one hundred people from yachts every night in a gala atmosphere and with excellent food. It is fun to listen to the VHF during the afternoon as people call in their reservations and menu selections. (One lady once called in and asked, "What are your entries for tonight?") Sometimes the discussions become very involved over how the lobster is cooked or what "chicken native style" means, and everyone builds up an appetite just by listening.

222

The Bitter End, Gorda Sound

Our favorite stop of all, though, is the Last Resort, that very casual affair on a little island called Bellamy Cay in the middle of Trellis Bay, which is a fine, protected anchorage just off the Beef Island Airport (the airport for Tortola). It is a shallow, protected harbor, with no surge and good holding ground, and transfers can be made directly to the planes by rowing ashore. It is a bit noisy because of the air traffic, but this subsides by mid-evening. Aside from these advantages, the Last Resort is great fun. The building is a rambling stone shed that covers most of the cay, and dinner is served by reservation at a single sitting about 2030 (after everybody has mingled at cocktails, comparing notes and swapping stories). Sometimes there is a choice of meat or fish, at a sit-down service. When the crowd is too big, everything is buffet style. The food is usually good and plentiful, with pumpkin soup a favorite as a starter and then native-style fish or chicken, cooked with vegetables and spices. If there is roast beef, there is also Yorkshire pudding, as Tony and Jackie Snell, who run the Last Resort and live there with their two children, are very British indeed.

It is the after-dinner hour, though, that gives the Last Resort its distinction, as Tony, a professional entertainer, puts on the only "floor show" in all the out-island clubs of the BVI. Over the years we have been there several times, including our visit in May, when *Brunelle* had just made it there, and we never tire of going back. Tony's show does not change much, and after a while it got to be almost a "sing-along" for us, but his presentation is unique, the satire is marvelous, and it bears up under repeated hearings. We wanted each set of our guests to see him, and everyone enjoyed it tremendously.

Tony is tall and compelling, with a strong voice, a casual, offhand British manner, and very mobile features that are handsome in repose. Aside from clever words and parodies to familiar tunes, with a few ribald jokes thrown in, told in his most exaggerated British accent, he does all sorts of tricks with electronic sound. His stage looks like the set for a one-man band from Mars, with an impressive array of microphones, tape recorders, and amplifiers, and he works double and triple playbacks and all sorts of special effects for a montage of sheer idiocy in sound that is hilarious. He uses it to particularly amusing effect in an original number called "The Bermuda Triangle" that ends with eerie whistles and crashing sounds echoing and re-echoing to a thunderous climax. He has a delightful ditty about "the world's simplest piece of machinery, the British Seagull. It only has one moving part: the man pulling the string!" Other songs poke fun at the foibles of charter folk "who go to Peter Island and stay there a week, or perhaps to Virgin Gorda if they're very brave." His electronic wizardry is also perfect for putting down hecklers. Sometimes a customer who has spent too long at the bar thinks he is funnier than Tony and interrupts with his own witticisms; Tony puts them on his re-recorder and plays them back faster and faster till they end up as Donald Duck gibberish.

It would be a masterful performance in any nightclub or musical show anywhere, and in this setting it has a very special impact. Sometimes Jackie, with a light, appealing voice, sings duets with him. We came back so often that Tony began to kid me during the show, calling me "the last of the big spenders" and "a glutton for punishment." In time we became friends enough for them to ask us for dinner one night with an interesting couple, Dr. Robin Tattersall and his wife, Jill. Robin is a plastic surgeon who has achieved a world reputation despite his relative isolation. He is a tall, dark, and strikingly handsome man with a friendly manner and originally came out to the BVI by answering an ad in a British medical journal because he knew it would mean good sailing. His wife, attractive, blonde, and drily quick-spoken, is a historical novelist who has written many books about a special period at the beginning of the nineteenth century that she has made her own province. She has now expanded her work and does research for novels about the early days of the British Virgins.

It was fascinating to talk to them, and Robin is one of the most enthusiastic sailors I have ever met in my long career of meeting enthusiastic sailors. Before we left the Virgins, we traded visits. Their house is an imposing villa, a landmark painted lavender that really stands out on a hill overlooking Road Town. Robin was also very helpful with advice on crossing Anegada Passage, which he has done many times.

On nights when we stayed aboard *Brunelle* for dinner, Jane would do her best to make me cook on the hibachi, a chore I do not enjoy. Fortunately it always turned out that our male guest would take over, through my using a culinary version of my Friendly Yacht Service technique. Both the Livengoods and Haights came back again despite

225

their misadventures with us in Florida, and both Hugh and Doc were masters of the grill. Nev Conyers said he begs for the opportunity at home, and even our Greek friend, George Legakis, with whom we had sailed in the Aegean and who was returning the visit, admitted to a certain expertise.

After dinner, the favorite entertainment was music on a portable tape recorder that Alice had given us for Christmas, with such generational choices as Glenn Miller, Benny Goodman, Ella Fitzgerald, Mildred Bailey, and Edith Piaf; Debby Haight actually managed to dance in the cockpit when she just couldn't sit still to Miller's "In the Mood." Martha had made a special tape of our personal "hit parade" at home that was great fun—it had everything from Marlene Dietrich to Flanders and Swan, George Symonette, and Janis Joplin.

George Legakis had an amusing experience when he arrived in Road Town on the Grumman Goose from St. Thomas. The only other passengers were a young couple in scruffy denim cutoffs and dirty T-shirts, with the usual hirsute disarray that goes with the costume, and the immigration officer, a dignified black gentleman, gave them a real talking to.

"You are rude to come to our country looking like that," he lectured them. "Why don't you dress neatly like this gentleman," he said, pointing to George, who was standing innocently by in a polo shirt and slacks.

Speaking of clothing, there was a silly episode with Alice one night when we rendezvoused with her and her crew at Cooper Island for cocktails aboard *Brunelle* and then dinner ashore at the friendly little beach bar and restaurant. It was a pleasant, convivial evening, and we all went back to our respective boats and turned in before midnight. Alice's cabin mate was an old friend, Smitty, who had never been cruising before but was enjoying herself thoroughly, except when Alice started to snore heavily after they turned in. Smitty couldn't sleep, so she moved out to the cockpit, and after a while she happened to notice that *Brunelle* was in the opposite direction from where she had been earlier in the evening.

The Last Resort

She went below and woke Alice, asking timidly, "Alice; is it all right if your father's boat is on the other side of us now?"

Alice popped up from her sleep like the good skipper she is, took a look at the situation, and determined that we were dragging. Just

The Cooper Island anchorage

before turning in, I had thought we were riding a bit too close, and I had shortened the rode a bit, probably breaking the anchor out. This is an uneasy anchorage anyway, where boats ride every which way in the backwind effect.

Dutifully, Alice rowed over to *Brunelle* and whispered down our hatch, "Dad; it's Alice. I think you're dragging."

This of course got me up in a hurry. I went up on deck and quickly realized that she was right, so we went about starting the engine and resetting the anchor, with Alice working along with me, and me in my sleeping costume. This happens to be a black nylon T-shirt and jockey shorts that I originally bought as a local joke to go with the slinky black nightgowns that Jane always wears in bed. Joke or no, this rig turned out to be the most comfortable outfit I've ever slept in. I now use my "Vietcong pajamas," as Jane calls them, all the time—but never before this in public.

Right in the middle of all the *tohu-bohu* of working the anchor, Alice suddenly stopped heaving in with me and gave me an astonished stare.

"Dad! What in HELL have you got on?" she cried.

We had gotten to feel like oldest residents of the BVI community by now. We knew our way around the stores and markets, the harbors and landmarks were all familiar to us, we had our special taxi driver, we knew that the Lagoon Plaza Drugstore was the best place to buy those wonderful little sugar bananas, and we had made some good friends among the CSY personnel and the local residents. It was the kind of life that could go on forever with no strain, and it had been one of the pleasantest episodes in my cruising career, but there were many more islands waiting to loom over the horizon between us and Venezuela. We had spent the time alloted for the BVI as January drew to a close.

Daughter Martha left her growing family in her "single-parent" ménage to a sitter they knew well, closed up my financial books for a week, and came down to join us for the next onward leg in the direction of Antigua. She miraculously had her luggage when she arrived. (Alice's had gotten to Beef Island all right on her trip down, but her duffel had fallen off the bus on the way in from the airport—a new wrinkle. Fortunately, it was found the next day.)

To celebrate Martha's arrival and as a farewell to Road Town, we took her to dinner at an unusual restaurant called the Cloud Room. It is high atop one of the mountains ringing Road Harbour and can only be reached by four-wheel vehicle. When you make a reservation, arrangements are made for you to be picked up in their special jeep, and the ride up the steep trail is enough to make a goat dizzy. The restaurant hangs over the brow of the hill, with a magnificent view across the nearby islands and out to St. Croix, whose lights twinkle on the horizon forty miles away, and Road Town spreads out almost directly below you.

Everything, from driving the jeep to bartending, to cooking, to serving is done by members of one Tortolan family, with no European or Americans on the staff; it is beautifully handled, with very good food

The view from shore, Cooper Island

to go with the remarkable atmosphere. The final, special touch comes halfway through dinner, when the roof slides back to reveal the open sky, as the diners burst into spontaneous applause. The night we were there just happened to have a full moon.

We would welcome that moon, we thought, when we set out across Anegada Passage.

21. Anegada Passage

~~~~~~

On the night of February 1 there was that rarity for the Virgin Islands, a flat calm. At anchor in Trellis Bay, we were bathed in the softly diffused light of the moon, round and white and sailing high over head in a cloudless sky. Not a ripple stirred on the smooth sheen of the harbor, and even Anegada Passage would be flat on a night like this. Too bad we could not be out there, once more getting past a worry box by powering through a calm, but we were again prisoners of a schedule. John Yeoman was joining us for the passage, and he was not due until the next morning.

We had had a leisurely day after saying good-bye and thank you at CSY, with a snorkeling-and-lunch stop on the CCA mooring at Little Harbour, where the coral heads along the shore were protected enough to have escaped the ravages of Hurricane David. From there we had reached on to Trellis Bay in a light southeaster and had caught Tony's second show after dinner.

John arrived the next morning with luggage (because he carried it on himself), and he was already at the pier when Martha and I rowed ashore to meet him—his plane had been half an hour early. One never knows about airline schedules in this part of the world! The best way to cross Anegada Passage is to make an evening departure from the Virgins for a morning landfall on the other side, eighty miles away, so while the calm still held we powered across the five miles to Virgin Gorda Yacht Harbour, which was then the only marina in the BVI outside of Road Town. We could get our customs and immigration clearance at the airport there and do a final laundry and some shopping before taking off.

This is an incredibly busy spot, with constant traffic in and out, as almost every boat cruising the area stops in at least once for these

services, or to eat ashore. The dockmasters are a bit gruff and uncooperative, but, after watching the performance of boat after boat ignoring
their instructions in trying to make a slip or anchor stern-to the service
bulkhead, one can perhaps sympathize with their attitude.

In general, BVI natives are quiet, shy, and basically polite, though
they have shown the effects of increased contact with tourists in the
past few years, and their shy charm is sometimes more akin to surly
diffidence; often, however, this can be attributed more to an uncertainty over what is expected of them than to any true resentment. The
great boom in yacht chartering has created so many new jobs that there
is virtually no unemployment.

Anegada Passage, eighty miles from Virgin Gorda to St. Martin
and fringed with unmarked reefs, is one of the famous challenges in
Caribbean cruising. I had read up on it in the various guides and
accounts of personal experience, and there seemed to be complete
agreement that it is a unique body of water, with a character all its own
that differs markedly from surrounding waters. The single characteristic pointed out most often is that it is completely unpredictable; the
second point of agreement concerns sea conditions, which are supposed
to be confused, rough, and ever changing. This is the meeting place
for weather from the open Atlantic, the Caribbean, and the last gasp
of continental influences from North America. Their clash creates the
unpredictability, and the mix of tidal and wind currents from the two
great bodies of water is the cause for the odd behavior of the waves and
for odd sets in unpredictable directions, complicating dead reckoning
navigation.

Everything I have ever read says, and everyone I have ever talked
to about it agrees, that it is a passage to be gotten over with as quickly
as possible: not a place to linger in and contemplate nature. It ranks
with the Florida Straits and Mona Passage in the "treat with respect"
category. Robin Tattersall said that his favorite route was to go north-
about Virgin Gorda and exit into Anegada Passage at a pass in the reef
near Necker Island, as this kept you in protected water for the longest
time possible. It was a general expectation that the wind would be on
the nose, but slants in it from the northeast or southeast should deter-

mine in which direction you headed. If there was a southeast slant, you could take starboard tack and aim for Anguilla, perhaps making a landfall at Dog Island—a small, deserted piece of sand with good protection (and diving) among its reefs that lies a few miles northwest of Anguilla. With a northerly bias in the wind, the port tack becomes dominant, and St. Martin is the more likely target.

As we sat at Virgin Gorda Yacht Harbour, I tried to gauge the wind coming over the hill; it seemed to have a definite southeast slant, which meant that we should start from as far south as possible at Round Rock Passage, rather than at Necker Island. A weather report from San Juan talked about a front, with northwest winds behind it, headed for the Virgin Islands, but I knew from experience that most of these lose their thrust before they get that far. There had only been one norther in all the time we had been there. It was too much to hope that this one would push as far as Anegada Passage and bring us a northwester.

At 1500, we powered out the winding dredged channel to St. Thomas Bay and set sail to reach down to Round Rock in a gentle breeze, one of the lightest of the winter. The sheer walls of Round Rock had a restless lacing of white around them when we eased past to the open waters of Anegada Passage, but the sea outside was remarkably smooth. The breeze was no longer from the southeast. There was enough north in it for us to lay 135°, gradually lifting to 120°, and the sailing was delightful at a lazy four knots. This would be a long, slow trip at that speed, but everything was so pleasant that I had no desire to hear the engine's rumble. As the sun slid down astern, turning the receding islands to dark silhouettes, it was more like sailing in Gorda Sound than the notorious Passage.

It was so calm that dinner was served on the cockpit table while a mauve twilight enveloped us. A good-sized cutter came up astern with sails set but motorsailing as well and moved steadily by us, obviously "getting there" with despatch. I knew we would have to do the same if the breze dropped off any more but I wanted to delay the moment as long as possible. We were going to stand four-and-four for the night, and Jane and I came on at 2000 just as the moon broke clear of the horizon over the bow and began to spread its path of silver toward us.

Seas from a norther breaking on Virgin Gorda

This was going to be a lovely night for sailing, or so it seemed.

So it seemed for about an hour. By 2100, a big, black bank of clouds in the east had built up from nowhere with startling speed, blotting out the moon. Soon afterward, cold rain was dashing across us on a strengthening breeze, and we were headed off to 160°. I was just beginning to think about shortening sail, when the breeze lost its weight, and we slowed to a wallow very quickly. The squall had been enough, though, to kick up a sea, and the waves leapt and crested around us without a discernible pattern, continuing after the wind dropped off. So it was on with the engine and set course 115° for St. Martin (or rather Sint Maarten, since we would be entering at the Dutch side of this split-nationality island).

The moon made brief appearances through splits in the clouds, and the rain stopped as quickly as it had started. Powering with the main up as a steadying sail, we would run into sudden bursts of breeze, and I would break out the jib—so easy to do with the roller-reefer—and kill the engine in hopes of some more sailing. Never did the breeze last longer than fifteen minutes, though, and all that these strange puffs accomplished was to stir up an incredible slop of sea. We bobbled and bounced every which way, and the sea condition reminded me of those scenes in a movie that are supposed to show a storm at sea but were obviously shot in the studio tank, with model ships heaving crazily in the kind of directionless waves kids make when they are splashing around in a bathtub.

While the breeze played its fitful jokes, coming in from anywhere between south and northeast in its brief appearances, rainy blackness alternated with quicksilver moments of brilliance when the moon would find an opening in the clouds. The only consistency was inconsistency, but the odd bobble of sea stayed with us and built up, often bringing sets of waves from opposite directions to meet and destroy each other in crazy spray tossings. They were not big waves, and *Brunelle* plowed on without too much discomfort, though it was bouncy enough for me to put the mattress on the cabin sole again when we went off watch.

There was some other traffic around us, both in boats on our course and the reverse and in large ships crossing our path, and we were disturbed to find that our bow running lights went out soon after dark. No vessels came very close, but we kept an extra careful watch, with a flashlight handy to light up the main if necessary.

In the bursts of breeze, we managed perhaps an hour of sailing without the engine, but with the dawn at 0600, the breeze freshened and steadied from absolutely dead ahead. In the growing light, St. Martin appeared in dark outline against the horizon, and a course change of ten degrees to port brought it onto the bow, proving that we had been set south a bit. Off to starboard, the dramatic, bluish-gray cone of Saba broke into the clear from a rain squall, and heavy black clouds ringed the horizon in all directions, showing, in the morning light, what we had been going through all night since the moon first blotted out.

Anegada Passage had predictably lived up to its reputation for unpredictability.

22.   Hideaways?

Even though we were back in an "onward" psychology, with Venezuela as a target at the nether end of this four-hundred-mile chain of islands, we were not yet in a hurry. We had a few months to make our way down the islands, landfall by landfall, without ever being out of sight of land (in good visibility) until there would be that last ninety miles from Grenada to the mainland of South America. It was an intriguing prospect, and a far different type of cruising from the laziness of zig-zagging through the cozy confines of the BVI.

Here, even though the legs are never more than fifty miles, the sailing is either in the open ocean over big, cresting seas rolling unimpeded from Africa under the full sweep of the trades, or in the fitful backwinds in the lee of the mountainous islands. The choice of harbors is thin, and there is always a sense of going somewhere, as the last island drops astern, bright green in the morning sun, and the next landfall looms dimly on the horizon ahead, a faint, purple outline. Gradually, as the day wears on, and (southward bound) the sun marches across from port beam to starboard beam in its convoy of swiftly moving, puffy clouds, there is a slow, subtle exchange of color values between the island astern and the one over the bow. By late afternoon, as the new destination draws near, the sun lowering in the west spreads a golden glow over its now-green hills, dappled in cloud shadows, and the island astern has faded to a misty memory. During the day, a massive buildup of cumulus over the peaks of both islands has shrouded them in shadow, and the late sun slants through the cloud towers, highlighting their roiled blacks and whites.

It is a glorious experience for the most part, though even here, where the trade-wind weather has an almost metronomic reliability, there are variations that bring unexpected challenges. For anyone who loves the feel of a boat under sail in the open sea, though, with the scend of waves sweeping under her in a rhythmic pattern of swish and surge, punctuated by the white parentheses of bow waves (and an occasional dollop of straying spray), this is sailing at its best—unmatched in the world's top cruising areas.

We had a lot of this to look forward to after our long slug from Florida, but first there was this little group of "in-between" islands to explore. For years, Anguilla, St. Martin, St. Bart's and the separate string of Saba, Statia, St. Kitts, Nevis, and Montserrat had been almost a no-man's land for cruising yachts because of Anegada Passage on one side and, very often, a tough thrash to windward to get back the other way to Antigua. Charter crews based in the Virgins or Antigua were not too enamored of going there, and there was no bareboat service in the area. Write-ups of these islands called them remote, unspoiled, seldom-visited, and I had a left-over impression that this was still the case. Also, I had gone to St. Martin by air in 1958, when it truly was unspoiled and undiscovered—two small hotels on the Dutch side and none on the French—and I still had that mental image of it.

It was a shock, then, as we powered along its south coast toward Phillipsburg, the main town of Dutch Sint Maarten, to see an array of fancy hotels lining the beach on the low western half of the island, with big jets roaring in and out of the airport. I knew it had been thoroughly "discovered" in the intervening years, but the extent of the development was still a surprise. Phillipsburg is a junior Charlotte Amalie now. Two white cruise ships, *Cunard Princess* and *Amerikanis*, bulked large in the wide, shallow bay of Phillipsburg as we moved into it, and the anchorage was chock-a-block with yachts. We were quite familiar with *Cunard Princess*, as she had been making weekly visits to Road Town all the time we were there. She is not a particularly large ship, but she towered over that harbor like a white mountain, the first cruise ship to make the BVI a regular stop.

In Phillipsburg, she looked impressive too. Her passengers and those from *Amerikanis* were swarming all over the narrow little main street of the town when I went ashore to clear in at the police station after we had anchored far up in the northeast corner of the bay to get

The harbor at Phillipsburg, Sint Maarten. Vigor *in center*

out of its persistent surge as much as possible. In 1958 this street had been a somnolent dirt lane with native stores, one small guest house, a few public buildings, and hardly a vehicle in sight. Now it resembled the equally narrow Main St. of Charlotte Amalie—one of the classic tourist traps in the world—in its rows of boutiques, gift shops, bars, and restaurants, (all emblazoned with credit card signs) and the taxis, Mini-Mokes, rental cars, and trucks were bumper to bumper. Changes like this are inevitable under the pressures of jet-age development and should not be so surprising. It was just that all this was such a clash with my memory of a sleepy West Indian backwater.

We were not about to fight it, in any event. We took a taxi ride around the island, where it is still an amusing experience to switch from the high-pressure development of Sint Maarten to the comparative rural peace and somnolence of St. Martin simply by going past a small cairn of stones on the narrow Macadam road that crosses the island to the French town of Marigot. France and Holland have shared the island peacefully since the seventeenth century, when they divided it

238

by having a representative of each power walk around it in opposite directions from a given point. Where they met on the other side established the opposite end of the boundary, and international amity has reigned ever since. There is absolute freedom of access between the two sides, but all of this amicable intercourse has not wiped out the very distinctive national characteristics that prevail in the two sections.

Most of the restaurants are on the Dutch side, but not all, and French entrepreneurs have moved into the act in Phillipsburg, with such establishment names as La Grenouille and Antoine's, as well as Chinese, Indonesian, and West Indian places. We tried La Grenouille to celebrate our arrival, and we could have been in New York's Upper East Side as to menu and quality of food (and price), except for the view out through palm trees to the harbor. John and Martha later bravely tried one of Sint Maarten's casinos, ruining their budgets for the rest of the cruise.

There were a few nautical problems by now. The running lights were one, but, more disturbing, we had taken a great amount of water into the bilge while powering in at the end of our Anegada Passage crossing, and I figured that the stuffing box must be leaking. There was an establishment called Bobby's Marina with a single pier sticking out from the beach in the northeast corner of the harbor and some fairly impressive vessels moored stern-to the pier. We investigated in the dink and found that there was room to come in and take a berth, and that we could get fuel and have the stuffing box looked at. On one side, our neighbor was a large Pacemaker motor yacht, with an Airedale aboard who whined almost constantly; on the other side there was a twenty-foot sport runabout, a Riva from Italy, owned by the Italian owner of one of the bigger hotels on the western end of the island. The sleekly contoured mahogany beauty was as sexy as a *Playboy* centerfold and seemed even more so when we heard that it had cost $140,000. What had I been thinking about the quaint, native charm of Sint Maarten?

"Bobby" turned out to be an engaging local named Bobby Velasquez, a large, solidly built, dark-haired man with olive skin, a dashing moustache, an engaging manner, and an accent that was an odd mix-

239

The $140,000 plaything

ture of Bermudian, Barbadan, and something distinctively his own. He had studied marine engineering at the University of Miami and in Curaçao, and, clad in a form-fitting suit of immaculate dark blue coveralls, he came aboard to check on our stuffing-box problem. The CSY 37 has a Vee drive transmission, with the engine facing aft in a space under the cockpit and the removable stairs that lead down from the cockpit into the cabin. The drive unit is in an extremely snug position in the shallow bilge, and Bobby, his muscular shoulders filling our companionway as he studied the situation, shook his head.

"Man! That's no place for someone my size," he said. "I've got a smaller boy who will have to do this job."

It was done and done well by a silent young man, of whom we saw very little except his ass poking high into the companionway as he sweated over the awkward box and occasionally gave out with a low moan. It was also very inexpensive, as dockage and the repairs came to twenty-one dollars, and we were able to buy new bulbs for the running lights in the marina chandlery.

I have a gimmick of bringing one hundred dollars in singles with me on the boat so that we will always have small-denomination cash with us if a problem arises (American money is the official currency of the BVI and readily accepted everywhere else except in the Dominican Republic). I had gotten this in a wrapped packet of new bills from the bank before I left home, and I paid for the running light bulbs with several of the new bills. The young man at the cashier's desk of the chandlery was absolutely fascinated by the pristine bills with successive serial numbers, and he fingered their crisp newness and studied the numbers.

"I've never seen anything like that before," he said, and I think he had a strong suspicion that I had made them myself.

Bobby came aboard to see the work that had been done, and we had a pleasant visit over a couple of beers as he told us of the vicissitudes of running a marina in the islands, such as the problems of finding competent help, getting supplies and parts, and the assault of hurricanes like David, which had almost demolished his pier. His was a relatively new venture, growing as more and more boats moved into the area, and he seemed like the kind of guy who could make it go.

The boats in the harbor were an odd mix of scruffy, shoestring, long-voyager types, modern American yachts, oddball vessels from Europe, and a few Panamanian-registered minesweeper conversions and derelict ex-luxury yachts that looked as though they were on a hunt for sunken treasure but had run out of fuel. A local specialty is multihulls—long, lean, futuristic-looking craft with sharp hulls, catamaran or tri, and ultra-modern high-aspect rigs. Many of them are built in Sint Maarten, and a long ocean race for them is a special local event.

There was also another CSY, *Argo,* a 44, privately owned by Judy and Bill Sena from Ohio, who put her out on charter for much of the year under a professional captain, Basil Hazell from St. Vincent, but who currently were using her themselves for a month-long cruise. We had several good visits with them comparing notes over cocktails on both boats. Basil, from a family that seems to be represented in all walks of life in St. Vincent, had been a CSY employee for a while, knows all sorts of people throughout the islands, and is a mine of helpful information as well as a drily entertaining raconteur in a Calypso-tinged accent. I even enlisted him in the Friendly Yacht Service to take down our winches and grease them at the price of a few beers.

Ever since the west coast of Florida, we had enjoyed this come-and-go camarderie of the world of cruising boats. The Rabows, Jean-Louis and Claudine, Jeremy, Don and Olive and other pier companions at Puerto Plata and Samana, the man who bled our injectors at San Juan, and many more whose paths had crossed with ours at some point, all added a human touch to our own adventures: it was always interesting to see the diversity of people who were wandering the world in small boats. All had a story of some sort in what had brought them to leave the routines of life ashore for adventures afloat. Most would be known briefly, with the normal patterns of friendship quickened by knowledge of the inevitable evanescence of the relationship, but another side of this camaraderie is the extra pleasure of surprise meetings many months later in some new area with sailors who had been brief friends in another port.

One of our pleasantest encounters had been with the Dutch family, Karl, Luise, and Joe, in Puerto Plata and, for a quick hello, in the Virgins; now, nine months later, it was not really surprising to find them in Sint Maarten, where they would obviously feel at home. Luise had a job as a teacher, Karl did free-lance boat work, and Joe had gone back to Holland to school. In catching up with them, we had an amusing postscript to the story of the lady-in-distress hitchhiker. After we left Samana, it seems that she finally arranged a ride, and it was with the American cabin cruiser that had arrived there in reverse. Somehow, they had made repairs, and they left for St. Croix with her aboard. As they entered the harbor in St. Croix and made for the quay where they intended to land, they could see that customs and immigration officials happened to be standing right there waiting for them. In a panic, they told the girl that she would have to jump over on the outboard side of the boat and swim to the shore, which was quite close, but she refused, so they picked her up and threw her in. Some day we may hear the rest of the story!

Hideaways?

I have always wanted to see St. Bart's (officially St. Barthelemey), but in all my previous visits to the Caribbean it was one place that had eluded me. I had heard for years from the few people I knew who had been there that it was the true hideaway, unspoiled and very different from the other islands—also a picturesque haven for smugglers where booze could be bought for the best prices in the West Indies.

It is an easy fifteen-mile sail from Phillipsburg, and we reached over on course 120 degrees in a morning's jaunt in a gentle northeaster, watching the steady parade of little STOL planes from St. Martin that are the only air link for St. Bart's. As they approach its coastal hills, they slide down at an angle of 45 degrees to its tiny airport.

The only port is Gustavia, whose name is a reminder that the island was under Swedish rule for many years before it was sold to the French in 1877 for £11,000. It is a small, rectangular harbor on the west side, almost land-locked, and has the look of a northern European fishing village with its tightly-packed houses and shops lining the quays. The Stone and Hart guide, written five years previously, referred to it as a lonely, untouched place, where one could tie up stern-to the quay anywhere and have the whole harbor to one's self and a few native sloops loading or unloading cases of smuggled liquor.

It was something of a surprise, therefore, to find the roadstead outside the inner harbor filled with yachts at anchor; Gustavia's narrow confines looked like Edgartown, Massachusetts, in mid-July with the jam of boats at anchor and moored stern-to all along the harbor's edge. In this "secret hideaway" that I had been expecting, I don't think I have ever seen a more crowded harbor this side of the French Riviera. We ranged around the shores looking for some spot to tie up, but there did not seem to be an open place. At a fancy new restaurant called the Yacht Club, a balconied building of natural wood with a quay in front, there were a couple of openings, but a man in a bikini bottom told us, in a strong French accent, that these were for charter boats. There was a long concrete quay that only had one motorboat, a Maine lobsterman-type hull with flared sheer and a small deckhouse, lying alongside and blocking it. We finally found a spot in the middle of the harbor—which meant we were only a couple of hundred feet from shore—where we

The crowded inner harbor at Gustavia

could anchor fore-and-aft, as all the other boats were, to keep them from swinging. This was the first time we had broken out our Danforth since we had been aboard.

Not too long after we were settled, the motorboat pulled away from its berth at the concrete quay, but I didn't want the bother of moving and we stayed where we were. Soon a big sloop we had seen in Phillipsburg, came in and executed a stern-to mooring to the now-empty quay as though she owned the joint, and I rowed over and asked her skipper what the story was.

"I don't know," he answered. "I just saw this open place and took it."

Half an hour later, he was on the move again. The motorboat came back, and the sloop was shooed away. Seems the quay is owned by David Rockefeller as the landing for the launch which services the vacation house he has on a remote point of the island.

Hideaways?

The harbor was an active boat-show-afloat for the rest of the afternoon, with a varied mix of vessels on the move. Along the main commercial quay there was a glossy one-hundred-foot power yacht from London (but owned by an Arab, as we found out later) with her crew all in snappy uniforms, near a scruffy native sloop—with a great long bowsprit and boom and almost no paint showing anywhere—unloading vegetables. There was a schooner yacht on charter and a mammoth orange catamaran that brings day-trippers over from Phillipsburg, a sport fisherman, and a native sloop or two—as catholic a mix as could be imagined. The day-sailing charter yachts from the Yacht Club came back into the harbor in late afternoon, and there was a great deal of fuss and shouting as they maneuvered to back into the openings, with everyone in the harbor enjoying the show. These boats had signs in their rigging saying "Haircuts and sail repairs" (not with the same scissors one would trust), "electrical repairs," and "Cruzan Rum." Despite the commercialism, none of them seemed in very good repair.

Most of the anchored yachts were private cruising boats with European flags dominating. Some with French flags were no doubt local, but many countries were represented, and there were a few American boats. We had had a crisis with a French courtesy flag for St. Bart's. I thought we had one, but I couldn't locate it anywhere, and there had been a facetious suggestion to turn the Dutch one for Sint Maarten sideways. This would not work because of the shape and the sequence of the colors, and we finally solved the problem by cutting the Dominican Republic flag in half. This made a proper French tri-color, albeit the smallest one in the harbor, after Jane sewed grommets on it and hemmed the part that had been cut. As for clearing in, customs, in a government building up a steep hill overlooking the harbor, was closed when we arrived; it opened for a while later in the afternoon, and a young French-speaking girl took a crew list from me with complete lack of interest.

Ashore, St. Bart's is very different from any other Caribbean island, as it is over 90 percent white, and French speaking. Blacks, who predominate on every other island, are hardly in evidence at all, and clerks in customs and the post office, people in shops and restaurants,

A real mix of vessels at the quay in Gustavia

truck drivers, fishermen, and street laborers are all white. Typical of any French area, there is little attempt made to speak English, but since my French is better than my Spanish (which doesn't mean it is strong), I find it fun to struggle along.

Martha found a young man she had known in the States who was the captain of a big Bertram sportfisherman based in St. Bart's, and we all had a pleasant dinner at the Yacht Club, with good food—except that the piped disco music had an overly loud, pervasive insistence. I don't like disco music anywhere, and I find it especially annoying with meals. This didn't seem to be the atmosphere for it, either.

We also had another connection at St. Bart's, Benji Doniger, a cousin of Jane's brother-in-law. He retired as a professional movie cameraman in the sixties and lived in Puerto Rico with his wife, Margot, a Latvian artist, for several years until conditions there became discouraging. They picked St. Bart's in 1967 for the hideaway it then was and built a house on a deserted hillside on the northeast side of the island at a bay called Marigot (every West Indian island seems to have a Marigot). There was not another house in sight when they built it, but now they can see twenty-two from their veranda, which soars out over the hillside and a garden of dense tropical growth that Margot has developed. Bananaquits, dainty yellow birds with wings that quiver into invisibility, swarmed around a feeding station like bees at a pot of honey; below us on the clear blue of the bay, heaving with trade-wind surge, fishermen worked bright red nets in a big circle. The Donigers still love it, but they feel that the world is catching up with them again, and they always travel for a month or two in the fall to avoid the sultry weather of hurricane season and fight off incipient "island fever."

The harbor at Gustavia comes awake about as early as Potter's Cay in Nassau, and almost as noisily. At 0500 there was hymn singing dimly heard from a distance, and, close at hand on the commercial quay, sawing, hammering, and shouting, mixed with blasts of radio music. Fishermen in outboards skimmed through the anchorage, and there was no sleep after a very early hour.

Shopping is easy in Gustavia. The supermarket, Service Libre, is right at the waterfront, with better parking for dinghies than for cars. There had been American brand names in most of the supermarkets on our way through the islands, but everything here was in unfamiliar French packages. I have a failing for Fig Newton cookies, always a subject of great amusement to my family and to guests aboard, so we always look for them while marketing. Everyone creates a great fetish out of making sure I have them. Here, there did not seem to be any, and I was crying crocodile tears and complaining about the uncivilized French, when some were discovered behind a gruesome-looking package of marshmallow treats. Eureka, and much celebrating.

Food was expensive in St. Bart's, but its reputation for cheap liquor still held true. I bought Mount Gay for 8 francs 50 (about $2.15), the best price anywhere in the islands, but nothing like it was in the old days here, or in Barbados for 75¢ a bottle—or like the case we had bought in bond in Grenada, 1965, for $7.50.

As we sat in the cockpit in the hot sun of morning, with trade-wind puffs gusting through the tightly packed boats at anchor, we watched a big minesweeper conversion and the orange catamaran unload the daily invasion of day-trippers from Phillipsburg, while plane after plane swooped down on a steep glide to the airport. St. Bart's is lively fun and different, but I had more than just an impression that the world now had one less place left in which to hide.

23. *Something Different*

Anguilla, though, was different. This is one of the least known Caribbean islands. It sits at the very top of the Windward-Leeward chain that strings from Anegada Passage to South America. North of it is the open Atlantic, and, though it is only six miles from St. Martin, there is a sense of isolation and of days gone by in its sleepy settlements, miles of deserted beaches, and low-keyed pace of life.

It is even different physically from most of the Windwards and Leewards. While St. Martin and St. Bart's have junior-grade mountains to lend bulk to their profiles, and the islands farther south are truly mountainous, Anguilla's highest point is less than three hundred feet. The island is sixteen miles long and never more than three-and-one-half miles wide; its name, Spanish for eel, reflects these proportions.

Jane and I had been interested in it ever since reading the book *Under an English Heaven* by Donald Westlake, which told of the odd series of events in the late 1960s when Anguilla was involved in a "reverse revolution." For a few years, it had been part of a newly created self-governing political entity known in the British Empire as an Associated State, with St. Kitts and Nevis—sixty miles to the south on the other side of St. Martin. This association did not please Anguillans, however, because they suffered from the physical distance, and from being a "poor relation" in the island trio. St. Kitts dominated, under its premier, Robert Bradshaw, who ran a form of bossism that could be compared to the days of Mayor Hague of Jersey City or Mayor Daley of Chicago. Anguillans took the short end of the stick in every relationship.

They wanted to sever this connection and either go independent, a hard road for a resourceless island of six thousand people, or rejoin the British Empire as a colony. This might have seemed like a fairly simple situation, but it ended up in impossibly involved comic-opera shenanigans, including an "invasion" by British paratroopers and London Bobbies in winter uniforms. Eventually, Anguillans had their way and it is again a British colony. Although Westlake, a comic novelist with a gift for the absurd, made an hilarious account of all this, it was also obvious that it had not been very funny for the Anguillans while it was going on. He had made the island and the people seem very real, and we were not about to leave the area without a visit.

We checked out for Anguilla from Phillipsburg, where entering and clearing is done at the police station in the heart of town. When I had entered on a Sunday, only one young man was on duty, in street clothes; I had had to wait for almost half an hour after completing the various forms while he dashed off in a police car to handle some emergency—a berserk merchant seaman, he said, when he finally came back. To check out on a weekday, there was a routine of visits to several offices where the rubber stamps banged furiously at the end of a wait in line with restlessly sweating natives who did not seem to enjoy the benefits of bureaucracy.

As we pulled away from Bobby's, several open work boats from the marina were bringing crowds of young American men in sports clothes in from seaward, and, in leaving the harbor, we went right by the source—an American submarine, *Finback,* anchored on the outer fringe of the bay. Black and mean looking, she rode low in the water, with no motion of her own and the surge sloshing up and down on her rounded hull, while more of her crew, dressed in civvies, lined the deck waiting for the next launch for shore liberty. She was a forceful contrast to the frivolity-dominated atmosphere of the area—a sudden reminder of the undercurrents of unrest and political uncertainty that lie quite close to the surface of Caribbean life outside the realm of tourism.

Leaving Sint Maarten's "Miami Beach row" behind, we had a brisk reach at hull speed from the islands western tip to Anguillita Point in a much smoother sea than the usual inter-island passage in the trades, since reefs and small islands to the east of Anguilla break up the rollers coming in from the open Atlantic. The port of entry on Anguilla is Road Bay, a third of the way up the north shore, and we powered toward it from Anguillita past low, limestone cliffs with a house or two showing now and then.

Entering Road Bay was a return to the Caribbean of forty years ago. At the inner end of its powder blue expanse, a village of small shacks and huts stretched behind a curve of pure white beach, with palms bending over the buildings. At the center of the town, one concrete and timber pier jutted out from the beach, with a light surge washing around its pilings; behind it, in a clearing, the wineglass hulls of several native boats were propped up under the palms. On a flagpole in the clearing, the British Union Jack fluttered and flopped in the uneven puffs of breeze.

Off to starboard, half a mile away at the end of the curving beach, there was a pier with several small island freight boats and native sloops alongside. In the harbor, one or two little native boats were moored out from the beach; there was one other cruising auxiliary besides *Brunelle*, plus a fine native schooner, painted a glossy black and named *Warspite*. She had the heavy, stubby rig, uncertain sheer line, and high freeboard so typical of island vessels.

In all this evocation of yesteryear there was just one discordant note. At anchor near *Warspite* was *Lac 5*, the biggest motor yacht we had seen anywhere in the islands, a gleaming white vessel with raked, futuristic radar mast, rows of portholes, and, on her stern, aft of several sports boats on davits, a red and gold helicopter. Young people in bikinis were swooping around her in Windsurfers, operating from her landing stage. We heard later that she was owned by an American who had developed a process for recapping tires. With *Warspite* close by, we saw two perfect symbols of the old and the new in the Caribbean.

The town is called Sandy Ground, and the flagpole marks the police station where you enter and clear. It is right back of a small sign that welcomes visitors to Anguilla. I made my way there from the pier through a "Little League" cricket game with cardboard boxes for wickets, slats of wood for bats, and a tennis ball as the pellet. Chickens and pigs were either team members or obstacles in the game. A shy young man in uniform was the only person on duty at the station, and he shuffled a few papers on the desk and handed me a plain piece of

Warspite *at anchor in Road Bay, Anguilla*

paper and a dim, fly-specked copy of some previous vessel's entrance declaration.

"Do the same he did" he said, pointing to the other paper, and when I did, formalities were complete.

Robin Tattersall had told me, when he was giving advice on crossing Anegada Passage, to be sure to look up a man named Emile Gumbs at Sandy Ground.

"He lives right near the police station," Robin had said. "He's a great sailor and I know you'd enjoy meeting him."

Gumbs was a name that had figured repeatedly in Westlake's book, though I was hazy now in my memory, since it was several years since I had read the book, of exactly how. On the land side of the narrow road, a two-story house almost drowned in flowers and blooming

252

Lac 5 *was quite a contrast to* Warspite

shrubs sat behind a picket fence in a neat yard. On the balcony, there was a bronzed man with iron gray hair. I called up to him, "I'm looking for Emile Gumbs."

"You've found him. That's me," was the answer, with a wide smile of flashing white teeth. "What can I do for you?"

"Robin Tattersall gave me your name," I said, and I explained who I was and that our boat was in the harbor.

"Oh. I saw her coming in," he answered. "Come on up and have a visit."

We sat on the veranda and were soon joined by his wife, Janice, a pretty, dark-haired woman with a touch of Canadian accent.

"We were about to have tea," she said. "Will you join us?"

While she was preparing the tea things, we started to chat about our cruise, and I began asking questions. Robin had told me only that Gumbs was "a sailor."

"Do you have a business here?" I asked. "What do you do?"

"Well, I'm the chief minister," Gumbs answered matter-of-factly.

"That keeps me pretty busy, but I also have a salt business that has been in our family for quite a while." He pointed out the back of the house to a shallow pond that confined the houses of Sandy Ground to a single row between it and the harbor. "Conditions aren't right for working it now," he went on. "We've had too much rain, and the flats have too much water on them."

The government in Anguilla is a legislature elected to represent local districts, and the chief minister is chosen by these representatives to be the top man in the government—as I found out through further conversation. When tea was over, they had errands to do, and I invited them and family to come to *Brunelle* for cocktails later so we could talk some more; they were obviously interested in seeing the boat. As twilight settled over the anchorage, I rowed to the pier to pick them up. Their pre-teen daughter, Cathy, was with them, and their son Larry was somewhere in the harbor in a small boat and would find us on his own, they said.

He soon zoomed up, his curly blond hair and tanned skin standing out in a Boston Whaler full of young blacks, and clambered aboard to join the group. He was fourteen, and his parents said that his one real interest was the harbor and the boats in it, where he spent much of his time. He and Cathy were practically the only white children on the whole island, not counting winter visitors, and Emile and Janice were a bit concerned about their education and the problems of mixing in. There did not seem to be any racial tension involved, however, and it would seem that the family's position was solid since Emile had been elected chief minister. Janice, as I had guessed, is a Canadian from Toronto, who originally came to Anguilla as a teacher.

The Gumbs family has been on Anguilla since the eighteenth century, and the name has been taken by many of the blacks who worked for the family over the years, so it is a fairly common one on the island. The house Emile and family live in now was built by his grandfather in the latter part of the nineteenth century, and *Warspite*, the big schooner in the harbor has been in the family since her launching in 1907. She was built as a sloop, was lengthened by having a mid-section added about ten years later, and was then converted from sloop to schooner. For years she traded through the islands—Emile had been her captain for a period when he was younger, before marrying and deciding to stay on the island. In addition to carrying cargo, one of her major tasks was to transport Anguillan workers to and from the Dominican Republic, where they went as temporary field hands during the sugar harvest. Several Anguillan schooners did this, and there was always a race to see who could be first home with the returning workers, who were eager to get back to their families. Evidently *Warspite* usually did pretty well.

Anguillans are no longer imported in the Dominican Republic, and the inter-island freight traffic is mostly under power. *Warspite* still earns her keep as the supply vessel for Sombrero Light, which the British government maintains on a lonely islet in the Anegada Passage thirty miles northwest of Anguilla. It was obvious that Emile was very proud of the old ship, and she made a fine sight sitting at anchor with the tracery of her rigging outlined against the sunset. He and Larry were particularly interested in the picture of the old *Brunelle* in the main cabin and the story behind it which I showed them during a "tour" of the boat. The children were a bit shy, but very polite and extremely interested in everything on board.

The subject of the "revolution" in the 1960s came up, but we didn't dwell on it in detail. They had read Westlake's book and had met him, and they said that it was a fair picture of what had gone on.

"I'll bet it didn't seem as funny at the time as he makes it sound in the book," I said; they agreed heartily.

"A lot of it was funny, and we could laugh about some of it," Janice said, "but it isn't so funny when people start shooting, which they did one night, and when you really wonder what is going to happen in the place where you live. I have to admit we were very worried for a while, and we were glad when it was over."

It was a pleasant session of talking about the places where we had been, many of which Emile had hit in his seafaring career, and to hear how interested they were in the yachts that came into Road Bay. Larry knew something about every one of them, it seemed, and he had been able to talk his way aboard the big motor yacht with the helicopter, a major coup. As I rowed them ashore—a full load for the Avon—we made plans for a tour of the island the next day, which Janice had offered to do in the family car.

"I'm the minister of tourism without portfolio," she said with a laugh.

It was a fine way to see the island. Its rolling hills, with open vistas of fields and seascapes, reminded me of Cape Cod or Martha's Vineyard as she took us to the main settlement, called the Valley, in the center of the island, where the government buildings and biggest stores are. It was a bright, breezy day, with whitecaps lacing the channel between Anguilla and St. Martin when we looked out over some of the lovely bays and beaches of the south shore. We saw one hotel under construction on a south shore bay, a moderate-sized affair with units strung along the beach; Janice said that Anguilla was adjusting to the inroads of tourism at its own pace. There had been a high-pressure proposition to build a three hundred-room hotel and casino, and a jetport to go with it, but this would have meant importing workers— and an implied conflict with off-island interests who would then assume that they "owned" Anguilla. The decision had been to build only at a rate that Anguilla could handle with its own labor force. Eventually there would be a total of several hundred rooms in a few resorts on different parts of the island, and air service might be expanded, but would still be in small planes from St. Martin (for the forseeable future).

On Fort Hill, which is the highest point on the island and has a commanding view, Janice told us of an involvement she had had there during the "troubles." There was a meeting at the police station there between Ronald Webster, one of the leaders of the Anguillan cause, and some of his henchmen, and the British representatives who were trying to arrive at a solution. It was during some of the tensest moments of the negotiations. Janice had been asked to provide a luncheon for the negotiators, and, thinking that the luncheon would be at the police station, she drove there, only to find that she was supposed to have taken the food to a nearby house. In backing out of the parking place, she hooked bumpers with Webster's car just as he came out in a tearing

Lobster boats at East End, Anguilla

hurry to go somewhere else before ending up at the luncheon, with one of the great decisions of the whole affair hanging fire and dependent on his getting wherever it was he was going. The fate of the revolution, then, hung in the balance as members of both negotiating teams bounced up and down on the bumpers of the cars until they disengaged. History is probably full of the incidence of such human sidelights popping up at critical moments. "For want of a nail——"

Janice could laugh about it now, but at the time she cowered down in her car and tried to pretend that she was not there at all, or at least was someone else.

At East End she showed us what she called the most prosperous part of Anguilla.

One of Anguilla's many gorgeous, empty beaches

"You can tell by all the TV antennas on the houses," she said. "This is where the lobstermen live, and they are making a lot of money. Everyone here has a TV and an antenna high enough to pick up St. Thomas and San Juan."

Their open outboard boats were all pulled up in a neat semi-circle that followed the beach of a little cove, with lobster traps piled all over the area; a few men were puttering around their boats on an off day. Lobstering, some farming, fishing, and seafaring are the main supports of Anguillan economy, with tourism slowly moving up in the picture.

On the way back from East End, we took side roads down to some of the most dazzlingly beautiful beaches I have ever seen, pure white sand extending for a tremendous distance, blinding in the midday sun and without a soul on them, while deep blue Atlantic rollers pounded a border of surf onto the fringing reefs offshore.

Anguilla has a lot to offer, but one can only hope that it does continue at its own pace, keeping what it has now—unique and irreplaceable in the growing pressures of the jet age.

24. *Night Passage*

~~~~~~

There are two possible routes from the "in-between islands" to Antigua, where we were headed to make plane connections for Martha and John and to pick up our next two crew changes. We could make a direct run for it from St. Bart's, seventy-five miles on a course of 140 degrees, or we could hop down the chain of St. Kitts, Nevis, and Montserrat—a great circle course with the longest leg about fifty miles. It all depended on the wind direction. With the wind anywhere south of east, it was a rugged slug to make the direct run—one reason Antiguan charter skippers seldom wanted to head into this area. Even the island-hopping route could mean plenty of hard thrashing to windward.

When it came time for our departure, we were in St. Bart's, and the wind was well north of east, just right for a straight reach. It was an opportunity not to be missed. The plan was an evening departure for a dawn landfall on Antigua, so we left the harbor of Gustavia at 1800 to clear its spider web of anchored boats before dark and then jogged around the outer roadstead under power while we had dinner in calm water. By 1915, it was completely dark, the dishes were done, and the trade was gusting off the hills in uneven puffs. We made sail, mainsail and jib, and headed out between the rounded rock called Pain de Sucre (Sugarloaf) and the main island on course for Antigua.

As soon as we cleared the lee of the island, there was real, steady heft to the wind, and I felt that a reefed main and both headsails would be the best combination. Reefing the main would do little to cut our speed in a breeze over sixteen, it reduced a touch of weather helm, and there was easy flexibility in the two headsails. It was a dark, clear night, with that full, horizon-to-horizon display of stars that is always so startling to someone who has spent most of his life around cities.

We cleared Gustavia before dark; the entrance is the only place devoid of anchored boats

As ever, our friend Orion, the easiest constellation to identify in all the vast panoply, was up there as a focal point, and at this time of year there was that wonderful juxtaposition in late evening of the Southern Cross on one horizon and Polaris and the Big Dipper above the other one.

There were periods of darkness when a batch of clouds would scud swiftly in from the northeast and blot out the stars. We would charge on through a blackness broken only by the phosphorescent rush of whitecaps on the port quarter, shining briefly as they hissed under us, the unearthly glow of the starboard running light flashing against the rhythm of the bow wave, and the little circle of white from our stern light spreading over the nearest foam in our wake. The lights of St. Bart's dimmed rapidly astern, and, well off to starboard, faint pinpricks in the gloom showed where St. Kitts was.

To me, emotions and perceptions are always heightened in night sailing, perhaps because of that primeval fear of the dark that crawls through our sensibilities no matter how matter-of-fact the surface approach might be. Whitecaps, ignored in the noonday sun, have an ominous authority as they suddenly burst out of the void with a swooshing crash, waves look blacker and bigger, and sound is magnified. The rush of water alongside, the hiss of waves and wake and their slap against the hulls, and the orchestration of wind in the rigging are heightened; the sense of speed is intensified; and euphoria is tinged with an anxiety, a presentiment fostered by darkness that something unknown is lurking just beyond the borders of consciousness.

Since our memorable thrash to the Caicos, our night passages had all been under power; this sailing was a wonderful contrast and one of the most exhilarating sails I have ever had, with the pleasures sharpened by that anticipation of the mysteries that might be hidden in the black of night.

There was also a warm spot of encouragement glowing behind the sense of blank blackness, in the knowledge that the late moon would be up before the night was over. Somehow, this prospect makes night watches in darkness better than the ones that follow the setting of a waxing moon half way through the night. On those, dawn seems so far away, but dawn loses its importance when the late moon lights the long hours after midnight.

By the change of watch, the breeze had come up, perhaps to eighteen or a bit more, and I felt that she would do better minus the staysail and still not lose speed significantly, so we doused that and swept on under reefed main and jib at about the same clip. Jane and I were off for the midwatch, and, while it was bouncy and noisy below, there was a marked contrast to the sense of strain and urgency there had been on the passage to Caicos. Just the few degrees change in wind direction, from a close reach to a beam reach, made all the difference.

The moon was up when we came back on at 0400. We were still tearing along at close to hull speed, but the sense of rushing blindly through blankness, alone with the little circle of our own running lights and the nearest breaking waves, had been washed away in the silver flood of light that glittered and danced across the wavetops out to the horizon. The lights of St. Kitts and Nevis, faint at best, had faded in the moonlight, and it was an empty ocean under the moon for a short spell until the first lights of Antigua came up on the bow at 0430.

As we approached them, a new set of lights came into view on the starboard quarter; we realized that they were not from an island, since they were closing with us rapidly and looming brighter as they did. Soon the red and green of running lights could be seen too. With the earliest glimmer of dawn across the water, the big white hull of a cruise ship took shape around the lights, and we could see the distinctive athwartships twin stacks of the *Doric,* a ship we had taken from New York to Bermuda several times. She passed about half a mile off on her way into St. John's, the deep-water port of Antigua, looming over the waves like a great, mobile apartment house. She was a majestic sight in the growing light when she swept on by, and before long her lights had blended with those on Antigua as she closed with the shore.

Rather than envying her passengers their luxury, I pitied them for being asleep at such a beautiful moment. Sunrise at sea, with its message of reassurance and renewal, is a lovely time of day—the freshness of new light on damp decks making you forget the dry, chalky taste in your mouth and the grainy feel in your eyes—and this was one of the most beautiful dawns I have ever seen. Antigua had a crown of clouds on its southern end, and Montserrat, off to leeward and more mountainous, had collected a great tower of cumulus. Smaller puffs of trade-wind scud were marching in from the east, and the sun, still below the horizon from our height of eye, was already sending shafts of color against the masses of clouds over the islands. Its slanting angle on Antigua picked glints of gold and paler yellow out of tumbled black and white, while Montserrat's cover, more down-sun, was bathed in glowing salmon. The colors shifted, grew brighter, faded, and glowed again, while the sun fought its way through small clouds on the eastern rim of the sea, and Antigua went through mutations of misty mauve and darker grays under the cloud shadows, gradually turning to tropical green as the sun rose and the day broadened.

We had Sandy Island off St. John's abeam at 0700, seventy-five miles in just over eleven and a half hours, and the pace of the passage slowed noticeably in the full light of day as we moved out of the

We anchored outside English Harbour in Freeman Bay (foreground) to await customs clearance; the Dockyard is center, and Falmouth Harbour is beyond

trade-wind seas into the protection of the island and the lighter wind of its leeward side.

I had just relaxed in preparation for going off watch, and Jane was taking the last of her wheel trick, when I felt a strange lethargy overtake *Brunelle*, as though she were caught in molasses. I looked over the stern, and, sure enough, there was a Clorox bottle float bobbing around abaft the rudder. Shades of the Gulf of Mexico! We had caught another pot. Under sail, this is nothing like the problem of getting one on the prop under power. We killed the jib and let the main luff, and John and I took turns at cutting away. He made the crucial deep dive to get the last two turns from around the prop, and we were free again. A shallow shelf extends well to leeward of Antigua, and it is liberally speckled with pots. From then on, we kept a good lookout for them as we sailed around the southwestern tip of the island and beat our way eastward along the south shore inside Cade Reef.

Through previous cruises here and two sessions in Antigua Race Week, I was familiar with the waters. Such familiarity is always a reassurance, especially since Cade Reef, which extends for several miles and is less than a mile offshore, is a wicked collection of coral that has trapped many a vessel on the approach to English Harbour. The passage inside the reef avoids the impressive trade-wind rollers that sweep by outside it; we short tacked in smooth water past the familiar promontory of Curtain Bluff and then moved out to the big waves of the open sea for the last few miles to English Harbour.

The entrance to it is marked by a strange natural sculpture on the high cliffs outside. A set of columns that look manmade, called the Pillars of Hercules, are set deeply into the cliff face, and if it were not for their distinctive profile, it would be easy to sail right by the narrow dogleg that leads into English Harbour. In the days of colonial warfare, when Lord Nelson based the British fleet here, this hidden entrance, and the ease of fortifying the heights around it, made it one of the best naval bases in the West Indies. Now, under the pressure of the yachting boom, boats spill over from the inner harbor and fill up Freeman Bay, the outer end of the dogleg, and the approach is not so secret any more.

One of the big, scruffy, rust-pocked schooners that run "dude cruises" through the islands was anchored on the outer edge of Freeman Bay, giving an instant identification. The rest of the bay was chock-a-block with boats at anchor when we nosed in and picked an empty spot off the beach in the officially designated quarantine anchorage. Still glowing in the pleasures of one of the more memorable sails of a lifetime, we put up our Q flag and settled down to wait for the port officials to come give us clearance.

25. *The Social Scene*

〰〰〰〰〰〰〰〰〰〰〰〰〰〰〰〰〰

It was 0500 according to my watch, which I fumbled for on the chart rack next to our bunk. As yet there was no light from the new day, but Jane and I had both been wakened by the clink of bottles and rattle of cans as someone or something worked at the garbage bin a few paces off our stern. We were moored stern-to the quay at the Dockyard in English Harbour, the restored naval station where Admiral Horatio Nelson had based the British fleet almost two hundred years ago. To port we had the replica schooner *America*, 103 feet of gleaming spit and polish; to starboard, we were dwarfed by a mammoth modern schooner, almost as big as *America*, named *Julie Mother* (is there any accounting for boat names?). *Brunelle* had never been in such fancy company, and all around the semi-circular quay there were equally impressive yachts in sail and power, up to a 150-foot motor yacht with tenders on davits that looked as big as *Brunelle*. There had been an open berth alongside her, but I did not like the prospect of being next to her perpetually burbling and rumbling generators and had moved on to a spot among sailboats when we came into the harbor.

To see what was making the noise in the garbage, I poked my head out the hatch—we had had no showers that night, for a change, and it was still open—and there at the garbage bin, a man and a woman, their dark features barely visible in the gloom, were tearing apart the plastic bags that yachtsmen had carefully encased their garbage in and were strewing the contents all through the bin as they culled out bottles. Bottles earn a deposit return of a few cents in Antigua, and this was found money.

There was poignant irony in the sight of this predawn scavenging a few feet away from millions of dollars of luxury yachts—a symbol of Caribbean contrasts and contradictions, of the uneasy juxtaposition of

The Dockyard in 1961 on our first visit

joyous hedonism and the raw realities of existence for the natives who are anxious to work out their own destiny on islands that no longer can support themselves without tourism. The next dawn in which we woke to a rustling in the garbage, there was added irony in the fact that the noise this time was being made by goats.

From these early disturbances on through the day, a berth near the garbage bin put us in the social center of English Harbour, as there was a steady parade of contributors all day long, many of whom stopped to chat and swap yarns. It was also the center of the considerable fly population of the area, and we were kept busy dealing with them, too.

Aside from the garbage bin, the background at the Dockyard is colorfully distinctive. The mellowed brick buildings that date from Nelson's day have been restored as an inn, museum, apartment building, chandlery, restaurant-bar, and market, and the ancient windlasses used for careening the ships are still in place. Upended cannon imbedded in the ground serve as bollards, and the quay, which runs in a large semi-circle around a point that almost divides English Harbour's nar-

A contrast: 1981 and the luxury yachts of today

row confines in two, has the same stone facing that the ships of the British Navy used to tie up to. The whole place reeks with tradition and atmosphere and is absolutely unique in the yachting world as a marina. The marine services include a sail loft, electronic shop, and engine repair shop; the chandlery and market take care of rudimentary shopping. In addition, local women set up open-air stands of vegetables and fruit each day in front of the historic buildings. There is never any lack of limes, tomatoes, cabbage, bananas, eggs, bread, lettuce, cucumbers, cristofine, and yams. The only problem is that almost every purchase must be accompanied by a donation to the church of the wizened, carpet-slippered salesladies, who never miss a trick.

Since World War II, English Harbour has been the yachting hub of the Lesser Antilles. Nelson chose wisely when he made it his base, as it is a completely secure hurricane hole, surrounded by high hills, with deep water right up to its mangrove-lined shores. Malaria and other tropical diseases were a scourge before modern medicine discovered their causes, and one can still imagine the problems of health and

The Dockyard is unique as a marina

sanitation in colonial times, as the harbor is situated so far down between the hills that there is little circulation of air. The trade must be quite boisterous to make an impression inside English Harbour.

In addition to berthing stern-to at the quay, which can take perhaps fifty to sixty boats in its full perimeter, many boats anchor out in Freeman Bay or in the two arms of the inner harbor, and many more are left in wet storage, simply tied up securely to the mangroves when owners have to interrupt their cruising. A boatyard with slipway is on a smaller point on the eastern side of the harbor, opposite the Dockyard.

On the brow of the hill on that side is Clarence House, built as a royal residence in the eighteenth century when the young Duke of Clarence, later King William IV, was on naval duty there, and far up on Shirley Heights, off to the eastward, the ruined battlements of fortifications from that era can be seen against the skyline.

There is no shore power in English Harbour, so the musical hum of generators (and their exhaust) fills the air at all hours. Fuel and water

Brunelle *berthed stern-to; Clarence House is on hill (left)*

are available at the boatyard, and there are a couple of hose connections at the Dockyard. A police officer opens the metered water outlets each morning, precipitating a mad scramble for possession of the hoses. The shower rooms ashore are a damp invitation to athlete's foot or allied fungi in the soapy swill of their lack of drainage.

We first saw English Harbour in 1961, not too long after Commander Vernon Nicholson, a retired British naval officer, and his family had pioneered in establishing yacht chartering there. He, his wife, and two teen-age sons were on their way from the British Isles to Australia for resettlement after World War II, sailing the seventy-foot teak schooner *Mollihawk,* and they stopped in English Harbour, then in a state of ruin, for rest and replenishment. A hotel proprietor asked them if they would be interested in taking some of his guests out for a sail, which they did, and an industry was born. They never moved on.

The commander, whose bluff, hearty manner and outgoing personality had much to do with the early success of the operation, has retired and gone "home," but his sons, Rodney and Desmond, are carrying on; V.E.B. Nicholson & Sons is a dominant force in the area. There were eleven charter yachts when we took our first two cruises in a converted North Sea trawler called *Viking* in 1961 and in *Mollihawk* in 1962. Now there are hundreds of crewed boats, bareboats as well, and a burgeoning fleet, flying the flags of many nations, of private yachts. English Harbour is a crossroads for world voyagers, for the swarms of people who slide over on the trade-wind milk run from Europe in everything from orange crates to luxury yachts, and for a growing fleet of Americans who have made their way down as we did, or on the offshore passage from Moorhead City, North Carolina, or from New England via Bermuda.

I walked around the perimeter of the quay at the Dockyard one day and catalogued the hailing ports. They included: Helsinki, Mombassa, Aqaba, Gothenburg, Sete, Cyprus, Basel, Hamburg, Valparaiso, Lisbon, Pôrto Alegre, Amsterdam, Rotterdam, Antwerp, Southampton, Cowes, London, Beaulieu, Auckland, Montreal, Vancouver, Panama, British Virgins, Honduras, Bermuda, and Buenos Aires. And of course, Rumson, New Jersey, for *Brunelle,* and many other American ports.

After waiting four hours and finally clearing through the very formal entry procedures and being allowed to make our way from the quarantine anchorage to the inner harbor on arrival day, we had managed to squeeze ourselves between the daunting presences of *America* and *Julie Mother.* I asked the customs officers if there was any routine to tying up at the Dockyard and they just laughed and said, "No, man. You just push in anywhere you can find a place." There were fees, including mandatory membership in the Friends of English Harbour, an organization that handled the restoration of the old buildings and maintains them, plus a very nominal charge for dockage and water.

We had almost a week to gather forces until the Gagnebins arrived as our next crew, and it was a fascinating interlude. Too much could wear you down, but it was great fun for a few days to watch the flow of boat traffic and mix with the heterogeneous crews. While moored there, you are as much on public display as a panda in the zoo; there is a steady stream of "lookers" from other boats and a daily influx of tourists from cruise ships or the island's hotels on guided tours. Buses or taxis deposit them at the Dockyard gate, and they wander by on a counter-clockwise circuit of the quay, tripping over stern lines and snapping pictures left and right. It was a revealing study of the dress habits, and the results of the eating habits, of Americans who travel. Between *America* and *Julie Mother* we were in the thick of it, but we did not arouse quite as many "oohs" and "aahs" as they did.

We did, however, live with a running gag that never ceased to give us a laugh, as Rumson, a suburban town of about nine thousand people, seemed to be one of the best known spots in the world. Time and again, someone would stop and say, "Rumson, eh? Do you know the so-and-sos?" Or, "We're from Freehold. We know Rumson." Usually we did know the people they asked about, and in this way we also met a Rumson couple staying nearby who live less than a mile from us at home. They were having a drink with us one noon, and I was just telling them how many people had come up to us the way they had, and someone stopped and said, "Rumson? Do you know so-and-so?" We didn't but our new friends did, much to their amusement. A boat with Philadelphia as hailing port was berthed nearby, but we never once saw anyone come play "do-you-know?" with her crew.

One day I heard an English voice say, "Oh look, Mum, another *Brunelle.*" I hopped ashore and asked them where they knew of another one, but all they could say was that they had seen a yacht with that name in the Channel Islands. So we are not alone, but the mystery of the name remains unsolved.

It was a time for catching up with old friends, like the Nicholson brothers and Jolyon Byerly, stocky, smiling, with a shock of curly reddish hair, who was a charter captain out of Antigua for years and *Yachting*'s correspondent for the area, and who is now a yacht broker. He had written the Caribbean section of the Stone and Hart book and was just beginning to rewrite it for an update, as the five years since it had been written have seen more changes in the area than any similar previous period. Jol has one of the drollest senses of humor that ever survived an adult lifetime in the tropics, and his columns were always eagerly anticipated at *Yachting* for their little touches of local color and their continuous references to his favorite, semi-fictional characters, Auntie Mabel and Uncle Albert, who seem to have had a genius for experiencing all the difficulties possible in yachting in the tropics. Our daughter Alice, fresh out of college, spent a winter working in the Nicholson brokerage office at English Harbour several years ago, while living next to Jol in the rather informal atmosphere of the apartments in the Officer's Quarters (which have since fallen into disrepair and have been closed again). He would often add a postscript to the covering note he sent to me at *Yachting* with his column, with some such information as "Don't worry, Pop. Alice is fine. She and the Chinaman and the three children are all doing very well, considering."

Now, he filled us in on the best cruising harbors on Antigua and on conditions to the south, which were deteriorating politically day by day. Grenada had joined the Castro-Nicaragua orbit, with troops swarming over its southern hills, including a half-acre of land we own (owned?) in Calivigny that had become part of a military base, and Cubans were building a big jet port nearby. There was also news of a "revolt" on Union Island in the Grenadines, where a score or so of Rastafarians had taken over the airport and radio station and were raising a ruckus. Somehow, with our consciousness of scavengers vying with goats for the garbage each morning, and the steady news of ferment in the southern islands and in Central America, the mental image of a carefree area given over to joyous reaching across the trade wind had dimmed somewhat. There was the unavoidable fact that all these islands, professing to want independence (with England all too ready to slough off having to support their deficit economies), were totally incapable of supporting themselves. They needed tourism yet resented it, and many times greeted visitors with a "Yankee Go Home" approach, or something rougher in the way of direct physical assault.

Newly independent Antigua, which had gone through a manifestation of black power several years before, seemed to have settled into a matter-of-fact approach to dealing with tourists, which, to them, includes yachtsmen of all descriptions. Individuals we met working around the boats, or as taxi drivers, waiters, or shopkeepers, were mainly businesslike and polite. The only evidence of officiousness was in some of the customs and immigration officials, who seemed to take the banging of rubber stamps too seriously.

We felt at home in Antigua, but the rumors of unrest farther down the Windwards and on around the mainland shores of the Caribbean were disturbing. Perhaps they were exaggerated, but it was something to think about as we headed that way.

We had a delightful visit with Desmond Nicholson and his tall, willowy, dark-haired wife, Lisa, who have lived on the same hilltop overlooking Falmouth Harbour, one bay west of English Harbour, since before our first visit in 1961. From their terrace we saw the green flash at sunset, framed in trees. A few days later, Desmond, who has become deeply involved with the history and archaeology of Antigua, took us on one of the field trips he conducts every Thursday afternoon to a museum of Arawak Indian artifacts he has collected and to the site of the old fortifications from Nelson's day on Shirley Heights, overlooking, and at one time guarding, the entrance to English Harbour. There were nineteen of us on one pickup truck as we lurched over the rutted two-track roads; it was like a lark of college days, with Desmond as the kindly professor (and truck driver). Tall, curly-haired and lanky, with a precise English drawl, he is the perfect embodiment of an absent-minded academic, but he manages to run the chandlery and market at English Harbour along with his academic and historical interests. His brother Rodney, a carbon copy of their father, runs the charter business.

In the Dockyard, there was constant trading back and forth between the boats, amid the excitement of comings and goings. *America* and *Julie Mother* both left to go cruising, and boats somewhat nearer our size took over their berths. I had spotted a Cruising Club burgee on a small boat at the other side of the Dockyard, and this led to a pleasant exchange of late-afternoon visits with Dick Kerry of Boston, who had recently sailed his Ericson 35 over from Europe and now had two CCA members with him for a cruise through the nearby islands.

America, *now painted white, left to go cruising*

Argo came in from Sint Maarten, and we had a reunion with the Senas, while Martha went out discoing with Captain Basil in the evenings. The Admiral's Inn, restored as an attractive hostelry, is the central spa for English Harbour yachtsmen, and evenings there are lively. The food is good, there is a Calypso band on some nights, and it is a constant challenge to get to the Men's Room without taking a hypodermic in the ear from the dart game that is perpetually in action at the bar.

For Jane and me it was also a chance to catch up with ourselves, as we were alone on the boat for the first time since Thanksgiving after John and Martha flew off. I can't settle down to read for any length of time on a boat, so my system is to force myself into a long novel like

275

Garp, Chesapeake, or the Herman Wouk "War" books and to let them carry me along a few pages a day without letting them become too hard to put down. When I finally finish one of these tomes after living with it for weeks, I feel deserted and bereft of old friends. Jane's literary club paper for this year, to be given when we were home in March, was to be on Willa Cather, and, when she wasn't doing her needlepoint, she had been steeped in the foothills of Nebraska ever since New Year's. I couldn't think of a more incompatible atmosphere for delving into Cather country, but she kept at it valiantly. (Womanfully?) This session at the Dockyard, between the visits from Rumson's public, was a good chance to catch up on reading.

One of our Rumson visitors was the young daughter of people we knew slightly who lived quite near us, and she invited us to crew aboard the yacht she was working on in one of the weekly late-afternoon races that are open to anybody. The boat was a twenty-six-year-old ocean racer that had been very successful in her day, and the crew consisted of the skipper, a husky, friendly young Greek-American, the Rumson girl, two native hands who had never raced, and Jane and me. It was a fascinating contrast to compare the cockpit and cabin of this classic fifty-footer with *Brunelle,* as she had about half the room below, in a cut up layout; the cockpit was a constricted nightmare with everyone poking elbows in everyone else's eyes and ribs while we tried to handle sheets and winches. (We came in last in a five-mile race to Falmouth and back.) The skipper confessed that he kept her in Antigua because there was no place else that he knew where a wooden boat could be maintained so cheaply, with the availability of labor in the Dockyard.

This was certainly the case, as we had a steady visitation of young men stopping by our gangplank and asking, "Hey, Skip. Got any work for me to do? Wash your topsides? Wax the boat? I do good work for you, Skip."

I did want the topsides washed and waxed, so I signed on an eager lad named Desmond, all smiles and happiness, who worked as diligently as anyone I have ever seen for a daily rate that was less than the usual hourly rate at our local yard at home and thought it hilarious when I asked him if he was any connection of Desmond Nicholson's. There were several bareboats berthed near us, all tended by a shyly smiling man named Lester Brooks, who loved to talk about yachts and yachting and knew more about the Bermuda Race and the America's Cup than most sailors in the States. Lester looked solemn while he was working, as he shuffled around in scruffy cutoffs and an old shirt, but his smile, when it came, was wide and bright, and he was very knowledgeable and helpful in an offhand way. At the end of the day's work, he loved to talk boats by the hour over a beer.

Most Marine services are available in the Dockyard. In addition to freelance day workers and laundresses who steep your clothes in Clorox, there are a sail loft, several mechanics, and an electronics shop. I wanted the SSB radio and the tachometer checked. I happened to be wearing a T-shirt that said "Antigua Race Committee" in big red letters across the front when I went to the electronics shop to inquire about service, and a thin, pale Englishwoman at the desk there greeted me coldly, in very down-the-nose Limey fashion, with "Where did you get that shirt?"

"I was on the committee," I answered.

"You certainly were not," she said, in tones calculated to put down a naughty third grader.

I let that sink in for a moment, bit my tongue, and said, "I'm sorry, but I was."

"That's impossible. I work with the committee and I know everyone on it."

"Well, you didn't know me when I was on it in nineteen seventy-seven, I guess."

"Nineteen seventy-seven?" she came back in that rising inflection the English put on a question. "Oh, perhaps you were then."

Having established my credentials, we went about the business of arranging for an electrician, who showed up two days later after I had made two more inquiries. He was Guy Dudley, a young Californian, tall, blond, and smiling; while shopping in a radio store in San Francisco, he had met a man who was leaving to sail a new boat back from Europe to the West Indies. The man started bopping questions about radio at Guy, whose field it was, and the upshot was that Guy joined him for the trip. Disillusion set in about half way from the Canaries to Antigua, and Guy was very happy to jump ship at English Harbour and get a job in the electronics shop. He eventually fixed our tachometer, spending hours beyond the time he charged us for simply because it was a challenge for him, and analyzed our SSB as not having a proper installation. Oh well; so it was a two-thousand-dollar mistake. We hadn't missed it.

In the Nicholson office in the ramshackle building called the purser's office, where everyone picks up mail addressed to them in care of Nicholson, there is a bulletin board with notices about people wanting crew berths, selling equipment, or wanting to exchange charts. I was not properly equipped with charts south of Antigua, and even though I would be back in New York and could get some when we went home for Jane's Willa Cather paper (and the Income Tax and my annual squash tournaments), I was looking for some now. There was a notice from a New Zealand vessel, *Havaiki,* that they would like to exchange Caribbean charts for United States East Coast, so I got together with her skipper, John McDaniel, and we managed a pretty good swap. His boat was an Alden 48-foot *Lady Helen*-class ketch; they had come west-about from New Zealand and were headed for the Northeast United States. His wife was from Bermuda, and we ended up in a good old "Do you know?" and "Have you been to?" session over cocktails and chart-swapping.

Day after day could go by like this very easily. Except for the hot sun overhead and the occasional rain clouds that doused us, usually at night when we had gone to sleep with the hatches open, we were snug in the tight little harbor and hardly concerned with the weather or the breeze. The boats around us, the crews walking around in cutoffs or bikinis, the constant traffic at the garbage bin, the flies, noise, and chatter of radios, the cooking smells from the Galley Shop, generator exhausts, dogs, sanders, outboards, passersby, tourists ogling at us, and the beat of Calypso music pulsing across the water to us from Admiral's Inn in the evenings, all made a compact community that seemed to shut out the rest of the world. There was a dreamy timelessness to the days as they drifted by. But it was not sailing, and we were glad when it was time for the Gagnebins to arrive so that we could shake the dust of the quay off our transom and get underway again. There was a lot more to Antigua than the colorful introverted scene at English Harbour.

26. *One-Island Cruise*

Unlike most of the Windwards and Leewards, which only have one or two good harbors, Antigua is ringed with them. Physically, it is distinctive, a contrast to the rest of the chain. While most of them are longer in a north-south direction than they are wide and have mountains that dominate them, rising almost as high as 5,000 feet in several cases, Antigua is roughly circular—54 miles in circumference, about 20 miles north-south—and covers 108 square miles. In the north, there are rolling hills and open plains, quite dry and brown, and only at the southwest tip is there anything like a mountain, Boggy Peak, which is 1319 feet.

Also—in contrast to such islands as Dominica, St. Kitts, Nevis, Martinique, and St. Vincent, and many others where there are long stretches of straight coast line—Antigua is indented with bays and coves every few miles, and there are perhaps two dozen anchorages with good protection in most conditions. Almost every one of them is bordered by a gorgeous white sand beach or a series of them set between rocky headlands, and good snorkeling lies in nearby shallow-water reefs at many of them. In addition, once you have paid your fee for a one-month cruising permit, there is the dividend of being able to visit another island without having to go through clearing and entering formalities. Barbuda, a lonely, low, sandy island twenty miles north of Antigua, belongs to it politically and can be visited as part of an Antiguan cruise. In Barbuda, however, because of its isolation and primitive surroundings, a situation has developed similar to Anguilla's, in which the islanders claim to be mistreated by the big island, and they, which means a population of about three hundred, have been making noises about separation. If Barbuda should ever become independent, I'm sure it could go into the *Guiness Book of Records* as the

Antigua's coastline is well indented with bays and coves

world's smallest nation.

On the day after we collected Al and Gen at the airport, the morning weather was rainy and blustery. We did chores and shopped, waiting for the agent for the rental car we had been using to come pick it up. By the time he did, it was lunch hour, and Al suggested making a party out of it at the Admiral's Inn. The rain had stopped, and it was very pleasant on the terrace under feathery trees and hibiscus blooms. Looking up we could see the smoky pink walls of the ancient building and the big brick pillars edging the lawn. These once were supports for a building containing a sail loft and spar shed, which has long since disappeared. Now they add to the drama of the setting in their reminder of days long gone, and they make an effective frame for the view of the hulls and spars glittering in the sunshine at the quay—a view which we enjoyed from the shaded peace of the terrace.

In many islands, the next harbor would be a run of twenty to fifty miles, but here we could get underway at 1445 when the weather cleared and—just for the sake of changing the scene—sail to Falmouth Harbour, a short walk outside the Dockyard gate but a five-mile sail around one headland. The anchor rode, after its long residence on the harbor bottom, came up gray with mud as we eased away from the quay between neighboring boats, so I left it on deck instead of lowering it to the forepeak so that it could be washed in the cleaner waters of Falmouth Harbour when we anchored there.

The trade was strong as we cut the engine and sailed out of Freeman Bay, and we had the heave of big rollers under us while we ran west around the point toward Falmouth's wide mouth. Falmouth is as open and broad as English Harbour is confined and narrow, and there is a good anchorage in its northeast corner off the informal little Antigua Y.C. in about fifteen feet of water. It is breezier and cooler than English Harbour, and many owners prefer to stay here if they are basing in Antigua for a while. It is still just a few minutes walk to the Dockyard from the dinghy landing at the yacht club, but the open, breezy atmosphere is a sharp contrast to the pent-in feeling at the quay. The Yacht Club and the native-run Catamaran Club across the bay are good places to eat. There were perhaps twenty yachts at anchor as we beat lazily past the reefs at Falmouth's entrance. Youngsters from a Morgan OI51 were riding a spinnaker off her stern, screaming and laughing as the sail soared and dipped. A luxury motor yacht bulked over the rest of the boats like a large mother hen, with her generators rumbling and splashing, and along the shore at the head of the harbor, native boys were racing toy sailboats along the beach. Their excited cries carried out to mingle with the shouts of the spinnaker riders. The breeze was cool, the rain had stopped, and the late sun glowed over the scene as we relaxed over cocktails and enjoyed the rewards of one of the shortest cruising passages we had ever made.

For the rest of our two weeks of cruising Antigua, every day was very much in this "as the spirit moves" mode. We stayed on the leeward side a good part of the time; Antigua has better sailing in its lee than most islands, since its low hills do not block the trades. The breeze is sometimes erratic and gusty, but there are no great cones of flat calm extending for several miles, as under Martinique's Mont Pelée, Guadeloupe's Soufrière, St. Lucia's Pitons, or Dominica's Morne Diablotin, and there is very seldom that confusing backwind from the west that is often found in the lee of the high islands.

Falmouth has its steady overflow from English Harbour, but it was amazing to us, aware as we were of the tremendous concentration of boats just a few miles away, to find that most of Antigua's very fine anchorages were virtually deserted. Perhaps one boat would be in them when we were, but in places like Five Islands, Deep Bay, and Carlisle Bay, we could have been thousands of miles off the beaten track for all the fellow cruising boats we saw. Once boats make it to English Harbour they seem to be magnetized in place for weeks on end, as we had seen.

From Falmouth, we ran west to Curtain Bluff for a lunch stop after exploring nearby Carlisle Bay, where a straight white beach at the head of the bay is backed by a row of palms that looks as though someone arranging a travel poster had planted them. Curtain Bluff sticks out from the shore on a narrow neck, and the best hotel on the island—at least from what we have seen, and we have been to many of them—covers the point. Its central building, with bar, dining room, and offices set amid gorgeous tropical plantings, is on the saddle in the middle. The bedroom units string along the windward beach in a two-story building, some separate units crown the bluff of a dramatic rise at the end of the point, and tennis courts and another beach line the leeward-side harbor. Jane and I have stayed at Curtain Bluff several times and consider it the pleasantest place we have been in the islands; it is always old home week to pop in there and see the Howard Hulfords and Ed Sheerins, who have managed it for many years.

Howard, a retired pilot with bald pate and Count Otto von Bismarck handlebar moustache, runs Curtain Bluff with the seeming air of a Prussian autocrat, insisting on high standards but with a twinkle in his eye and a genuine concern for his guests; his staff belies the manner and it all results in a remarkably well-run place. The standards include jacket and tie for dinner in a dining room that I hold largely responsible for the state of my waistline. When we had dinner there later in the cruise, it was the first time I had worn a tie since the last week in December.

On our first visit we had a swim and lunch aboard but had no desire to linger, as the wind was well to the south of east, and a big surge was rolling around the point and agitating the harbor. When we came back later, the wind was more in the north, and the harbor was peaceful enough for an overnight stay.

Five Islands, where we ended up after the lunch stop at Curtain Bluff, is an enormous indentation that cuts into the middle of the west coast of Antigua for almost three miles and could be in the Tuamotus for all the signs of civilization—although St. John's, the capital and a noisy, dirty little city of twenty-five thousand, is only a couple of miles across the hills at the head of the bay. The best anchorage is just inside the entrance to starboard, though there are others farther inside, and we dropped the hook in sixteen feet off a deserted stretch of pure white sand with one other boat, a motorsailer from California, a few hundred yards away. Her crew was taking turns water skiing behind a Whaler as we came to anchor; they had the decency to come by after a while and apologize for the disturbance, which really hadn't bothered us at all.

As a peaceful twilight settled in, the western horizon became very sharp, and Nevis and the little isolated lump of Redonda, hidden in clouds and haze all afternoon, stood out sharply against the deepening colors of the sunset. The only jarring note in a lovely scene was a terrible time in getting damp charcoal to light in the hibachi, but we persisted, in a storm of four letter words, and finally had steak and cristofine for dinner.

Dickinson Bay, at the northwest tip, where we ended up the next night after a fast reach close along the beach, is the only other populated harbor on Antigua. There are a few hotels along its several miles of hard sand, and the anchorage, wide open to the west, is a pleasant one if the surge is not too heavy. We had a quiet night there before heading for Barbuda, an open-water sail of twenty-two miles. It was one of the better sails of the winter, complete with needlepoint by Jane and Gen. The wind was a bit aft of the beam, and we set main, staysail,

Dickinson Bay, at the northwest tip of Antigua

and jib and took off for the empty horizon over steep, cresting white-caps—not as long and high as the seas of most inter-island passages, as we were in relatively shallow water, dotted with lobster pots and with reefs and banks to windward. *Brunelle* was at her best, grooving along like an express train. I probably should have reduced sail a bit as the breeze gained weight with the warmth of the morning, but she was handling it well, and we made our best speed of her career to date by covering twenty-two miles in three hours.

The Barbuda landfall took us back to the Bahamas, as the island is low, sandy, and scrubby and can only be seen from about seven miles off. A Martello Tower was described in Stone and Hart as the major landmark, and it appeared as a tiny white dot in the featureless line of the land. It is used as a bearing to avoid Codrington Shoal to the eastward of the approach course; once we were clear of that and inside the bight at the bottom end of Barbuda, we rolled up the jib and started beating eastward to Coco Point, the nearest anchorage. The trade was now gusting to thirty (confirmed by the Barbuda airport later), but

Barbuda's beach curves away into the distance

Brunelle had no trouble with it under main and staysail, and we had an easy sail in smooth water while we ate lunch.

A Camper & Nicholson 40 bareboat from English Harbour was anchored off the endless stretch of beach that curved away into the distance north from Coco Point. I thought she was a bit far from what looked like the best anchorage—a spot between two reefs directly in front of Coco Point Lodge, which is a hotel at the southern end of the point making the bight. Jol Byerly's description in Stone and Hart, written five years previously, said that Coco Point Lodge, which had been difficult in the past, "now welcomed yachtsmen," so we headed along the beach toward it and the anchorage I had picked out.

While we were taking off sail and preparing to anchor, a native in a Whaler came out to us from the Lodge and called over.

"Anchor back by de odder boat. Can't anchor up here. We uses

286

this for water skiing."

I bridled a bit and said that the indicated anchorage had too much surge, and he just shrugged.

"Dat's what dey tells me to tell you."

Rather than get him in trouble, I turned her around and anchored near the C & N close to the powdery beach, where the surge made lacework patterns on the wet sand.

Coco Point Lodge trades on being extremely secluded and exclusive. Various friends had stayed there in the past and reported a fine time. One very high fee takes care of all charges, including bar and water activities, so there is no grubby exchange of hard cash during one's stay. The presumption that they could stop someone from anchoring in navigable waters agreed with rumors of their attitude toward visiting yachts. I gathered that Jol Byerly's word about their friendliness was somewhat out of date.

To find out more, I rowed ashore and walked the half mile or so along the beach past the individual units lining the waterfront north of the Lodge's main building. Almost everyone seemed to be asleep in deck chairs in front of their units, except for one group playing bridge, and I saw no one who would appear to have been on water skis in the past twenty-five years. I asked for the manager at the reception desk and was told to wait. Eventually I was ushered in to a trim, coolly handsome, youngish man extremely self-possessed in a Lacoste shirt and Ivy League manner, and handed him my business card.

"I'm writing about cruising in this area for the magazine," I said, "and I wanted to find out about yachts coming in here."

There was a long pause as he studied my card. A "Hmmmm" was his only answer as he placed it down as though I had given him a dead mouse. Finally he said, "The best thing would be for you not to mention us at all. We don't want any yachts coming in here."

"But you're going to get them anyway, and I just thought it would be helpful to know how you handle the situation."

He sighed and looked at his watch. "I'm really very busy right now. If you come back at seven o'clock I'll buy you a drink and we can talk about it."

"There are three other people on board," I said. "I wouldn't like to leave them at that time of day."

"I'm sorry, but you'd have to come by yourself," was his answer. "Our guests would be very upset to have a yachting group come in."

I declined the invitation, said I thought I had a clear message already, and made my way back to the boat. The crew from the C & N had also rowed ashore while I was on my way back, and they returned, passing close by *Brunelle,* just before the sunset of a gorgeous clear evening with an early moon.

"Friendly bastards, aren't they?" came a very British voice across the water. "Won't even let a man buy a drink."

"Seems they don't like us," I agreed, as we exchanged ironic laughs.

We had just finished breakfast about 0900 the next morning and were thinking about getting under way, when the Whaler came toward us again. I muttered, "I wonder what we've done now," to Al, who had been highly amused at my account of the manager's greeting. In his travels around the world Al has stayed in a great many top hotels and resorts under red-carpet treatment, and he knows the type.

There was a white man as passenger in the boat, middle-aged and sandy haired. As they came alongside he called up, "Are you Bill Robinson? My name is Bill Kelly, owner of the Lodge. May I come aboard?"

With introductions all around, he settled on a cockpit seat, refusing a cup of coffee.

"I'm so sorry I wasn't there when you came ashore yesterday," he started. "I didn't see your card until after dark because I was away from the Lodge. It's a funny coincidence, because I just wrote you a letter last week to tell you how much I enjoyed your articles about bringing your boat down here. This is the boat, isn't it?" He stopped and indicated *Brunelle* with a sweep of his arm.

"Yes. That's right."

"Well we brought our fifty-eight-foot Hatteras down the same route this fall, and we found your articles very helpful."

"Great," I murmured.

288

"I'd like to show you around on shore," he went on. "We have a marina around the point I'd like you to see."

"Thanks, but we're about to head back for Antigua," I said. "I think I got the picture from your manager yesterday about visiting yachts."

"Sure. Well, I hope you understand. We have a lot of trouble with yachts coming in here and littering our beach. The French are especially bad, with topless women walking along, and we just can't have our guests disturbed that way. We have some very high-powered people staying here, and they want privacy." He went on to drop the names of several corporate bigwigs who were there at the moment, and I couldn't resist the opportunity to drop one myself.

"Oh yes," I said. "Incidentally, Mr. Gagnebin here was the chairman of International Nickel."

He stopped with mouth open, looked at Al closely for the first time, and then said brightly, "Oh. Inco! Yes. Of Course. Inco."

He went on to explain a bit lamely that their facilities were just barely big enough to take care of their guests, and they could not take extras in the bar or dining room. And the guests became very uneasy, he said, if unidentified people showed up in the bar.

"We have a Mrs. duPont here who just froths at the mouth if she sees a yachtsman." He laughed apologetically.

"Her cousin Pete is in Antigua right now," I said, "Maybe he'll come up here and scare her. He's cruising in his yacht." Pete duPont (Pierre S. III) is a former director of *Yachting* with whom I had been in two Bermuda Races and many other shorter ones in his beautiful seventy-two-foot ketch *Barlovento.* I wanted to see how Mr. Kelly would react to this news—and was amused at the thought of how Coco Point would handle *duPont* vs. *duPont,* should *Barlovento* ever appear.

With many protestations of how sorry he was we wouldn't come ashore, Kelly left. We again made ready to sail, and I resisted a perverse temptation to throw our garbage overboard. Kelly had confirmed that the wind had been gusting to thirty the day before, at least at the Coco Point airstrip, but it was much lighter and more in the east on this bright, cloudless morning. The reach back to Antigua, standing clear on the horizon, was a perfect sail and an easier slide than the trip up. The breeze was about fourteen, and yet we made within a fraction of the same time as we had the day before, anchoring again in Dickinson Bay.

This seemed to be our week to have trouble with shore establishments. I rowed ashore in mid-afternoon and made a dinner reservation at Hyatt Halcyon Cove Hotel, whose dining room sits on a hill overlooking the beach and the bay, and I was not told of any "dress code." When we appeared at the maître d's station that evening with Albert and me in shorts, the very cool native officiating there, who was incredibly dolled up in a white tuxedo and ruffled shirt, refused to seat us because of our shorts. I apologized and explained that we were from a yacht and had not been told of any rule, and that it would now be very awkward to row back out to the boat for dinner. He remained superciliously adamant until an American from the hotel staff, much less flashily dressed, came up to see what the trouble was and overruled the censor. We humbly promised that we wouldn't stand up once at table, which got a laugh from him as he seated us.

Our other brush with civilization was in St. John's, three miles from Dickinson Bay, where we went to do some shopping. The crew of a day-sailing charter schooner at Dickinson said that we could get fuel and water in St. John's by inquiring at the deep-water pier, so I called the harbormaster on VHF as we powered up the dredged channel. I was told to report to his office. The only way I could get onto the high bulkhead, whose proportions were designed for cruise ships, was to tie alongside a tugboat and then go ashore across her. Her crew happened to be chipping rust with an electric hammer, and the noise and dust were cataclysmic.

The harbormaster, a cold-eyed and unbending man, insisted that I had to enter the port formally, even though I had entered at English Harbour and had my cruising permit, which is supposedly good for all Antiguan ports. There was no arguing with him, and this abortive visit cost me eleven dollars E.C. (Eastern Caribbean currency) or about four dollars U.S., only to learn that the minimum water order was one thousand gallons and that a man had to be called from town to open the diesel pump. I didn't think my twenty to twenty-five gallons would make this worth his while, so the whole thing was a live-and-learn bust. Jane, Gen, and Al were practically deaf and shell-shocked when I climbed back across the tug in a cloud of rust dust. They had also been talked out of some paperback books and magazines by the tugboat crew. I hoped they enjoyed back issues of *Yachting*.

The supermarket in St. John's is a short walk from the boat landing at the head of the harbor, so we anchored as close in as possible, and Jane, Al, and I rowed to the pier, leaving Gen with her needlepoint to guard the boat. St. John's is not exactly the garden spot of the Caribbean. It is undistinguished in architecture, hot, dusty, and smelly in the glare of the sun, with the usual gutters running with sewage and a traffic tangle that would give a New York City "gridlock" some competition. The stores are well stocked though, and I have become partial to a type of shorts known as "jams" made especially for the Coco Shop. They are lined bathing suits of Bermuda-shorts length, and they are very comfortable for wear as regular shorts or for swimming. I spend most of my time in them afloat and ashore and have become used to the rather wild patterns they come in.

The market has mostly American brands and is fairly well stocked, but the fresh produce and meat departments are hit or miss. Al was buying on this trip, and he stood by the register worrying about the E.C.–U.S. conversion as it made digital beeps and blips. There was consternation all around, especially on the face of the young male clerk, when the red, computerized numbers lit up at $2,376.72. Even in E.C. and in inflationary times, we all knew that was a little much. Eventually, it was all straightened out at $2,300 less, but the clerk was still in shock when we collected our bundles and headed back to the boat landing.

Back in Dickinson Bay for the Gagnebins' last evening, after a sail of a couple of hours off to leeward and back into the anchorage, we were having cocktails, fussing with the hibachi, and enjoying a green flash sunset with Redonda and Nevis standing clear against it, when a small sloop flying a Q flag and a strange ensign beat her way in from offshore and anchored near us. Two men—one white, one black—got in a small rubber boat and rowed over. I looked up her ensign and found it was Chilean, but the white man asked, "Parlez-vous français?" when he came alongside. Al responded to this like the proverbial fire horse, and we invited them aboard.

"Is this Antigua?" was the first question, and we allowed as how it was. It seems that they were nineteen days out of Dakar, West Africa, and had only the big general chart of the Caribbean for making their landfall. They had anxiously eyeballed through the great number of reefs off the north end of Antigua and headed for the first place they saw yachts anchored. The owner was a Chileno who had been working for the United Nations in Africa and had bought the twenty-seven-foot sloop as a means of getting home. His crew had never been in a boat before they set sail and had suffered badly from seasickness for a few days before getting his sea legs. They were headed for Panama and on to Chile as soon as they could obtain supplies, so we showed them our chart of St. John, where they would head in the morning. Strangely, for some reason he lapsed slowly into hesitant English as he talked to us, and that was all he spoke the next morning while checking with us before heading in to St. John's.

Between the Gagnebins' leaving and the arrival of the Freemans, we had two days to ourselves, and they happened to be the windiest ones we had gone through since early January. Deep Bay, between St. John's and Five Islands, seemed like a good spot for holing up, and we reached over like a runaway truck and anchored in the farthest northeast corner of Deep Bay after skirting the wreck of an old schooner that lies just under the surface in the middle of the entrance. The harbor was bustling with day-trippers from a big, red-sailed Thames barge from Dickinson Bay and a high, old-fashioned tug named *Tugboat Annie*. A large, native picnic occupied much of the beach to windward, but we were the only humans left at sunset—a cloudy one with low scud flying swiftly by overhead. There were spits of rain, and the wind played a high-pitched tune in the rigging as we charged around our anchor for two days. None of the day-trippers came back, and not a light shone at night. Two miles from St. John's, just across the hill at the head of the bay, we seemed as alone as we had been at West Caicos, except

The anchorage at Green Island

for the fact that we were on the direct approach path to Antigua's busy airport, and jumbo jets lumbered in at low altitude quite frequently.

It was a snug interlude of reading and napping, a good place to be until the trade moderated, and I was actually able to finish *Chesapeake* after more than a month of dipping into it. Jane, with Willa Cather pretty well in hand, used the time to dredge up some long-frozen meats from the freezer and to work up a couple of special dishes from them.

The Freemans brought calmer weather when we picked them up

293

at Dickinson Bay, and we reversed our itinerary back to English Harbour with stops at Five Islands and Curtain Bluff and a luncheon sail through Carlisle Bay, jogging easily under main and staysail instead of bothering to anchor while we ate. We had more time at the Dockyard and Falmouth—and a night in Freeman Bay when the backwind mixed the anchored boats in a great tangle. For a last Antiguan fling, we beat the nine miles up the east coast to Green Island under jib, staysail, and main. It was a good deep-sea sail with constant sightseeing to port along the steep bluffs of Shirley Heights, the wide spread of reef-bound Willoughby Bay, and the impressive mansions of the Mill Reef Club perched in dramatic vantage points atop the cliffs.

Green Island is tucked behind the big reef that fringes most of Antigua's east coast and is easy to enter (though a French sloop was high and dry on the reef off its southeast point). The best anchorage is on the north side of Green Island, which is perhaps half a mile by a quarter of a mile and uninhabited. There is a little half moon of a beach there, with a good anchorage close in to it and a view to seaward of the tumble and boil of rollers ending their trip from Africa on the white line of the reef. Mill Reef's houses crown the hills and sprawl across the cliff tops in the other direction as a reminder that civilization is not too far away. We had last come here in *Viking* in 1961 on our first Caribbean cruise, and it was reassuring to find that, under Mill Reef's careful stewardship, it had not changed at all.

After a swim, snorkeling, and beachcombing, cocktails hit the spot while we got the hibachi to cooperate for a dinner of steak, cristofine, and mushrooms as a full moon flooded the anchorage and taped music flooded our cockpit. It was one of those perfect evenings of peace after a good sail that wraps up all the reasons why people cruise.

Back in English Harbour, we made arrangements for Lester Brooks to be *Brunelle*'s boatkeeper while we went home for a month. When we came back, it would be time to press onward again, headed for Venezuela and a very different kind of cruising through the high islands to the south. With all the political uncertainty we had been hearing about, the prospect was not an entirely bright one. I would have to confirm final arrangements for leaving *Brunelle* in Venezuela while

Beachcombing on Green Island—between snorkels

we were back in New York. So far, we had just had a "Fine! come ahead; we'd love to see you," sort of thing, and I was a bit uneasy about it.

I was even uneasier when we came back to Antigua from New York after Easter, as phone calls, letters, and Telex messages to Venezuela had all gone unacknowledged. I still intended to press southward and try to make contact as we drew closer, but there was suddenly a feeling of uncertainty, of being adrift in an unknown world, that set my nerves on edge. We had plane tickets home from Caracas on May

295

6 because I had two longstanding speaking engagements for the week after that. I also had a writing assignment and the Bermuda Race Committee to keep me busy in June, so we had a month in which to settle *Brunelle*'s summer arrangements. Those 0400 musings, which had not been bothering me very much, began to recur as I mentally turned over all the uncertainties and possibilities.

27. *Sailing Too Fast*

~~~~~~

Guadeloupe was a dim shape forty miles away on the horizon, and Antigua was shrouded in rain squalls as we made sail outside the harbour and headed south on 190 degrees in a perfect reaching breeze. With "all three" set—jib, staysail, and main—*Brunelle* charged across the trade-wind rollers, and her eagerness matched my feeling at being back aboard after our month north. Jim Lillie had signed up with us again, which solved all crew problems for the month ahead, and Lester had kept her in beautiful shape in her layup. Perhaps there were a few more cockroaches, but we could handle them. We were on our way to the high islands, and, possibly, Venezuela.

I had no idea whether we could work out arrangements for leaving the boat in Venezuela, but we had one commitment to head south, which we were fulfilling at the moment, and I really did want to range down the Windwards. Although the harbors are fewer and farther apart, and cruising is more a question of pressing onward in long, inter-island passages than poking around casually in the close-at-hand delights of the Virgins, the St. Martin area, or Antigua, the sailing is stimulating in these waters and the sights and scenes are magnificent. It would be a dereliction to come this far and not make the classic passage from Antigua to the Grenadines.

Our commitment of the moment was to take our old and dear friend Julia Gross to a rendezvous in Dominica with her Vassar '34 roommate, Mary Narodny, who had lived there since World War II. Julia and her late husband, Mason, had cruised with us in many waters over the years, and we had worked out this plan to get Julia and Mary together as part of our island cruise. Julia had never seen Dominica, although she had heard many tales of it over the years, and she was eager to get to it by sea, rather than the more conventional approach by air. Mary was then to join us and continue on to Martinique.

The gorgeous sailing as we reached swiftly from Antigua to Guadeloupe was not all that stimulating for Jim and Julie, since both were suffering from first-day stomach, but they revived gradually while Guadeloupe firmed up ahead of us. We were in bright sunshine as we sped along, and a school of killer whales added to the excitement when they charged across our wake in late morning, but clouds were building over both land masses. Antigua had all but disappeared in a dark jumble of clouds, and a great wall of black began to tower between us and Guadeloupe when we brought Tête à l'Anglais, a funny lump of rock off the north coast, abeam. We had averaged seven knots so far on a classic inter-island reach, but conditions were not to hold for the whole crossing. Swiftly, the darkness enveloped us as we moved into the front of clouds, and in no time at all we were inundated with a torrential downpour.

For a few minutes the rain killed the wind, and we wallowed on the flattened mounds of the waves, but it was a thin front, and we soon broke through to a gray sky and windy seascape on the other side. The sea was a hard black, contrasting with whitecaps marching in close order drill, and the trade was whistling in from the northeast with real authority. We killed the jib and shot forward under main and staysail and were in the harbor of DesHayes at the northwest tip of Guadeloupe by 1530. This was not just a local squall. It was a distinct change in the weather pattern, and the conditions that came in behind that wall of clouds stayed with us for many days.

In the lee of Guadeloupe's mountains, DesHayes, a sleepy little village on a broad bay, with a steeple as the focal point behind the town landing, was peaceful and sun-shot in late afternoon. I wasted an hour rowing ashore and walking a half mile to the *douane,* which was of course closed, since this was Saturday. So our Q flag and tiny French ensign were strictly for form's sake. There was the usual odd collection of reverse-sheer, scruffy looking European boats at anchor, plus a Morgan 41 and a Canadian ketch—the skipper of the latter gave us a special treat when he suddenly appeared alongside in his dinghy and presented us with a beautiful dolphin steak.

Sleepy DesHayes, Guadeloupe

"Too much for me to eat myself; caught it today," he said, as he waved off our thanks and rowed back to his boat. It made a wonderful dinner, and we all collapsed into the sack soon afterward.

The leeward coast of Guadeloupe has almost as many lobster pots as the Gulf of Mexico, and we spent an anxious morning powering through them and the wind cone of 4,869-foot Soufrière, the highest peak in the Lesser Antilles, alternating drenching rain squalls and occasional bursts of sunshine and backwind from the west. By the time we were off Basse-Terre, Guadeloupe's capital city at its southwest corner, we could see that the trade had the same authority we had felt the afternoon before. Looking beyond the slim white lighthouse at Pointe aux Vieux Forte, the southern tip of Guadeloupe, I could see large, cresting seas charging along close together—the whitecaps rearing and tumbling. It was only time for lunch, which we quickly got out of the way while still in the lee, and I didn't want to call it quits this early, but the prospect ahead was rough.

Leaving the southern tip of Guadeloupe, the prospect was rough

The Iles des Saintes were just twelve miles south of the point. I felt we could at least get that far, heading in there if it was too dusty, so we pulled down a reef and set the staysail and took off. *Brunelle* showed more confidence than we did, taking it beautifully. When we cleared the lee of the Saintes, I switched staysail for jib, since she was doing so well, and we roared toward Dominica on 160°, with the lee rail down and the boat driving just as fast as she could possibly go. There was an exhilarating sense of power in the rush of water along the side—a taut urgency that is only felt when a sailboat is taking the maximum the wind can give her and handling it well. Roiled clouds alternated with shafts of the westering sun, and the jagged, crumpled peaks of Dominica began to take definition over the bow, with two rounded lumps at the shoreline, Prince Rupert Bluff and Rollo Head, as special landmarks for the entrance to Portsmouth—the harbor at the northwest end that we were headed for.

As we came under the lee of Prince Rupert Bluff and the headlong rush subsided, we rolled in the jib in preparation for turning on the power, but all we got out of pressing the starter button was a single "Thunk" and dead silence. Something had happened to the engine. Amid curses and consternation, we put the jib back on and beat our way into the wide expanse of Prince Rupert Bay. On our approach to the recommended anchorage at the northeast corner, we were intercepted by a flotilla of rowboats manned by teen-age boys, who shouted at us as they pulled at their oars, offering all kinds of services. The first one to come close said his name was John, and I called over and told him we needed a mechanic.

"I get you mechanic, Skip," he cried. "I do good job for you!"

While I was concentrating on anchoring under sail, they swarmed all over us, grabbing the rails and getting in the way of everything we were doing; I began to lose my patience, none too well controlled anyway after the failure of the engine. For the half hour after we had come to anchor, we were besieged by the rowboat boys. I had told John that he was our agent, but this did not stop the others from pushing and pestering unmercifully. One, a flip, glib lad with a gold ring in his ear, was especially loquacious and insistent and finally became too much for me as he hung on the rail and jabbered at me.

"Look," I cried. "I'm in a bad mood. Leave me alone, will you?"

"It's okay, Skip," he said with a wide smile. "I make you good mood!"

When I made it clear that I would only deal with John, there was then a half-hour of water fights and smashing of oars on gunwales that I was sure would end in broken limbs, but they gradually evaporated. John said he would be back at eight in the morning to tend to our needs. Dinner was not the most joyous of occasions after all this fuss; the wind and rain howled all night; and we rode to an erratic surge on a long scope. I would say that this night ranked as a real low point. How could we get the engine fixed in this Godforsaken backwater, and what were we heading into farther south? My musings went on for most of the night, not just 0400, stirred by the uneasy rhythm of wind gusts in the rigging and the lurching of *Brunelle* in the surge. On most

301

nights, I had everything that could rattle or bang secured, but odd, unidentified knocks and bumps added to the disturbances of this restless night.

Great rain clouds swept down from the invisible peaks as we looked at the new day the next morning, and there was no sign of John at 0800 or for the next hour. Finally, Jim and I rowed ashore, fighting the wind gusts. We met John just as we landed on a black sand beach in front of a row of dismal shacks. Boys came running from every direction, shouting "Hey, Skip" at me. I left Jim to their mercies, with the garbage to dispose of.

John had another yachtsman in tow from a French ketch anchored near us. He had a bad starter motor, and John was going to get both of us together with a mechanic. We walked along the beach in a heavy downpour in a setting of utter poverty; I think the only worse conditions I have seen were in Haiti. Here, the usual ravages of poverty were added to by the still very evident effects of Hurricane David, which had completely devastated newly independent Dominica seven months before. Many of the buildings in town were roofless, and John told me that there had been no electricity or telephone at this end of the island since the storm. Groups of people stood around the sidewalks and storefronts in dull silence, watching without expression as we passed, and the stores seemed almost empty of things to sell. An occasional car or horse-and-wagon would splash by in the mud, and now and then voices would be raised in a typical high-pitched argument; the whole setting was as forlorn as any I have ever seen. Customs was tucked away in a stuffy corner of the post office at the far end of town, and the man at the desk was quietly polite but unresponsive. Immigration was at the police station—off the main street on the second floor of a ramshackle building. It smelled of mold and decay. A loud argument was going on when I walked in, and my forms were stamped while the clerk continued to argue vehemently without looking at me.

John had waited outside at each stop, and now he led me along muddy back alleys and through a huddle of tumbledown shacks to a small yard where children and chickens were scrambling in the mud. A man in coveralls was sitting in a van working on the Frenchman's starter motor with the Frenchman watching. This was the mechanic. I told him my problem; he nodded absently and said he would be out in "a couple of hours."

There was nothing to do but go back to *Brunelle,* so John and I headed for the beach. As we had moved around the town, his shyness had given way to evidence of an aware intelligence and a polite, friendly manner. I wanted him to do well for us for his own sake as well as mine. He promised to bring the mechanic out as soon as he was ready to come, and I broke Jim loose from his entourage of small fry for the row back to the boat. He said it had been a lively morning of lots of chatter in several languages, while they asked him all sorts of questions about who he was and where he was from and about the boat. Disposal of the garbage had been no problem, as it was a welcome gift for the nearest group of pigs. As a matter of fact, the whole town had given the impression of being littered with garbage.

As the day went on, the weather gradually brightened, and I kept an anxious eye on the shore for signs of John and the mechanic—but nothing happened. In midafternoon, a blond young man swam toward us from a sloop anchored nearby, and, while he was treading water, asked us in a marked Scandinavian accent if we knew anyone sailing for Europe who might need a crew. I said that we did not, and added offhandedly that we wouldn't be going anywhere ourselves till we had our engine fixed.

He swam back to the sloop, and very soon afterward the Scandinavian, a dark-haired young man, and a girl came back from the sloop in a dinghy.

"I understand you have engine trouble," the dark-haired one said. "I'm a mechanic. Would you like me to have a look at it?"

"Sure," I answered, happy to grasp at any straw." Come aboard. No harm in trying."

"Would ten dollars an hour be all right?" he asked as we pulled back the stairs.

"Fine with me. Go right ahead."

At first he thought it might be a loose ground when I described it to him, but there was nothing like this wrong. His second guess was

303

water in the cylinders. He opened up an injector, and we turned the starter on for its half a turn and "Thunk."

"Look at that!" he cried as clear liquid shot out of the injector. "That's what it is. You got water in there. It must have backed up through the exhaust when you were sailing fast."

In no time at all, he had all the injectors open and the engine turning over to bleed them of the water, which spurted out as the battery cranked the engine over. Tightening them up again, he said, "Let's give it a try."

After a tense interval while the starter churned the engine and there were coughs and burps, it suddenly roared to life. We all cheered, and I have to admit to a great sense of relief at such a simple solution. It had taken him all of ten minutes, but I considered it well worth a full hours pay, and we asked them to stay and celebrate over a beer.

Their stories were a capsule of the free-and-easy, island-hopping, boat-bumming life of the younger generation. Our hero's name was Carlo, and he had been running a bicycle shop in Queens in New York City before deciding to chuck it all and head for the islands. He bought *Otter*, a twenty-four-foot, strip-planked, centerboard, gaff-rigged sloop, in St. Thomas, and, ironically for a mechanic's boat, she had no engine.

"I didn't want to mess with one," he said with a laugh and shrug. "They're always trouble, and I'm in no hurry."

The girl with him was from France and had only been aboard for a few days. She had sailed over from Europe on another boat and was hitch-hiking her way around the islands. The Scandinavian was a vagabond Norwegian who had just made friends with them on shore the day before.

As for me, I could breathe a bit easier again, as trying to negotiate the lee side of the high islands without an engine would have been a tedious performance, we would have been without refrigeration, and I had no idea where I could have had the engine put back in working condition again. How the water had gotten in there remained a nagging mystery and I worried over a possible recurrence. *Brunelle* has a high

U-section in the exhaust that should prevent the problem. No shut-off valve was visible.

In any event, Friendly Yacht Service, even if it had cost the magnificent sum of ten bucks, had once again come to the rescue.

28.   The Roughest Yet

The wind never let up, and rain clouds swept us all night, but the sun was bright in the morning. John had not showed again, and I had a guilty twinge about not having paid him anything for his help the day before, even if he had not done all he said he would. This, however, was not about to keep us from leaving for Roseau, twenty miles south, where we were to meet Mary Narodny, as we were already a day late.

Otter started to get underway, but while she was still at anchor, a vicious gust ripped her main, and they were snugged down again and making repairs when we motorsailed out of Prince Rupert Bay and started down the lee of Dominica's incredibly rugged mountains. Columbus is said to have shown Queen Isabella what Dominica was like by crumpling a piece of paper and dropping it on the table—an aptly graphic description of this most mountainous of the Lesser Antilles. He named it for having sighted it on a Sunday. These peaks cause almost continuous rainfall when trade-wind clouds blow against their heights, and, because of its luxuriant jungle growth, Dominica has always been the hardest to cultivate and economically the poorest of the Lesser Antilles.

Morne Diablotin, only one hundred feet lower than Guadeloupe's Soufrière, is the main bastion of these awesome ramparts. It is capped by towering clouds, with curtains of rain sweeping blackly down from the green heights; leeward-side weather is an erratic mix of rain squalls, forty-knot wind gusts hurtling down the valleys, and contrasting periods of sunshine and pleasant west winds that suck back under the flow of air above the peaks. We made our way through all this under power with the main up. Marvelling at the savage scenery, we arrived off Roseau in the bright sun of noon.

There is no harbor at Roseau, just a roadstead (where I remem-

Morne Diablotin, Dominica

bered rolling our rails under at anchor in *Viking*), and we had arranged
to meet Mary at a hotel south of Roseau called the Anchorage. Yachts
anchor there on the narrow shelf of shallow water off its pebbly beach
or moor stern-to the bulkhead in front of it.

It was an awkward place to moor, because the anchor was in very
deep water, yet the boat was riding too close to the rocks of the beach
—with big boulders showing in the clear water under the keel. One of
the omnipresent "Hey Skip" fraternity swam out and took a stern line
in for us, and we were eventually settled in a none-too-secure berth and
shuttled the few feet to shore in the dinghy. The hotel, which was
supposed to have moorings, a boat landing, a swimming pool, and
tennis courts, had obviously suffered in the hurricane. The sea wall was
cracked and half falling down, the tennis courts had been washed away,
and the pool was empty and full of debris. Repairs were being made,
however, and the buildings were all in use. We found out later that the

The Anchorage recovering from hurricane David's damage

hotel had suffered a double inundation, with waves crashing in from the sea on an exceptionally high tide over the sea wall and into the ground floor, while massive floods from rain in the hills brought a torrent of water, followed by mud slides, in from the other direction. The wind had blown 150 miles an hour for almost half a day at this southern tip of Dominica.

I checked ashore and found that Mary had been looking for us for a day, since our engine trouble had held us up from our original arrival date. She lives high in the hills on a dairy farm, which she helps manage, and there is no phone there. The hotel management assured us she would be back soon. And she was, "Hoo-hooing" from the sea wall an hour after our arrival.

Mary is a proper Vassar Bostonian, with an accent and manner that belong at the Vincent Club for lunch or the weekly concerts of the symphony—and which almost forty years of living in Dominica have not changed a bit. She had married a Russian and together they had gone to Dominica during the war to grow food for the war effort, but he evaporated after a few years, leaving her with three young children. A predictable reaction would have been for her to return to security in Boston; instead, she stuck it out in this remote outpost, raising the children herself and sending them off to school in Barbados by trading schooner. She had held a variety of jobs, including newspaper work and running the local radio station, and now she was helping to manage the dairy farm where she lives, a twentieth-century version of the pioneer woman. The farm is owned by an English woman who had spent most of her life on the island.

Mary came aboard all enthusiasm and excitement and soon had Julie, Jim, and Jane on a sightseeing ride into the mountains of this most primitive of all West Indian islands. The unbelievably lush tropical growth, which Jane and I had seen when we were here nineteen years before, had been torn apart by the hurricane, but Jane reported that it was amazing how rapidly growth was appearing again on tree trunks stripped bare by the force of the wind.

Anthony Agar, the son of the woman who owns Mary's dairy farm, had come with her to help her get aboard; while they were off sightseeing, he took me the couple of miles into Roseau to clear out with customs, a two-minute formality here. He had operated a trading schooner for several years but had lost her when she dragged anchor off Roseau in a freak storm from the west. His house had been all but ruined by David. He was now living in one room of what had been a graceful plantation house dating from the eighteenth century, while repairs were being done to the rest of it. Roseau, even this long after David, looked like a town that had been bombed out in World War II. Many buildings were roofless, and wreckage was still lying in heaps between the half-ruined skeletons of most of the houses. It was an awesomely depressing sight, especially on an island that has long been known for its poverty and especially in contrast to the impervious grandeur of the mountain peaks towering into the clouds—a setting that greatly emphasized nature's power.

Despite his misfortunes, Anthony—dark-haired and soft-spoken, with a shy, quiet manner—seemed bucko about bouncing back. He had a very lively interest in everything to do with boats and was really appreciative of *Brunelle*. We had a pleasant evening of cocktails aboard and dinner at the Anchorage, as Mary and Julie caught up on the many years. We learned something about life on Dominica from Mary and Anthony. The poverty, lack of education, and inevitable growth of black-power sentiments had brought many difficulties, and the hurricane had been cataclysmic. For once, American help, which was prompt and voluminous, had been appreciated and had had some effect, as there was no longer half as much "Yankee Go Home" sentiment. The new, independent government had been incapable of handling the island's problems and the responsibilities of "freedom," but Mary and Anthony had hopes that the next election would bring a more responsible and efficient government into power. (P.S. They got their wish in July 1980.)

In the lee of the high mountains to windward, the weather looked moderately promising the next morning. The sun was out, though rain squalls were drifting off to leeward on both sides of us, and the wind seemed fairly gentle. The sky had the look of heavy weather, however, and it was not with any great confidence for a good passage to Martinique that we got underway at 0840 the next morning. One reason I was happy to be away from the berth was that one extra large swell of the surge had dropped us down enough to bounce—just once, but hard—on one of the boulders, evidently swept off the land as more evidence of David's ravages.

The south end of Dominica is famous for "white squalls," williwawlike gusts that swoop down from the steep mountains behind Scott's Head, the southern tip of the island. They hit with very little warning and with a special impact, since their thrust is downward with cooler air from the heights given added impetus by the trade wind bursting over the peaks. When these downdrafts hit the surface of the water, they churn up a maelstrom of eddies, whitecaps, and wind streaks—sometimes with miniature tornados swirling in their midst—and we began to experience them as we powered down the coast. While they were buffeting us, I could see up ahead, beyond the distinctive mound of Scott's Head, which is connected with the island by a stretch of low beach, that the trade was sweeping through Martinique Passage with extra authority. The sky had clouded over completely, and Mont Pelée, Martinique's infamous volcano, was almost lost in the swirl of gray around it. In the open passage, the seas were great, charging, white horses, and every instinct told me to turn back and the hell with it. This was no day to take three ladies in their sixties out for a sail.

But we weren't just going for a sail. Mary had not been off Dominica for months, and this was to be her big adventure. She had made her farewells, and I knew she felt it would have been ignominious for us to crawl back into port, tail between our legs, after the excitement of breaking away. She and Julie had plane reservations as well, and, after all, it was only twenty miles of open water before we would be in Pelée's lee. I warned all hands that it was going to be rough, and all agreed to "press on irregardless."

The wind was about thirty, with many higher gusts, which called for reefed main and staysail, and we charged out into it with the last of the white squalls giving us an extra shove. *Brunelle* made good weather of it, but there was, inevitably, a lot of spray in the air with that much wind. It was the roughest, wettest day we have had in her. The waves were much the biggest I have ever seen in an inter-island passage. I have trouble judging wave heights, but these towered well above us as they approached, with wind streaks making little furrows down the front of them when they reared up. The tops, roaring and crashing like surf, broke into scuds of foam that flew away on the wind. They must have been close to fifteen feet, with one of those monster "seventh waves" every so often plus oddballs that came in at an angle to the regular scend and broke in leaping collisions. These were the ones that would send bullets of spray across us, and odd slaps of secondary waves against the hull would spread more water around.

Flying fish were making heavy weather of it. They would break free to start their usual skimming flight, which can go on for hundreds of feet on a day of normal waves, only to slam quickly into the steep face of the next wave.

Julia, tall, slender, and almost fragile—not really an outdoor type but ever the good sport—was over her first-day blues and was hanging in there stalwartly. It was her suggestion that we play "Ghost" to take our minds off the wind and weather, so while we roller-coasted over great, gray-blue combers, ducking blasts of spray, we were thinking up words and letters and passing them verbally around the cockpit circle. Mary finally succumbed to first-day troubles, but she stayed in the game valiantly. She would bring her head up from a session at the rail, contribute the next letter, and return to the position again.

In the dense, steamy heat of the closed-up cabin, I managed the "over-the-yardarm" nooners, with Jane and me the only takers, and she handed up "finger food" for lunch—celery, carrots, hard-boiled eggs, and fruit. That sustained us in the long, slow process of making Dominica look smaller and Martinique bigger. For a while, when both were misty gray and distant-looking, there was that treadmill illusion, with no sense of progress at all. Pelée gradually took more definition, with green beginning to show on its slopes, and the long slug ended at 1500, when we abruptly slid into its cone of calm and wallowed to a halt on smooth-backed swells. Despite the strong reaching breeze, the reduced rig and violent ups-and-downs over the waves had cut our speed down to about four knots for the passage.

Now came the moment of truth for the engine. Had the same thing happened again? We had been heeled well over on port tack again, but we had not been going anything like as fast as on the sail from Guadeloupe to Portsmouth. With fingers crossed, bated breath, and so forth, I pressed the starter button, and there was the rewarding roar of the engine taking hold. From there we motorsailed the twenty-five miles to Fort de France through alternating calms, trade-wind gusts, backwinds from the west, and spits of rain, admiring the play of sun and shadow on Pelée's massive shoulders and tracing the path of lava, now a flat green slope, that poured down on the town of St. Pierre in 1902 and killed its forty thousand inhabitants in one of the world's worst natural disasters. It is a view and a thought to give one pause.

In the very last of a twilight made uncertain by a heavy cover of clouds that moved in with the sunset, we chugged around Pointe desNegres and its flasher into Baie des Flammands, the crowded yacht

Mont Pelée took a long time to come closer

anchorage of Fort de France, and found an open space not far off the customs office and boat landing.

The icy sharpness of martinis cut through the day-long salty thirst with authority and effect, before a quick dinner of corned beef hash and peas—my favorite cruising meal—and Mozart's Forty-first on tape sent us all early to bed, well relaxed from the brine-encrusted buffeting of the roughest day we had spent in *Brunelle*.

29. *Dilemma*

~~~~~~

It was April 17, and the question of *Brunelle*'s future was beginning to become a pressing one. We had delivered Julia and Mary to their plane connection and there were no more crew changes to consider, so it was strictly a matter of deciding whether to press on to Venezuela in the face of a lack of any confirmation of plans or to decide upon some alternative. The possibilities were the CSY base at St. Vincent, The Dockyard in Antigua, or all the way back to Tortola. There were no other places I would want to leave her for the summer.

In addition to the political uncertainty over Venezuela, I began to think about the return journey to Grenada of more than one hundred miles to windward—and Grenada itself had become a question mark since its new government had aligned itself with Cuba. Yachtsmen reported that they were well treated by Grenadians, always among the friendliest people in the West Indies, but cruising there was restricted to two ports, control was tight, and the future was iffy.

I decided to look up the Venezuelan consul in Fort de France to find out what I could from him. When I rowed in to the customs office, which is specially setup on the waterfront to take care of yachts, the considerable red tape was handled with great courtesy and friendliness by the officials, and when I inquired about the Venezuelan consul, I was told that he was a good friend of the owner of the restaurant which adjoined the customs shed. The *douanier* said that the owner would be most happy to get me together with the consul, and I made a date to go there with the restaurateur that afternoon.

The *douanier* also made arrangements for a mechanic to change our lube oil and offered help in many other ways—shopping advice, laundry, ice, and so forth. He was light-skinned and smiling, and his English, heavily accentuated à la Maurice Chevalier, was very serv-

Fort de France, with the customs office (center under white building)

iceable—more so than my French. The question of race and color consciousness is entirely different in Martinique from what it is in the other islands. Blacks are just as numerous—though there seems to have been more of a mixing of the races judging from the number of very handsome, light-skinned people one sees in Fort de France—but I detected none of the underlying tensions that are sensed in places like Dominica, St. Lucia, and St. Vincent. The city is a bustling metropolis of over sixty thousand people, with first-class shops, hotels, and restaurants, and a European ambience that almost overcomes the tropical touches. Everybody is very businesslike and matter-of-fact, and any sense of color distinction is soon lost in the easy-going atmosphere.

After the customs stop, I went to the American Express office to cash a check; the city streets seemed strangely deserted and somnolent. American Express is upstairs from Roger Albert (pronounced Row-jhay Al-bear, of course), the number one store for tourist shopping in Martinique. The store, with only half its lights on, was almost empty, and there were only a couple of clerks on duty. American Express was almost deserted, too, and I asked the pretty young lady who waited on me why things were so quiet.

"There is a strike, with *manifestations* today," she said. "Many places are closed."

Back at *Brunelle,* I found two mechanics ready to change the oil. With my noteworthy lack of mechanical knowledge, I even have difficulty talking to mechanics in English. Here the conversation was entirely in French. At least I remembered that *huile* was the word for oil, and I really concentrated on it; somehow the job got done. While the men, two cheerful lads in trim coveralls, were doing the work, one of the strike *manifestations* materialized on the waterfront boulevard in the form of a rhythmic chanting, which carried out over the water. When they heard it, the two mechanics burst into derisive laughter, and as they worked they mocked the chanting with exaggerated mimicry, making it sound like children playing a game. I gathered that the strike did not have the complete backing of all the workers of Fort de France.

It did, however, have the support of the Venezuelan consul. When I appeared at the restaurant for our three P.M. date, the restaurant manager informed me that the Venezuelan consul had closed his office because of the strike and had gone away for a week. Scratch one more communication with Venezuela.

Julia and Mary had spent the day checking on their plane reservations at the airport. Telephone service had been curtailed, so they had to go out there in person; since taxi service had been reduced, the only way they could get back to town was to share a cab with a glamorous gal from Trinidad in form-fitting white coveralls. She had flown to Fort de France to pick up some spare parts for the Puegot dealership in Port of Spain. Such was her effect on the taxi driver that he took her to the Puegot dealer first. Before they were brought back to the quay, Julia and Mary spent a good part of the day watching the Trinidad queen charm the locals into filling her order.

It had been a difficult trip all the way, since they had been unable to climb out of the Avon inflatable at the boat landing, which is about chest high. Jim, who had rowed them there, had then taken them to a more negotiable quay at a boat yard next door. They managed to get out of the dinghy okay but then found that they were locked in the boatyard, which was closed because of the strike. Jim finally found a way for them to crawl through a hedge to a hole in the fence.

Meanwhile, I was watching the lube oil change, and I figured that they had put too much in when they renewed it. I had riffled through the owner's manual, past all the lists of spare-parts depots in the Far East and diagrams that looked like the digestive system of the Rhodesian Ridgeback, and found a page that gave the lube oil capacity and said DO NOT OVERFILL, in no uncertain terms and letters.

"Trop d'huile," I said, showing them the book and pointing at the dipstick.

"Non, non, monsieur. C'est correct."

"Ah, non. Trop d'huile," I kept insisting and finally got the boss mechanic to look at the manual. With a very expressive shrug, he gave in, which then involved calling around the anchorage until he found a boat with the kind of pump he needed to reduce the amount of oil, so that we soon had a wide circle of concerned friends.

As a farewell to Julia and Mary we ventured ashore to a modern-looking restaurant called La Grande Voile at harborside and had the best shore meal of the entire cruise (at a price: twenty-six dollars per person). Everything was very good—paté, smoked salmon, veal, filet du boeuf, cheese tray, and fondu, and a Mâcon Blanc de Blancs that was the cheapest thing on the list at thirty-five francs, with everything else much higher. Jim had a little problem getting the ladies back in the Avon afterwards at the little boat landing in front of the restaurant, but the only mishap was a sudden swoosh of the boat as it slipped in under the pier. The ladies held on to the pier desperately, their knuckles turning white and their faces just showing above the edge of the pier. Slightly damp rear ends were the only casualties, and in contrast to our early collapse of the night before, we sat up late settling the affairs of the world over *chapeaux de nuit,* as nightcaps are sometimes called in our family.

Jim had to get Mary and Julia ashore at an ungodly hour of the morning, and he managed it without losing anybody or any luggage by dropping them at La Grande Voile and the luggage at the customs landing, where the taxis were.

The strike was over, and Fort de France was a madhouse as an aftermath. Jim went ashore to buy stamps and stood in line for an hour at the post office, but he did manage to find two days of the Paris *Herald Tribune* (which carries the *New York Times* crossword); we felt we were right back in the swing of things. In the afternoon, we all went shopping and finally found a supermarket on the second floor of a sort of five-and-ten, Korvettes, general-store affair called Prisunic. Shopping was an adventure, as the packaging was all French, and the system was confusing—with locals shouldering knowledgeably by—but we did moderately well. Jim was particularly proud of having found a package of bacon in an obscure corner, since we were fresh out on board.

To get vegetables and meat, we wandered through the open-air market in a square in the middle of town—an overwhelming mélange of gory sights, noise, and a pungent gamut of the strongest smells this side of the Chicago stockyards. Overall there was a wonderfully Caribbean-Gallic mixed ambience of shouts, shrugs, and laughs, and produce, entrails, fish, and unidentifiables being tossed about with abandon.

Back at the boat, a Valiant 40 we had seen in the Virgins and Antigua was anchored near us; we invited her crew, Roland, a German-American, and Lisa, thoroughly American, aboard for cocktails. They had been down as far as the Grenadines and were not taken with the lower islands, reporting swarms of rowboat ruffians in most anchorages and a general feeling of unrest. Combined with several reports we had had of really unpleasant encounters in St. Lucia, with overt resentment, racial epithets, and obscenities—especially from Rastafarians near the Pitons—my enthusiasm for continuing south was rapidly diminishing.

We had to do something, however. I was feeling more and more cast loose in the limbo, but riding at anchor in the persistent surge of the Baie des Flammands, surrounded by the strange-looking reverse sheer boats—with peeling topsides, odd color combinations in puce, lime green, and baby blue, and misfit deckhouses—that seem to be popular with European yachtsmen now, was not going to solve my problem.

In the end, I decided to go on to the CSY base at St. Vincent, where we could have some minor work done, and I could come to a final decision there. We would go straight through for ninety-five miles overnight, since such an unattractive picture had been painted of St. Lucia—we had been there several times in years past anyway. Saturday morning April 19 found the breeze just as strong as it had been ever since we went through the front off Guadeloupe one week before, with rain squalls sweeping through every so often.

I was making up the bunk while Jane was cooking breakfast, when through the closed door I began to smell a very strange, pungent odor that was a mix of dead animal and some of the mustier locker rooms I had been in during my football-playing days.

"What in hell is that?" I called. I thought of escaping gas, or some unspeakable mishap in the sewage system on shore.

"It's the French bacon," Jane said. "I just opened it." (She eventually discovered a note on the package about opening half an hour before use).

Jim and I were both brave enough to eat the stuff after Jane fried it; after all, it was his major find at Prisunic. I have no idea how the French cure their bacon, and I don't dare ask, but nobody suffered ill effects from eating it.

Our plan was to leave after lunch, which was spent watching a French sloop that looked moth-eaten—with a strange reverse sheer line, streaked black paint, and the appearance of having been resurrected from a gravel pit—come to anchor near us in a flying approach, in which the bearded, bikini-bottomed skipper tossed the anchor over like a shot put. He didn't wait to see if it even hit the water, much less the bottom, and the boat was still going forward. Without so much as a glance at the rode, he and a female, and two little children immediately piled into their inflatable and went to visit on a nearby boat. While they sat in the cockpit socializing, their boat was relentlessly moving out to sea. We called over to them, and they just shrugged. Jim figured that they perhaps did not understand English and rowed over

Lava's devastation on the top half of Soufrière, St. Vincent, where the smell of sulphur was strong

to make sure they saw what was happening. They told him that they knew the boat was dragging but that it would fetch up sooner or later, and they continued to drink with their friends. Not until the boat had gone another couple of hundred yards and ended up in a tangle with an anchored vessel, did they get in the dink and go back to her. *C'est la vie!*

It was still blowing fresh when we motorsailed across the bay toward the south end of Martinique. When we came out of the lee into St. Lucia Channel, we killed the motor. It was great sailing, not as rough as our last passage by any means, and we zipped toward St. Lucia

320

The CSY base at Blue Lagoon, St. Vincent

at close to seven knots through moderate seas, while the sunset light over Martinique bathed the hills in a lovely golden glow beneath the blue-black castles of rain clouds above the peaks. It was fast sailing until we slid under the lee of the Pitons, the twin peaks that are St. Lucia's trademark, and we lazed along in the dark over easy swells until close to 0400, when the trade came back freshly. We then made six and a half knots under jib, staysail, and main on the crossing of St. Vincent Passage.

St. Vincent's Soufrière (there are almost as many Soufrières as there are Marigots in the Caribbean), at 4,048 feet, is one of the major peaks in the islands. As we closed with it, we could see the gray, wasted spread of lava all around its cone—grim evidence of its eruption a year previously. When we came under its lee, the smell of sulphur was very strong.

By lunchtime we had rounded the south end of St. Vincent, skirting Kingstown, the main port, and poked through the narrow dynamited cut in the reef, which was marked by little stakes and leads to Blue Lagoon anchorage, where CSY has its base. It was like being back in the Virgins again to see all the American boats in the harbor, with CSYs on one side and Heritages and Gulf Stars across the way at Heritage Charters. Beyond us, in a misty haze that looked more like a smoky sou'wester in New England than the bright seascape of the Caribbean, the Grenadines—one of the prime cruising areas in the Hemisphere—stretched into the distance, with Venezuela, ninety miles beyond their southern limit. We anchored in deep water with very little room for proper scope because of all the anchored yachts, and gusts from the open Atlantic on the other side of the hill played nervously around us.

I rowed ashore and checked with Allen Hooper, CSY's manager, and made arrangements for coming in to the marina in the morning. This was a lazy Sunday afternoon and everything was in suspension. We felt that way, too, as we gazed across Bequia Channel to the south and wondered whether we would be heading that way soon—or what we would be doing. After all the months and months of planning that had gone into this cruise, it seemed frustrating to be in such a question-fraught limbo at what should have been the climax.

30. The Long Voyage "Home"

It was very soon evident that one of our choices would not be to leave *Brunelle* at Blue Lagoon. The bulkhead at the CSY marina was already too small for the number of boats being serviced there and was being expanded, and the harbor was no place to leave an untended boat. It is not a big one, and its center is quite deep. The only anchorage is in the northeast corner, still in more than twenty feet, and the holding ground is iffy. There are no moorings, as there are at CSY's Road Town base, and the anchorage is so crowded that there is no room to put out sufficient scope. Scratch one possibility.

This decision had nothing to do with the amount of cooperation at the base, as everyone was extremely helpful. At breakfast time the next morning, Eddy, a wiry Vincentian from the CSY crew, came aboard with a sidekick and moved *Brunelle* in to a stern-to berth. I didn't object to being treated like a charterer; on the contrary, it was pleasant to sit back and have them do the work. As soon as we were in, we were overwhelmed by workmen ready to do the few minor repairs that we needed; it was good to see how well they knew their stuff.

My main worry was the possibility of getting water in the engine again, but this was no mystery to the chief CSY mechanic. He explained that there is an anti-siphon valve at the top of the loop in the exhaust pipe, high up under the starboard cockpit locker—something that I, in my ignorance, did not know existed. He got in at it in a very awkward corner and soon had it out, confirming that it was stuck open. Evidently this is nothing extraordinary and can often be a problem. He loosened it up and put it back in. The only other problem of note was a squeak in the steering system, which Eddy finally tracked down to the rudder post itself (I had been lubricating the quadrants, chain, and so forth without having any effect). Meanwhile, Jane provisioned from CSY's commissary.

While all this was going on, I put in hours trying to call Venezuela in a final effort to confirm arrangements. St. Vincent is not the ideal place from which to communicate with the rest of the world, as to start with, it takes a long time to get an operator. Then a call to Caracas had to go via Jacksonville, Florida, through all sorts of bleeping, booping, and humming, and lots of operator chatter—all with the same result as before. The number I had as a contact did not answer. I was able to get through to my office in New York to have them send a Telex, giving the Venezuelans the CSY number in St. Vincent and asking them to call, but all efforts struck out. Whether the numbers had been changed or the company had ceased operations, I still do not know, as later letters went unanswered as well.

When all this was added up, it seemed foolish to push on into the unknown for the arbitary goal of getting to South America. I would have to come up with an alternate plan fairly quickly, since by now it was April 23, and my commitments back home were creeping up on us. The only possibilities were to go back to Antigua or all the way to Road Town. Antigua is used by a great many people to leave their vessels under a boatkeeper's care, and Lester had certainly done a good job for us in March. The physical security was all right, though a direct swipe by a hurricane could be a problem. The main drawback was that Antigua Race Week was on at the end of the month, with hundreds of boats jammed into English Harbour, and all normal services would be overwhelmingly overtaxed. We had been to Race Week twice in the past, and it is great sailing and a great party, but I had no desire to tangle with its complications under the present situation; Road Town seemed the answer, even if it was almost five hundred miles back there.

A call to Albie Stewart at Tortola Yacht Services, which only took about half an hour to get through, turned up the information that he was absolutely fully booked for the summer, with a waiting list of boats that were anchored right off his bulkhead hoping for a cancellation. This meant I was down to my last chance, wet storage at Village Cay, and the rigamarole of another call there brought an affirmative. They could take care of *Brunelle* for the summer, and there was a professional boatkeeping service available. That had to be the answer. It was going to be a long push to get there in time, but it should be all down wind, and the murky, squally weather that had been with us ever since we went through that front off Guadeloupe seemed to be breaking up.

Instead of looking misty and lost, the Grenadines loomed up more sharply across Bequia Channel in the brightening weather, and I hated to miss cruising in them. We had been there six times in the past, however, and there were also reports that they had become very crowded and that the rowboat brigades in the harbors had grown unpleasantly demanding, so the disappointment was not as sharp as it might have been.

We had time to poke around St. Vincent a little, with dinner one night at the Sugar Mill—a steep walk from the harbor to its hilltop location. As a farewell, we had dinner with Allen Hooper and his Grenadian wife, Shirley, at a new restaurant called the Umbrella on the waterfront opposite the fancy offshore resort of Young Island. Shirley and Allen had met while she was in school in England, and she was the reason for his being in this part of the world, which he didn't seem to mind in the least.

In talking to some Vincentians I met a white man with the same name as a sailor from St. Vincent whom I had seen farther up the islands and who was a light-skinned black. I asked if there was any connection.

"Oh, yes," the man said. "He's a cousin. He's Uncle Albert's 'outside child.' " It seems there are several grades of familyhood. An "outside child" is acknowledged but not brought into the home, a "yard child" is allowed to play at the family home but does not live there, and the regular family has "inside children," who live at home.

Whereas Dominica had been recovering from Hurricane David, St. Vincent was still struggling back from the disastrous eruption of Soufrière the previous spring. It had wiped out most of the vegetation on the northern half of the island, ruining thousands of houses and causing mass relocation as it covered the whole area with a dusting of ashes. Both these islands have been at the bottom of the economic scale in the Caribbean, and these natural disasters have been particularly cruel.

And so this was our turnaround point, the end of the line in the south. From now on we would be northbound on the other tack (and at least the heads would be to leeward); we would have to make some long, fast passages to keep schedule. My worries of being homeless were over, but there was still a tension in having to move on so rapidly. It was lucky we had Jim with us to share the watch standing, and he was his usual accommodating self and very glad to be having what for him was an all-new experience of seeing these islands and their people.

Again we would bypass St. Lucia and overnight it the ninety-five miles to Fort de France, which would give us a good jump on the route. The sail back there after an 1100-departure in bright sun was an easy slide, one of the nicest inter-island passages so far after we powered past Soufrière's wind cone and the odorous reminder of its activity, which smelled even stronger than on the way down. The waves were gentle in a twelve-to-sixteen-knot breeze on the beam, and we slid past St. Lucia by 2130 and were under Martinique's lee by 0100, where we shortened down to staysail to delay our arrival in Fort de France until daylight. Once gun shy with lobster pots you tend to think about them, and there are some in the bay at Fort de France.

We crept slowly across the wide mouth of the bay in the growing light and anchored off the customs dock at 0600. I immediately hit the sack for a short nap but was ready to go ashore at 0900 to enter with the friendly customs people at the landing. When they went through my papers, they realized that I had not cleared out when we left on our way southbound. I received a mild chiding, but I apologized for my ignorance, and everything was smiles as the last rubber stamp was banged on the last form.

A cruise ship, *Carla C,* was in the harbor, and the town was crawling with her passengers when I made my way to the American Express office at Roger Albert to arrange new air tickets home. The last time I had been there it was morguelike in dim-lit stillness during the strike, but now, with cruise passengers on the loose, the main store at street level had the cacaphony of a chicken yard, with dozens of clerks in uniform to wait on the swarm of shoppers. I was getting tickets here because I knew that Air BVI at Tortola did not accept credit cards, and I did not have enough cash left to buy three tickets to the States. Here, there was an Eastern Airlines computer, since EAL serves Martinique, and I could get San Juan-New York tickets on my Amex card. The process took all morning, and we napped and read during the afternoon, as heavy surge agitated the anchorage. We had dinner ashore in a restaurant overlooking the Savanna in the heart of town, with its white statue of Empress Josephine, who was born across the bay at Trois Ilets.

When we got back to the boat, Jane and then Jim folded rather quickly, but I was not ready for bed after my afternoon nap. I sat in the cockpit drinking Mount Gay on the rocks and listening to tapes of the late George Symonette, the Calypso laureate of the Bahamas, whose distinctive style has never been matched in this kind of music. The songs had a strong nostalgic ring for me, taking me back twenty years to our first cruises in the Bahamas, when the whole atmosphere had been new to us and we would stay up all night every night to seek out the whole experience—listening to George in person or going "over the hill" for more excitement. Now, with his lilting rhythms and wonderful touches of humor filling the cockpit, I couldn't help but compare those days with my willingness now to sit quietly and enjoy where I was—even though one of the most sophisticated cities in the Western world was there over the bow for the adventuring. Maybe it was déjà vu, but I was thoroughly happy with the setting as it was and with the memories of the sailing we had done to get here. Or, by any chance, could it be age?

A burglar alarm in a shop along the waterfront woke us at 0530 on a clear, pleasant morning, and under the continuing sense of urgency to be on our way we were rounding Pointe des Negres by 0710, powering along the lee shore with main up until we finally hit the trade at 1000—three miles north of Cap St. Martin at the northern tip of Martinique. The main had been reefed since April 13, but we shook it out now and had a glorious reach across to Scott's Head in moderate seas and bright sun, a vivid contrast to our rough day coming down.

By 1330 we were under Dominica. We had been figuring on Roseau, but we were so early that we powered on to Portsmouth and got there at 1730, sixty-five miles in ten hours. The rowboat armada was not as much in evidence, though the local boys swarmed over us again as we anchored; forewarned from our previous stop, I bought off two of them with one dollar each as encouragement to stay away and to tell everybody else we were taken care of. It worked.

We asked about John, and the boys said that he had gone to Guadeloupe on the French yacht whose starter motor had been under repair. I figured that giving them money for him would be throwing it down the drain. My guilt from not having paid him on our previous stop was still with me when he suddenly appeared alongside, grinning shyly, in his old beat-up blue boat with a spritsail sailing rig added. He had just gotten back from Guadeloupe that day and was a bit disillusioned by the trip as it had been rough without much wind. He was genuinely surprised when I slipped him a few bucks and told him it was for his help last time, and he apologized, explaining that the mechanic had been working on the starter motor all day.

We had a good dinner of chicken and eggplant, but the anchorage had one of the worst surges we had felt on the cruise: a restless, intermittent rhythm in which *Brunelle* would lie quietly for a few minutes and then go into a crazy pendulum motion that was very hard to adjust to. The night was otherwise lovely, with a three-quarter moon, and it was more pleasant to be on deck than to be fighting the surge in a bunk. Portsmouth was almost completely blacked out under the shadow of the mountains behind it, but we could hear one generator humming on the beach. From somewhere in the almost-dark town, where just a few dull glimmers showed, a disco beat carried its incongruous rhythm out to us.

Before we left in the morning, John brought us a dozen bananas for one dollar, and an engaging nine-year-old named Glenroy in a home-made raft that was more underwater than on it, took our garbage away for a fee after a conversation in which he promised to be in charge of the anchorage the next time we came back.

It took us an hour to get out of the wind shadow of Morne

328

John with the sailing rig for his boat

Diablotin, and we then had another easy reach to the Saintes, arriving at noon. These little islands off Guadeloupe had charmed us in 1961 as something really different, with descendants of Breton fisherman operating lovely little sailing canoes of a most graceful design and a lively mingling of the townspeople in the waterfront square as the men came in from fishing in late afternoon, but the Saintes, like St. Martin and St. Bart's, are no longer something special. They are just as touristed and junked up as any of the major islands. We were quickly disillusioned by a walk on shore and were soon back aboard. Ahead of us was a twenty-one-foot sloop with a self-steering vane that had come in just after us; the crew was a lone woman, running around her tiny deck like a chicken performing all the tasks of getting off sail and anchoring.

We asked her over for a drink, and she came with alacrity. Her name was Margaret Hicks, and she had participated in the Mini-Transat single-handed race for small boats to Antigua a few months previously and was now ranging the islands on a cruise. In her forties, she was a high-school English teacher who was taking a sabbatical this way. Like all single-handers when they finally get someone to talk to, she was a nonstop monologuist as she sipped a beer. She had very strong opinions on everything and was full of tales of the difficulty of being a woman alone in this unusual world she had chosen to enter. She said that the inter-island passages had been much rougher and much more of a challenge than anything that happened on the race; she was not happy about the treatment she had received in Antigua, St. Lucia, and Roseau.

She was not discouraged though and was already planning her single-handed passage home in late spring via Bermuda. While her story would have been unique and amazing a few years ago, she was now just one more example of the explosion in long-range passaging that has taken place in the last decade, filling the once lonely harbors of the Caribbean with assorted craft.

On another delightful day, we made fast time across to Guadeloupe and were able to carry sail well past Basse-Terre along the leeward coast since the wind had some southeast in it and was bending around

Leaving the Saintes astern

the point and its distinctive white lighthouse. Almost without a lull, we then ran into a fresh westerly that carried us northward for two hours at a good clip. As we ran out of it, we came upon *Anonymous Bay,* Margaret's little sloop, wallowing in the calm. She had left the Saintes about 0300 and had made good progress so far, but the calm stretched well into the distance ahead, so we offered her a tow; an hour-and-a-half later we pulled into DesHayes at 1615. This was a Sunday, so I didn't try the *Douane* at all this time. Margaret came for dinner, which was marred by my failure to get the hibachi going at all, as we ran out of lighter fluid and all our cardboard-encased briquettes were wet. Jane finally, under protest, had to do the chops in a pan on the stove; they tasted fine to me. The night was absolutely calm in the lee, with few clouds, and the moon was almost full.

The dawn was equally as beautiful as we got underway at 0600. This was going to be a long day. The obvious passage was to Antigua,

Margaret Hicks and her single-handed Anonymous Bay

but I had no desire to tangle with Race Week, so we were instead headed more to the northwest for Nevis, with Montserrat as a possibility on the way if we were running out of time. *Anonymous Bay* again left at 0300, and I heard her little Seagull outboard clattering past us

332

as she bravely headed for the Antigua shambles. When we left, the ketch *Auralyn II* was also on her way out. She was the boat, now owned by someone else, that Marilyn and Maurice Bailey had built for cruising to the Cape Horn area following their incredible ordeal in a lifeboat in the Pacific—after a whale sank their first *Auralyn!*

Although the sailing had been delightful on the northbound inter-island jaunts, and the weather was a marked contrast to our southern passage, I was beginning to feel the pressure of time on these long days; this was to be the longest of all—the one that would break the back of the push northward if we could manage to get to Nevis. I had never been there, and the guidebooks were not encouraging about the anchorage, so it was one of those days of anxiety and an uneasiness over what we were headed for as we set course of 325° for Montserrat, which was standing boldly on the horizon. Montserrat, still a British colony, is mountainous and virtually harborless, and I hoped that we could move on by without trying to anchor in its lee—famous for a heavy surge. We had had enough of that in Portsmouth.

We started out on a broad reach, but the breeze gradually veered to the south. By the time we came under its southern point, we were on a direct run. All winter long we had been listening to Radio Antilles, a powerful station that covers the whole Caribbean from Montserrat, and now we slid by the bleak point where its towers stand and moved into the lee off the main settlement, Plymouth, which did not look appealing as an anchorage. It was only 1300, so we powered through the wind shadow and into the trade again, reaching rapidly to Redonda, halfway between Montserrat and Nevis. This one-thousand-foot-high rock is starkly lonely; it is hard to believe that people have lived on it in the past. It is now uninhabited, and there is a story of a man who claims to own it, had his son made king and appointed all his friends dukes and counts of Redonda—even though none of them have ever been there. From the look of it, I would not want to be dog catcher. Off to windward, Antigua was a dim shape on the horizon, and I could imagine the goings-on there.

For the last four hours, from Redonda on, we had the wind dead aft, and we wung-out the staysail with a preventer rigged forward as the

333

The "snow cap" on Nevis

best we could do straight downwind. The Flasher does not stay full with the wind dead aft, so the staysail is the best wing-and-wing candidate we have.

Nevis, named by Columbus because the perpetual white cap of clouds on its 3,600-foot cone reminded him of snow, was bathed in a greenish-gold glow while we closed with it on steepening seas, and it was hard to pick out landmarks in approaching a completely round island. Perspectives are difficult to judge, and it seems to take a terribly long time to pass a given point in this kind of landfall. The full moon came up at 1800, the sun went down at 1825 in a glowing bank of clouds, and we slid along the barren shores of Nevis in the last glimmers of twilight, finally rounding the low point that gives some protection to the roadstead off Charlestown—the main settlement on Nevis—at 1850. Several boats were at anchor inside the point, heaving gently in a mild surge, and two more straggled in, running lights aglow, after we did.

After dinner, Jane and I sat in the cockpit watching the moon break free from the cone of Nevis, bathing us in pale silver; Jim was reading below. I was relatively at peace with the world, since we now had plenty of time to make schedule without rushing. The long day behind us, dawn twilight to evening twilight, had been a major step. As we chatted, it began to come out, though, that Jane had been increasingly unhappy over the past few weeks.

"All we've been doing is push, push, push," she said. "A lot of the passages haven't been much fun. I don't really like this kind of cruising."

I admitted we had been under some strain and that the big islands south of Antigua do not make for as good cruising as the ones north of there.

"You don't have any time for me any more," she went on. "You're so wrapped up in the boat that I might as well not exist except to give you meals when you're ready."

I was surprised and taken aback, but, on thinking it over, I could see her point, recalling how preoccupied I had been with the problems of getting to Venezuela, the engine trouble at Portsmouth, and negotiating the rough passages. Even after making the decision to head for Tortola, I had been thinking mainly about keeping schedule and the choice of stops to make the most efficient day's runs. I had not been much of a husband, I had to admit, and it was good that Jane had cleared the atmosphere by speaking up; otherwise, our cruise might have had a negative wind up.

It was true that we had not enjoyed this past month of cruising as much as all the previous ones. The lower Windwards as far as St. Vincent, not counting the Grenadines, have magnificent scenery and some interesting sightseeing, but the harbors leave something to be desired in most cases. They are very crowded, and there are not very many of them, making for long runs each day. Most of them have a persistent surge that keeps you on edge through the night as well. When the inter-island channels are rough, as on our southward trip, it is a question of hanging on and hoping everything holds together— and that your anti-siphon valve works, once you know you have one. The northbound sailing had been much closer to the picture-postcard ideal of blue seas, purple islands, and easy going, but by then the mood had been set, and we had probably not enjoyed the passages as much as we should.

Now Jane's frankness had put things in perspective, and the situation was pretty well smoothed over by the time we went to bed, with the help of Mount Gay, a Mildred Bailey tape, and my promise to be more thoughtful.

Feeling renewed and more cheerful, we were greeted by a dramatic dawn that turned the snow cap of Nevis blue-black and saffron. Curtains of rain drifted away from the cone and crossed The Narrows to cast shadows across the golden slant of sun on the fields of St. Kitts, bright green patterns of sugar cane covering well up the slopes toward Mount Misery, its 4,314-foot peak. We ran along the lee of St. Kitts directly before the fresh trade, admiring the play of light and dark on the neatly laid out fields, with a good look at the old fortress on Brimstone Hill. These islands were the most important ones in the Lesser Antilles in the seventeenth and eighteenth centuries and games of empire were played around them constantly between the Spanish, French, Dutch, and English. Statia (St. Eustatius), nine miles northwest of St. Kitts, was a staging depot for material for American forces during the Revolution and one of the busiest spots in the West Indies. It was at Oranjestad, on Statia (Dutch), that the flag of the new American Republic received its first formal recognition by a foreign power when the fort there answered a salute from the naval vessel *Andrew Doria*. President Franklin Roosevelt sent a plaque to Statia to commemorate this, and it is mounted near the waterfront. Admiral Rodney eventually punished Statia for its role in aiding the Revolution by raiding it and laying the town waste, making off, for his own personal profit, with most of the booty stored in warehouses there. Evidently the island never recovered. I have never been there, but I understand it is the sleepiest, least-active backwater in the Lesser Antilles. The anchorage is an open roadstead, poor for yachts.

While we powered through Mount Misery's wind shadow, massive isolated squalls—their tumbled heights shining white in the sun over a black shroud of rain—moved across Statia's flat-topped cone, all but blotting it out; a waterspout spun tenuously out of one squall only to dissipate in a few minutes. We remained in bright sun, picking up a fresh blast of trade as abruptly as if we had gone through a door into a wind tunnel when we moved out of the lee at 1010. St. Bart's was a dim shape thirty miles away to the north, and we enjoyed one of our better sails of the winter on a broad reach; the flying fish were having an active day around us, skittering and splashing over the sunlit waves. The mood aboard was much better.

Astern, St. Kitts's green fields, marked off in patterns, held their bright color under the sun long after most islands would have misted into pale blue, and Saba's distinctive cone loomed beyond squall-shrouded Statia. This is one of the more dramatic seascapes in all the islands, and it was a day to see it at its best. Our passage down had been at night, with the dim lights of St. Kitts as the only visible reminder of the presence of land.

St. Bart's was as crowded as ever when we poked into the narrow confines of Gustavia, but we managed a fore-and-aft anchoring in almost exactly the same spot we had been in in February. It was now noticeably warmer in the harbor than it had been in mid-winter, and we were content to relax aboard while Jim explored ashore. Dinner was good old hash and peas, and bedtime was early after a few tapes of music.

The morning was noisy, as remembered, with little sleep after 0500 amid the buzzing of outboards and clatter of work on the quay—backed by music, both sacred and profane. With the supermarket right there at the dinghy landing, we took the opportunity to stock up, probably for the last time, and were off for St. Martin by mid-

337

Dramatic rain squalls around Statia

morning. It was a straight downwind run past the isolated collections of rocks that almost make a slalom out of this route, and we were in Phillipsburg for a late lunch.

We now had enough time to spare to take a "lay day" here, and I had always wanted to see Saba, which is not practical in a yacht because of the almost nonexistent landing facilities, so Jim and I rowed ashore to see if we could arrange an air trip for the next day. STOL planes serve Saba from St. Martin, and the landing on the short strip cut out of the face of the mountain is supposed to be one of the thrills of a lifetime.

Phillipsburg was not itself, however. All the shops were shut, the airport telephone did not answer, and crowds lined the narrow main street looking expectantly westward, where the liquid rhythms of a steel band could be heard in the distance. It was Carnival, the Queen of Holland's birthday, but also a special one this time—Juliana was abdicating, turning the throne over to her daughter Beatrix, just as her mother, Whilhelmina, had done for her. The crowd was a mix of whole families of natives—their children holding balloons and jumping around in anticipation—tourists bedecked with cameras and sweat, and boating people in beards, tank tops, faded jeans, and T-shirts. Everyone was holding a beer or something stronger, and there was a holiday restlessness in the air.

As the first float came in sight, I took a chance that things would go slowly and rowed back to the boat to get Jane so she could see it. Things were going so slowly that the front of the snail's-pace parade was barely past the dinghy landing when we got back. There were elaborate floats of space craft and pirate ships, and trucks with steel bands and calypso combines playing their heads off. There was a strong element of commercialism, with Marlboro hats on almost everyone, along with hats and shirts from Guiness, Don Q, and local stores.

Each float or truck was surrounded by dancers of both sexes and all ages, costumed in bright satins doing the basic shuffle-and-bounce Calypso step, sweat gleaming on their faces and darkening their clothes. Each truck seemed to have one man whose main duty was to pour beer on anyone nearby. A big pirate ship float caused screams and surprised scrambling when its gun ports suddenly blasted clouds of "gunpowder" (flour) over the tightly packed crowd.

It was a hurricane of noise and laughter, of teeth flashing in the afternoon sun, of sweat streaming over glistening faces, and under it all the pervasive beat of the music, clashing and blending as one band moved along and another could be heard approaching from the west. The street, a narrow canyon between the closely bunched buildings, was an echo chamber for the cacaphony.

Finally, the tail-end truck inched along, with, wisely I'm sure, an ambulance following; in no time the town was somnolently quiet while the beat of the last band receded slowly, far down the street. The crowds melted away, probably to private revels with the paraders, and we repaired to the nearest restaurant, Antoine's. Our table was at the corner on a balcony directly over the harborfront beach, with a grand view of the curving shoreline and anchored yachts and, later, of the moon breaking from behind the hills east of the harbor. My snapper Meunière was as good as any I have ever had, and the fine dinner after the crazy Carnival made the day an unexpected dividend—a coda to the down-island adventures. Tonight the surge hissed softly on the sand below us, with the tracery of foam glinting in the moonlight, and palms rustled above us. Tomorrow we would cross the Anegada Passage back to the Virgins.

A downwind crossing is quite different from an eastbound one. We had the wind absolutely dead aft, with the staysail wung-out, and we swooped along in easy fashion from our afternoon departure, with the lowering sun glowing on St. Martin, St. Bart's, and Saba, and the seas sliding under the transom in easy rhythm. The moon kept us company after 2000, and it looked like a delightfully straightforward passage until 0330, when Anegada Passage had to assert itself with its reputation for changeable unpredictability. From then until we rolled by Round Rock into calm water at 1000, having averaged 4.7 knots, we had clouds, heavy downpours, and a fitful wind that finally settled in the south. The squalls had little weight to them, but there is always an ominous feeling in being alone on deck when black clouds mount to the zenith and blot out the moon—you are not sure whether a distant hissing on the water is just rain approaching or a wind line too, especially in Anegada Passage.

And so we were back in the Virgins with a few days to spare. A night of rest in hot, airless conditions at Virgin Gorda Yacht Harbour caught us up with lost sleep, though downwind sleeping the night before had been the easiest yet on a night passage. I took a taxi to enter customs at the airport, the first formality we had gone through since

A last tingler of a reach in the "home" waters of the BVI

Martinique. All the other stops had been on a weekend, after hours, or during Carnival, and it made the whole business of entering and clearing seem like the silly red-tape nonsense that it really is. I'm sure you could sail the islands for months with no one being the wiser, except at English Harbour, but it is not a good idea to take the chance.

A brisk reach under Flasher took us to Trellis Bay to arrange plane tickets to San Juan; then we made a farewell visit to the Last Resort. There was a big Saturday-night crowd, and Tony was in specially fine form. Perhaps it was being back in the BVI or a reaction to the month of stress and strain, but I went beyond my usual limits at the bar and could possibly have been accused of drunken rowing on the way back to *Brunelle.*

The aspect of the islands in May was very different from the mid-winter atmosphere. It was much warmer and there was a gauzy haze over everything, brought in by the unaccustomed south wind.

There was a definite end-of-season feel to things as we took our last sail, a tingler of a hull-speed reach up Francis Drake Channel to Road Town, past all the familiar landmarks of what now seemed like home waters, to the berth we had arranged at Village Cay Marina.

It was strange to leave *Brunelle* after having had her as the hub of our universe, our home, our plaything, and the means of realizing our dreams for so many months. We were leaving her with a professional boatkeeper who would turn over the engine, check the batteries, keep her aired out, and tend the lines in the long hot months of summer; it seemed as secure a setup as could be imagined. And we would be back to her in the fall for some more cruising here, and perhaps a return to the Bahamas and the States.

Now, however, it seemed hard to grasp that breakfast would be at a dining-room table, that we would be sleeping in a Queen-sized bed that was fully assembled at all times, that we would be getting around by plane, train and automobile and walking paved streets in hard-soled shoes and dressed in city clothes.

We would be living that way, though, amid special memories of morning sun flooding the cockpit at breakfast, of islands luring us on across the trade-wind seas, of hull-speed reaches scattering the flying fish, of moonlight bathing an anchorage, of boats and sailors we had met, of anchor cups of rum after a fast passage, of the companionship of our crews, of the hours we had been able to spend together, and yes, of rough seas, tensions, and dark times too that only served to make the good ones better.

Brunelle had brought us all these memories and many more. This part of her story had ended: mission accomplished. But there was more to come. The dream, fulfilled for now, still lived on—it was too good a one to stop.